Implementing VMware vCenter Server

A practical guide for deploying and using VMware vCenter, suitable for IT professionals

Konstantin Kuminsky

BIRMINGHAM - MUMBAI

Implementing VMware vCenter Server

First published: October 2013

Production Reference: 1211013

Published by Packt Publishing Ltd.
Livery Place
35 Livery Street
Birmingham B3 2PB, UK.

ISBN 978-1-84968-998-4

www.packtpub.com

Credits

Author
Konstantin Kuminsky

Reviewers
Erik Nielsen
Mario Russo
Anish Varghese (Panthalani)

Acquisition Editor
Akram Hussain

Lead Technical Editor
Susmita Panda

Technical Editors
Nadeem Bagban
Aparna Chand
Venu Manthena
Kanhucharan Panda
Vivek Pillai
Amit Singh

Copy Editors
Roshni Banerjee
Tanvi Gaitonde
Mradula Hegde
Gladson Monteiro
Alfida Paiva

Project Coordinators
Venitha Cutinho
Arshad Sopariwala

Proofreaders
Simran Bhogal
Ameesha Green
Paul Hindle

Indexer
Hemangini Bari

Graphics
Disha Haria
Yuvraj Mannari
Abhinash Sahu

Production Coordinators
Aditi Gajjar
Kirtee Shingan

Cover Work
Kirtee Shingan

About the Author

Konstantin Kuminsky (MCSE, MCSA, MCITP Enterprise, CCNA, and CCNA Security) is an IT professional with over 10 years of experience in different areas of the industry, including virtualization, networking, and security. His experience includes support of Tier 3 datacenters, management of private clouds, administration of second- and third-level help desks and on-call support, and the deployment and support of various redundant systems and environments with high security requirements.

This book wouldn't have been possible without the support of my family. I would like to thank all my family members for their patience and encouragement during this and other projects. Most importantly, I would like to thank my parents for all that they've done for me. This work is worth it because of their love and understanding.

About the Reviewers

Erik Nielsen is currently working for Harbor Freight Tools. He feels that working for a fast-growing company that is moving to become a 100 percent virtualized is challenging as the company is constantly moving to the latest and most stable configuration of an evolving software-defined datacenter platform.

NetApp and Dell|EMC are the two companies that allowed him to learn, as he previously worked for both these companies as a Professional Services Engineer.

You can read more about him at `http://www.linkedin.com/pub/erik-nielsen/6/a79/88`.

Mario Russo has worked as an IT Architect, a Senior Technical VMware Trainer, and in the pre-sales department. He has also worked on VMware Technology since 2004.

In 2005, he worked for IBM on the First Large Project Consolidation for Telecom Italia on the Virtual VMware Esx 2.5.1 platform in Italy with the Physical to Virtual (P2V) tool.

In 2007, he conducted a drafting course and training for BancoPosta, Italy, and project disaster and recovery (DR Open) for IBM and EMC.

In 2008, he worked for the Project Speed Up Consolidation BNP and the migration P2V on VI3 infrastructure at BNP Cardiff Insurance.

He is a VCI certified instructor of VMware and is certified in VCAP5-DCA.

He is also the owner of Business to Virtual, which specializes in virtualization solutions.

He was also the technical reviewer of the book *Implementing VMware Horizon View 5.2*, Packt Publishing.

> I would like to thank my wife Lina and my daughter Gaia. They're my strength.

Anish Varghese (Panthalani) has been working in the field of IT infrastructure for about a decade now, developing an expertise in VMware, Windows, Linux, and Web hosting. He has earned certifications/completed training in VCP, MSCE, RHCE, CCNA, and ITIL, and is an expert in many technologies. Whether it be IBM X series, Blade Centers, servers, or Enterprise applications; Anish has expert knowledge of all of them. He has expertise in VMware ESX/ESXi, vCenter, Windows Server 2000/2003/2008, Microsoft Active Directory, Exchange 2007/2010, MSSQL, DNS, DHCP, and so on. He is also well versed in backup solutions such as Symantec Netbackup, VEEAM, EVAULT, and PHD Backup.

After completing his B.Sc. degree in Electronics, he completed his postgraduate education at Cochin University of Science and Technology. Then, he joined Religare Securities of Ranbaxy Group, where he was in charge of the Kerala zone, and he later moved on to JRG Securities as an IT Officer. He currently works with UVJ Technologies, Calpine Group as Senior Systems Engineer, where he handles remote infrastructure management as a part of the Global IT team.

He has spent a lot of his time training people on the intricacies of VMware, sharing his valuable experience with fresh talents in the field. He has also been an expert technical blogger (`http://blog.techmaniac.in/`) for many years and has been the forefront of solving technical issues for the online world in the field of IT infrastructure.

I would like to thank all my friends and family members who have been a great encouragement and who have supported me in completing the reviewing of this book. I just can't imagine what I would have done without you all.

www.PacktPub.com

Support files, eBooks, discount offers and more

You might want to visit www.PacktPub.com for support files and downloads related to your book.

Did you know that Packt offers eBook versions of every book published, with PDF and ePub files available? You can upgrade to the eBook version at www.PacktPub.com and as a print book customer, you are entitled to a discount on the eBook copy. Get in touch with us at service@packtpub.com for more details.

At www.PacktPub.com, you can also read a collection of free technical articles, sign up for a range of free newsletters and receive exclusive discounts and offers on Packt books and eBooks.

http://PacktLib.PacktPub.com

Do you need instant solutions to your IT questions? PacktLib is Packt's online digital book library. Here, you can access, read and search across Packt's entire library of books.

Why Subscribe?

- Fully searchable across every book published by Packt
- Copy and paste, print and bookmark content
- On demand and accessible via web browser

Free Access for Packt account holders

If you have an account with Packt at www.PacktPub.com, you can use this to access PacktLib today and view nine entirely free books. Simply use your login credentials for immediate access.

Instant Updates on New Packt Books

Get notified! Find out when new books are published by following @PacktEnterprise on Twitter, or the *Packt Enterprise* Facebook page.

Table of Contents

Preface

Virtualization is a hot topic today. It saves the time and effort of IT professionals, helps to keep the infrastructure costs down, and helps to make the IT industry greener. VMware, one of the major players in the virtualization market, offer great scalability and reliability features, professional support, and constantly work for improvements in their products. VMware vCenter Server is a necessary component for any professional vSphere implementation. It offers a great variety of features and capabilities that simplify an administrator's day-to-day work.

This book is a practical and hands-on guide to VMware vCenter Server that provides descriptions of its features and capabilities as well as useful tips for performing day-to-day administrative tasks.

This book starts with an introduction to VMware vCenter Server, describing the requirements and deployment steps along the way. It then takes you through a description of product features and different aspects of administration, giving useful tips on day-to-day tasks. You will also learn how to deploy VMware vCenter Server and manage hosts and virtual machines. We will take a look at security features, availability, and resource management, and also discuss monitoring and automation topics.

The last two chapters describe additional products that can be used with VMware vCenter Server: VMware vCenter Operations and VMware vCenter Orchestrator. If you want to learn how VMware vCenter Server can help in managing your environment, then this is the book for you.

What this book covers

Chapter 1, vCenter Deployment, gives a brief overview of the features available in vCenter, the terminology used in VMware, vSphere architecture, and the licensing options available for vCenter. The second half of the chapter focuses on the vCenter installation process, including prerequisites and follow-up tasks.

Chapter 2, Managing ESXi Hosts, is devoted to different aspects of host management in vCenter, such as storage support and redundancy, networking concepts incorporated in vSphere, the options available for supporting hosts with different processors, and host profiles.

Chapter 3, Virtual Machine Management, focuses on managing virtual machines in vCenter, time synchronization challenges for a VM's operating system, and VM snapshots.

Chapter 4, Availability Management, describes the features in vCenter that allow you to reduce downtime and make sure your services are available for end users most of the time. The features are vSphere High Availability, Fault Tolerance including host and VM monitoring, datastore heartbeating, and Dynamic Resource Scheduler (DRS).

Chapter 5, Security Management, focuses on users and groups and the logic behind them, user authentication, and roles and permissions. The second part of this chapter is devoted to ESXi firewall, security certificates, and ESXi lockdown mode.

Chapter 6, Resource Management, discusses the different aspects of resource allocation such as shares, reservations, limits, and resource pools. This chapter also covers DRS and power management.

Chapter 7, Events, Alarms, and Automated Actions, focuses on the availability of automation and the monitoring options in vCenter, which includes performance and storage monitoring, possible response actions, scheduled tasks, and the Update Manager plugin.

Chapter 8, VMware vCenter Operations, describes the requirements, installation, and configuration of real-time performance monitoring and management offered by VMware. It also focuses on the way this software is organized and the logic behind it.

Chapter 9, VMware vCenter Orchestrator, gives a brief overview of VMware vCenter Orchestrator, its requirements, and the installation process—initial configurations, networking, LDAP, database connectivity, and SSL security. It also describes several administration aspects of vCenter Orchestrator, such as workflows, elements, and actions.

What you need for this book

You do not need to have prior experience with any software in order to read this book, but a working knowledge of the following would be good to have:

- ESXi 4.1 or later

- vCenter Server 4.1 or later

- VMware vCenter Orchestrator 4.2 or later

- VMware Operations 5 or later

Who this book is for

This book is useful for administrators and technicians who are only starting just getting started with VMware or who already have some experience with other virtualization products. It is beneficial for IT professionals who are working on expanding their existing environment and are concerned about being able to manage it better. IT managers will also find it helpful in terms of improving cost efficiency, ensuring required levels of service, and its reporting abilities.

Conventions

In this book, you will find a number of styles of text that distinguish between different kinds of information. Here are some examples of these styles, and an explanation of their meaning.

Code words in text are shown as follows: "The `.crt` file contains the certificate and the `.key` file contains the private key."

New terms and **important words** are shown in bold. Words that you see on the screen, in menus or dialog boxes for example, appear in the text like this: "To create a new connection, click on **Add**, select **SQL Native client**, and then click on **Finish**."

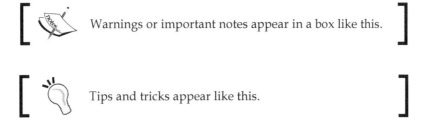

Warnings or important notes appear in a box like this.

Tips and tricks appear like this.

Reader feedback

Feedback from our readers is always welcome. Let us know what you think about this book—what you liked or may have disliked. Reader feedback is important for us to develop titles that you really get the most out of.

To send us general feedback, simply send an e-mail to feedback@packtpub.com, and mention the book title via the subject of your message.

If there is a topic that you have expertise in and you are interested in either writing or contributing to a book, see our author guide on www.packtpub.com/authors.

Customer support

Now that you are the proud owner of a Packt book, we have a number of things to help you to get the most from your purchase.

Errata

Although we have taken every care to ensure the accuracy of our content, mistakes do happen. If you find a mistake in one of our books—maybe a mistake in the text or the code—we would be grateful if you would report this to us. By doing so, you can save other readers from frustration and help us improve subsequent versions of this book. If you find any errata, please report them by visiting http://www.packtpub.com/submit-errata, selecting your book, clicking on the **errata submission form** link, and entering the details of your errata. Once your errata are verified, your submission will be accepted and the errata will be uploaded on our website, or added to any list of existing errata, under the Errata section of that title. Any existing errata can be viewed by selecting your title from http://www.packtpub.com/support..

Piracy

Piracy of copyright material on the Internet is an ongoing problem across all media. At Packt, we take the protection of our copyright and licenses very seriously. If you come across any illegal copies of our works, in any form, on the Internet, please provide us with the location address or website name immediately so that we can pursue a remedy.

Please contact us at `copyright@packtpub.com` with a link to the suspected pirated material.

We appreciate your help in protecting our authors, and our ability to bring you valuable content.

Questions

You can contact us at `questions@packtpub.com` if you are having a problem with any aspect of the book, and we will do our best to address it.

vCenter Deployment

1

This chapter gives a brief overview of the features available in vCenter. We will discuss the common terminologies used in VMware and vSphere architecture and the licensing options available for vCenter.

The second half of the chapter focuses on the vCenter installation process, prerequisites, and follow-up tasks.

In this chapter, we will cover:

- vCenter; its functions and capabilities
- vSphere, ESX, ESXi, hypervisor, and VMFS
- The VMware licensing model
- vCenter system requirements
- vSphere physical topology
- The installation process, Linked Mode groups, and database configuration
- How to access vCenter

vCenter is a tool for the centralized management of the **vSphere** suite. It allows managing multiple **ESX/ESXi** servers and VMs through a single console application. The tool makes it easier to manage large and complex virtual environments. A single administrator can manage hundreds of workloads and be more productive in managing physical infrastructure. vCenter is required for most of the famous and important vSphere features such as vMotion, Storage vMotion, Fault Tolerance, High Availability, and **Distributed Resource Scheduler** (**DRS**).

vCenter Orchestrator that comes with vCenter, gives the user the ability to easily create and manage workflows and automate tasks.

vCenter allows dynamically provisioning new services, balancing resources, and automating high availability. With its open-plugin architecture, it allows adding additional capabilities from VMware and its partners by integrating plugins that provide new features; for example, capacity management, compliance management, business continuity, and storage monitoring.

With vCenter Server APIs, it's possible to integrate third-party physical and virtual management tools.

Key vCenter functions and capabilities

vCenter performs the following three main functions:

- **Visibility**: vCenter allows configuring hosts and VMs and monitoring their performance. It provides an in-depth visibility into configuring all critical components on every level of your virtual infrastructure. Administrators can use events, alerts, and the scheduler. vCenter allows managing environment securely with users, groups, and roles.
- **Scalability**: Visibility is scalable across multiple hosts and virtual machines.
- **Automation**: With vCenter Server alerts, you can trigger actions. Orchestrator allows automation of hundreds of actions.

The main features of vCenter are:

- **vCenter Server Appliance (vCSA)**: It allows you to quickly deploy vCenter Server and manage vSphere using a Linux-based virtual appliance.
- **vSphere Web Client**: It allows you to manage vSphere from any supported web browser:
    - For vSphere Web Client 5.0: Internet Explorer 7, 8 and Mozilla Firefox 3.6
    - For vSphere Web Client 5.1: Internet Explorer 7, 8, and 9; Mozilla Firefox 3.6 or later; Google Chrome 14 or later.
- **Hardware monitoring**: Using the CIM SMASH technology, it provides information about physical and virtual server health and alarms when hardware failure occurs, including fan, system board, or power supply failure.
- **Storage maps and reports**: It provides information about storage usage, connectivity, and configuration.
- **Customizable topology views**: It provides visibility into storage infrastructure and assistance in diagnosis and troubleshooting of storage issues.
- **Host profiles**: It allows simplifying the host configuration and monitor compliance.

- **vCenter Single Sign-On**: It provides users the ability to log in once and then access all instances of vCenter Server and vCloud Director without the need for further authentication. This is a new feature in vCenter 5.1 and requires at least one vCenter 5.1 server.

- **Resource management**: It allows managing resource shares for CPU, memory, disk, and networking bandwidth; modifying allocations while virtual machines are running; and enabling applications to dynamically acquire more resources when needed.

- **Dynamic allocation of resources**: It provides the ability to continuously monitor resource utilization and automatically reallocate available resources among virtual machines according to predefined rules.

- **Energy efficient resource optimization**: It reduces power consumption by consolidating workloads and putting hosts in the standby mode and brings back powered-down hosts online when more resources are needed.

- **Automatic restart of virtual machines**: It provides an easy and cost-effective failover solution.

- **Fine-grained access control**: It allows securing environments with groups and fine-grained permissions.

- Microsoft Active Directory or **Network Information Service** (**NIS**) integration.

- **Custom roles and permissions**: It enhances security and flexibility for user-defined roles.

- **Audit trails**: It maintains a record of configuration changes and allows exporting reports for event tracking.

- **Session management**: It allows discovering and, if necessary, terminating VMware vCenter Server user sessions.

- **Patch management**: It provides the ability to install updates and upgrades through automated scanning and patching of online VMware ESXi hosts.

- **VMware vCenter Orchestrator**: It simplifies management by providing the ability to automate over 800 administrative tasks.

- **VMware vCenter Multi-Hypervisor Manager**: It extends centralized management to Hyper-V hosts. This feature can be added by installing an additional plugin, which can be downloaded from the Download VMware vSphere 5.1 Update 1 page.

- **VMware vCenter Operations Manager Foundation**: It provides additional visibility into performance and health of the vSphere infrastructure.

- **Linked Mode**: It provides additional scalability and visibility across multiple vCenter Server instances with roles, permissions, and licenses only replicated across the infrastructure.

VMware terminologies – vSphere, ESX, ESXi, hypervisor, and VMFS

There is a lot of confusion out there regarding VMware terminology. Part of the issue is that VMware has been changing terminology with every new version. In this section, we'll describe a few important terms that are widely used and which will also be used in this book.

VMware vSphere is VMware's server virtualization suite. This software bundle was called VMware Infrastructure 3 (VI3). When VMware Infrastructure 3.5 (VI3.5) was in development, vSphere was considered as an advanced suite of tools utilizing VMware ESX/ESXi4. At the same time, VMware was developing VMware Infrastructure 4 and eventually vSphere 4 was announced and released in May 2009 instead of VI4.

In November 2009, Update 1 for vSphere 4 was released with support for Windows 7 and Windows Server 2008 R2.

vSphere 4.1 became available in August 2010. This version included an updated vCenter Configuration Manager and vCenter Application Discovery Manager as well as vMotion capability.

Update 1 for vSphere 4.1 was released in February 2011 with added support for **Red Hat Enterprise Linux (RHEL)** 6, RHEL 5.6, SLES 11 SP1, Ubuntu 10.10, and Solaris 10 Update 9.

On July 12, 2011, VMware released Version 5 of VMware vSphere.

On August 27, 2012, VMware released its latest version of the suite; that is, VMware vSphere 5.1. This update extends vSphere to also include VMware vSphere Storage Appliance, vSphere Data Protection, vSphere Replication, and vShield Endpoint.

Depending on the version and license, vSphere includes, but is not limited to, the following features:

- ESX/ESXi hypervisor
- Distributed Resource Scheduler
- **High Availability (HA)**
- **Fault Tolerance (FT)**
- vMotion
- Storage vMotion
- vSphere Storage DRS

- **Virtual Machine File System (VMFS)**
- Resource Pools
- VMware Update Manager
- VMware View
- vCenter Server
- VMware vSphere Client
- VMware vSphere Web Client
- VMware vSphere SDKs
- Virtual SMP
- **vSphere Distributed Switch (VDS)**
- Host Profiles

More information on most of these features is available in the following chapters. In the following section, we will give their brief overview.

ESX/ESXi is a bare metal-embedded hypervisor. It runs on the virtualization layer that abstracts physical server resources, such as CPU, memory, and storage, into multiple virtual machines.

Hypervisor is a software or hardware that creates and runs virtual machines. The computer it's running on is called the host. Virtual machines are often referred to as guests. A hypervisor allows guest operating systems to run with an appearance of full access to underlying systems. During this process, the system's resources that are shared among multiple virtual machines and are accessed by VMs are under the complete control of the hypervisor.

There are two types of hypervisors:

- Type 1 or bare metal hypervisor, which runs directly on the host's hardware and controls hardware as well as manages virtual machines.
- Type 2 or hosted hypervisor runs on top of the conventional operating system. In this case, guest operating systems run at the third level above the hardware.

An embedded hypervisor is a type 1 hypervisor that supports the requirements of embedded systems development. Embedded systems, in contrast with general purpose computers that are supposed to meet a wide range of requirements, are designed for specific control functions within larger systems. Often, real-time constraints have to be addressed as well.

The hypervisor requirements suitable for embedded applications are quite different from the hypervisor requirements aimed at enterprise applications. These requirements are briefly summarized as follows:

- A small, fast type 1 hypervisor with support for multiple VMs
- Support for lightweight but secure encapsulation of medium-grain subsystem components that interact strongly
- High-bandwidth, low-latency communication between system components subject to a configurable, system-wide security policy
- Minimal impact on system resources and real-time performance
- Ability to implement a scheduling policy between VMs and provide support for real-time system components

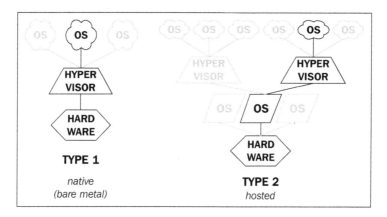

The description of the previously mentioned features of vSphere is as follows:

- **DRS** provides the ability to continuously monitor resource usage across environments and dynamically reallocate available resources between virtual machines. With DRS, administrators are able to dynamically reallocate resources according to business needs, balance computing capacity as well as reduce power consumption in the datacenter. Power consumption can be reduced using vSphere **Distributed Power Management** (**DPM**). It consolidates workloads onto fewer servers and turns off the rest. Later, when more resources are needed, DPM brings back these hosts online to utilize them.

- The **High Availability** feature automatically restarts VMs on other hosts in case of a host failure. This provides an easy and cost-effective availability solution.

- **Fault Tolerance** in turn provides continuous availability. With HA in case of a host failure, VMs are restarted on another host, which means that these VMs are not available for a short period of time. Fault Tolerance creates a shadow copy of a VM, which is used for failover in case of a failure.

- **vMotion** allows the migration of running virtual machines from one server (host) to another without downtime. These migrations are completely transparent for users and can be used for maintenance and optimizing the infrastructure without disrupting business operations.

- **Storage vMotion** allows the migration of running VMs to another storage array without any downtime. It simplifies storage upgrades and migrations, allows better and easier management of storage capacity, and storage I/O performance.

- **vSphere Storage DRS** offers load balancing mechanisms based on storage I/O and space usage. With Storage DRS, administrators are able to aggregate several datastores into a single cluster. This simplifies management and allows using available storage resources more efficiently.

- **VMFS** is used by ESX/ESXi servers to store virtual machine disks and snapshots. It is designed so that individual virtual machine files can be locked. This allows multiple servers to do read/write operations on the same filesystem simultaneously. Multiple VMFS volumes can be spanned together which allows you to logically grow volumes without losing any data stored on these volumes.

- **Resource Pool** is a logical group of CPU and memory resources. It allows having more control over partitioning available resources among virtual machines as well as meeting service levels.

- **VMware Update Manager** is a patch management software. With Update Manager, administrators can test and deploy updates for ESX/ESXi hosts as well as for guest operating systems.

- **VMware View** helps to simplify and automate management of multiple desktops and deliver them as a service to users from one central location. This solution addresses increased requirements for scalability and mobility for end users, allows having more control over desktops, and at the same time, decreases costs by centrally delivering services from your cloud.

- **vCenter Server**—the subject of this book—is a centralized management solution for vSphere suite.

- **VMware vSphere Client** enables access to vCenter or ESX/ESXi hosts from any Windows machine.

- **VMware vSphere Web Client** is a cross-platform client for vCenter so that users can access it using a web browser under different operating systems.

- **VMware vSphere SDKs** provide development tools for creating vSphere Client applications that use vSphere APIs and allow managing infrastructure components such as datacenters, datastores, and networks.

- **Virtual SMP** is the utility that allows a virtual machine to use two or more available host CPUs at the same time.

- **vSphere Distributed Switch** (**VDS**) simplifies virtual machine network configuration and offers advanced network monitoring and troubleshooting capabilities by providing a centralized interface for virtual machine access switching setup.

- **Host Profiles** allow administrators to define host configuration policies to simplify host configuration management for large datacenter environments.

The most important features previously mentioned are summarized in the following diagram:

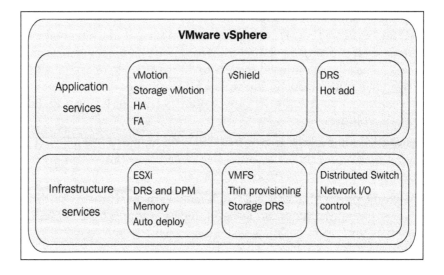

vSphere component layers

The VMware software stack consists of three layers: virtualization, management, and interface. The relationship between these layers is shown in the following figure:

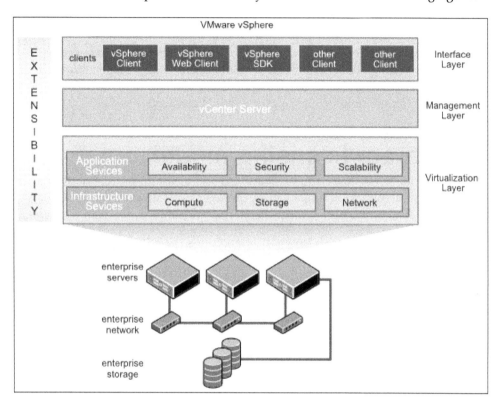

The virtualization layer of VMware vSphere consists of infrastructure services and application services. Infrastructure services abstract, aggregate, and allocate all hardware and other resources. Infrastructure services include:

- **Compute services**: These services are VMware capabilities that abstract away from underlying server resources. Compute services also aggregate these resources across many servers and assign them to consumers such as virtual machines.

- **Storage services**: These services are a set of technologies that are used to provide the most efficient use and management of storage resources across your virtual environment.

- **Network services**: These services are a set of technologies that simplify and enhance networking for virtual environments.

Application services are designed to ensure availability, security, and scalability for applications; for example, features such as vSphere High Availability and Fault Tolerance.

The management layer is represented by VMware vCenter Server, which is the main central point for configuring, provisioning, and managing your virtual environment.

The interface layer is where user access to vSphere happens. Users can access the environment using GUI clients such as vSphere Client or vSphere Web Client. Also, users can access the datacenter using command-line interfaces or SDKs for automated management or third-party product connections.

The VMware licensing model

vCenter Server comes in two editions: Standard and Foundation. Foundation is designed for small- and middle-sized environments and can manage up to three hosts. The Standard edition is for large vSphere deployments.

VMware vCenter Server Foundation edition includes the following capabilities:

- Management service
- Database server
- Inventory service
- VMware vSphere Clients
- VMware vCenter APIs and .NET
- vCenter Single Sign-On

VMware vCenter Server Standard Edition includes all the capabilities of vCenter Server Foundation plus the following capabilities:

- **vCenter Orchestrator**: It automates key processes.
- **vCenter Server Linked Mode**: It enables a common inventory view across multiple instances of vCenter Server

vCenter Server has to be purchased separately on a per-instance basis.

vCenter Server can also be purchased as part of VMware vSphere Essentials Kit. It supports up to three hosts with up to two processors per host, includes one license for vCenter Server Essentials, and is a great starter kit for small businesses.

VMware vSphere Essentials Bundle includes the following:

- VMFS
- 8-way Virtual SMP
- VMware Hypervisor
- VMware vStorage Thin Provisioning
- VMware Update Manager
- VMware vCenter Server Essentials

VMware vSphere Essentials Plus Kit includes all the benefits of Essentials and the following additional benefits:

- VMware vSphere Storage Appliance for Essentials Plus
- VMware Data Protection
- VMware High Availability
- VMware vMotion
- VMware vShield Zones
- VMware vShield Endpoint
- VMware Replication

There is an option to purchase the support plan along with the software. The basic support plan is meant for non-critical environments that require support only during business hours. The production plan offers global 24 x 7 support for production environments where a fast response time is required for critical issues.

Both plans include an unlimited number of support requests and remote support as well as product updates and upgrades.

It is important to remember that vCenter Server is an additional product that is licensed separately from vSphere on a per-instance basis, while vSphere is licensed per processor. vSphere 4.1 has additional restrictions for the number of cores per CPU as well as memory capacity per host (see the following list); vSphere 5 licensing removes all these restrictions.

vSphere 4.1 additional licensing restrictions are as follows:

- Cores per processor:
  - 6 cores for Standard, Enterprise, ESS, and ESS+ editions.
  - 12 cores for Advanced and Enterprise Plus editions.

- Physical RAM capacity per host:

    ○ 256 GB for Standard, Advanced, Enterprise, ESS, and ESS+ editions.
    ○ Unlimited for the Enterprise Plus edition

A review of vSphere editions is out of the scope of this book. More information can be found on the VMware website and in the *VMware vSphere Licensing, Pricing and Packaging* white paper in particular.

The VMware license key is a 25-character alphanumeric string that contains encrypted information about the software edition purchased and restrictions such as processor quantity for vSphere. It doesn't contain any server or hardware-specific information. This means that the same license key can be assigned to multiple vSphere hosts as long as the quantity of physical processor on these hosts doesn't exceed the quantity included with the license.

vCenter Server is the recommended interface for managing vSphere licenses. When a license key is installed in vCenter, it's copied to the host and kept there in the persistent format. The license key remains active after the host is rebooted or disconnected from vCenter Server. If a key needs to be removed or replaced, it has to be done manually by the administrator.

Planning the vSphere environment

According to VMware documentation, vCenter Server setup is an optional step for vSphere deployment. As you will see later in this book, however, vCenter offers a huge amount of features and options for managing the vSphere environment. It also simplifies management and adds flexibility. It's useful for any administrator and/or environment no matter how large or small. It's fair to say that vCenter is an essential component of every professional vSphere deployment and for each more or less critical environment.

vCenter 5.0 deployment consists of the following tasks:

- Setting up vCenter Server databases.
- Installing vCenter Server and vCenter Server support tools. Connecting to vCenter Server from the vSphere Client or the vSphere Web Client.
- As an optional step, creating a Linked Mode group or joining vCenter Server to a Linked Mode group.

vCenter 5.1 deployment consists of the following tasks:

- Setting up vCenter Server databases.
- Installing vCenter Single Sign-On, Inventory Service, vCenter Server, and vCenter Server support tools. Connecting to vCenter Server from the vSphere Client or the vSphere Web Client.
- As an optional step, creating a Linked Mode group or joining vCenter Server to a Linked Mode group.

More information on each of these steps will follow.

vCenter system requirements

Before starting vCenter deployment, you need to make sure that all prerequisites and requirements are met.

The vCenter Server hardware requirements are:

- At least two 64-bit CPUs or one 64-bit dual-core CPU.
- At least one 2 GHz CPU. This requirement will be higher if the database is running on the same server.
- An Intel or AMD processor. Itanium-based CPUs are not supported.
- At least 4 GB of memory. This requirement will be higher if the database is running on the same server.
- At least 4 GB of available disk space. This requirement will be higher if the database is running on the same server.
- An additional 2 GB of free space to decompress Microsoft SQL Server 2008 R2 Express temporary installation files.
- A gigabit network connection is recommended.

JVM heap requirements as well as memory, CPU, and disk requirements for vCenter Server, depending on the size of environment, can be found in the VMware documentation at `https://pubs.vmware.com/vsphere-50/index.jsp?topic=%2Fcom.vmware.vsphere.install.doc_50%2FGUID-67C4D2A0-10F7-4158-A249-D1B7D7B3BC99.html`.

If you choose to use VMware vCenter Server Appliance, make sure you have a host that is running at least Version 4 of ESX or ESXi system.

Hardware requirements for VMware vCenter Server Appliances are listed in the VMware documentation at `https://pubs.vmware.com/vsphere-50/index.jsp?topic=%2Fcom.vmware.vsphere.install.doc_50%2FGUID-67C4D2A0-10F7-4158-A249-D1B7D7B3BC99.html`.

Recommended JVM heap settings for VMware vCenter Server Appliances can also be found in the VMware documentation at `https://pubs.vmware.com/vsphere-50/index.jsp?topic=%2Fcom.vmware.vsphere.install.doc_50%2FGUID-67C4D2A0-10F7-4158-A249-D1B7D7B3BC99.html`.

The vCenter Server software requirements are as follows:

- A 64-bit operating system:
    ◦ Microsoft Windows Server 2003 Standard, Enterprise, or Datacenter SP2 64-bit
    ◦ Microsoft Windows Server 2003 Standard, Enterprise, or Datacenter R2 64-bit
    ◦ Microsoft Windows Server 2008 Standard, Enterprise, or Datacenter SP2 64-bit
    ◦ Microsoft Windows Server 2008 Standard, Enterprise, or Datacenter R2 SP1 64-bit
    ◦ Microsoft Windows Server 2008 Standard, Enterprise, or Datacenter R2 64-bit
    ◦ Microsoft Windows Server 2008 Standard, Enterprise, or Datacenter SP1 64-bit
- 64-bit DSN to connect to the database.
- Microsoft .NET 3.5 SP1 Framework (if missing, it will be installed by the vCenter Server installer automatically).
- For non-English operating systems, the Microsoft .NET Framework 3.5 Language Pack needs to be installed manually via Windows update. vCenter Server installer will not install it automatically.
- Microsoft Windows Installer Version 4.5 (MSI 4.5) is required if Microsoft SQL Server 2008 R2 Express database will be used.

vSphere physical topology

A common VMware vSphere datacenter physical topology is shown in the following figure. It may be useful for better understanding of the different vSphere components and the relationships between them.

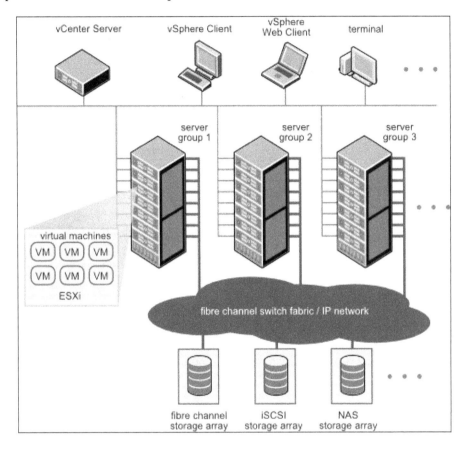

There are three interfaces that can be used to manage the vSphere environment and access virtual machines: VMware vSphere Client (vSphere Client), vSphere Web Client for access through a web browser, and vSphere Command-Line Interface (vSphere CLI). They are shown on top of the preceding figure.

Computing servers are shown at the center of the preceding figure. Each computing server is an ESX or ESXi host with one or multiple virtual machines running on it. When there are two or more hosts, they can be grouped into clusters to provide an aggregate set of resources and to take advantage of features such as fault tolerance, high availability, and so on.

Storage networks and arrays are shown at the bottom of the preceding figure. Depending on the environment, there may be Fibre Channel SAN arrays, iSCSI SAN arrays, NAS arrays, or their combinations. Storage arrays are usually connected to computing servers, and in most cases, they are connected through a separate network—**Storage Area Network** (**SAN**). This is often referred to as a third network after the management network, and it's also called the network or networks virtual machines are part of.

vCenter Server is shown as a separate physical server. Depending on how your infrastructure was designed, it can also be a virtual server located in one of the server groups. When vCenter is separate, computing servers continue to function in case vCenter Server becomes unreachable and the other way round. If one or few of the computing servers go down, you are still able to manage the rest of the environment using vCenter Server.

Virtual versus physical vCenter Server

There are two approaches to the deployment of vCenter Server: it can be deployed on a virtual server or on a physical server. As an alternative to installing vCenter on your own Windows server, vSphere 5.0 provides VMware vCenter Server Appliance. vCenter Server Appliance is a Linux-based virtual machine configured and optimized for running vCenter Server and its services.

If you choose to use it instead of building a server by yourself, make sure all prerequisites mentioned in the previous section are met, download the appliance, and import it using the Deploy OVF template option from the **File** menu. The import procedure is straightforward. You can deploy **Open Virtualization Format** (**OVF**) with thin provisioning if you are not able or don't want to commit 80 GB to the server.

For vCenter Server Appliance, the default username and password are:

- Username: `root`
- Password: `vmware`

It's important to know that vCenter Server Appliance does not support the following:

- Microsoft SQL Server and IBM DB2. Version 5.0.1 of the vCenter Server Appliance uses PostgreSQL for the embedded database instead of IBM DB2, which was used in vCenter Server Appliance 5.0.
- Linked Mode configuration.
- IPv6.

The embedded database cannot be used for managing more than five hosts and 50 virtual machines. If the embedded database is used with vCenter Server Appliance, it will exceed the limits mentioned earlier. Exceeding these limits can cause different performance issues; for example, vCenter Server may become unresponsive. Therefore, the embedded database is not supported for production environments.

The advantages of using virtual machines for vCenter Server are obvious and are listed as follows:

- Since no additional hardware is needed to run it, administrators don't need to buy a server and dedicate it to vCenter and are able to save on power and space in the datacenter

- Administrators will be able to provide high availability to vCenter Server with vSphere HA

- A vCenter Server virtual machine can be migrated from one host to another, giving administrators the flexibility to do maintenance and other activities

- Virtual machine snapshots can be used for backup, archiving, and so on

It is not recommended to use snapshots for long term backups as well as having many snapshots for a virtual machine. Large snapshots may decrease performance and cause other issues. See *Chapter 3, Virtual Machine Management*, for more details.

Virtual machines are easier to manage; so, in other words, you get all the advantages related to virtualization while deploying vCenter on a virtual server.

From the other side, running a virtualized vCenter has certain concerns. One of them is ESXi updates when there is only one host in your environment.

To be able to install updates, a host needs to be put into the maintenance mode. The host can't have any VMs running in the maintenance mode; therefore, all VMs need to be turned off or moved off the host. For environments with only one host, administrators have no choice other than turning all VMs off. However, Update Manager is a vCenter plugin, so you will not be able to run or install updates when vCenter Server is not online. In this case, you will have to download and install ESXi updates manually from the server's command-line interface. Many administrators find installing updates manually more time consuming and in certain cases more difficult.

Another concern with virtual vCenter Server is its accessibility in case of issues and failures. For example, if the host where the vCenter Server VM is currently running fails, and for some reason not all VMs were restarted on another host, vCenter Server becomes inaccessible until this host is back online or at least until its connectivity is restored. Thus, the administrator can move the vCenter VM manually to another host. Of course, the administrator can always connect to other hosts directly using vSphere Client; certain features, however, require vCenter, and it may be unacceptable for larger environments to not be able to manage vSphere and other hosts because of one host failure.

The bigger picture is that when you are running vCenter on a virtual machine, any issues with your vSphere environment are affecting vCenter as well. Many administrators will say that this is not desirable as in case of any issues, you still want to manage your environment and diagnose and troubleshoot these issues.

Installing the Management Suite

Once all hardware and software prerequisites are met, before running the installer, make sure that:

- The server's name complies with RFC 952 guidelines and contains not more than 15 characters.

- The server's **fully qualified domain name (FQDN)** can be resolved into an IP address using `ping` or `nslookup` and the server's name matches the DNS entry.

- There is an appropriate PTR record for the server's IP address so that it can be resolved back to FQDN.

- The server's IP address is assigned statically so that clients don't run into any issues trying to connect to vCenter.

 vCenter will use IPv6 if the server it's installed on is configured to use IPv6. In this case, the server's IP address should be specified in the IPv6 format when you connect to vCenter or install additional modules.

- The installation path you will use does not contain any of the following characters: non-ASCII characters, commas (,), periods (.), exclamation points (!), pound signs (#), at signs (@), or percentage signs (%).

- There is no **Network Address Translation (NAT)** between the network that vCenter Server will be a part of and the network where hosts will be managed.

- There is a connection between the server and the domain controller. vCenter can be installed on a server that is a part of a workgroup as well; however, not all functionality will be available in this case.

- The server is not a domain controller itself.

- The user account that is used to install vCenter has the following permissions:

  ○ Member of the Administrators group

  ○ Act as part of the operating system

  ○ Log on as a service

> It is recommended to use a Windows account to run vCenter Service. This account can be used to connect to the SQL database and also provides more security than the System account built into Windows. This user must be the local administrator on the server and the SQL server has to be configured to allow Windows authentication.

- The NETWORK SERVICE account has access to the folder where vCenter Server will be installed as well as to the HKLM registry branch.

vCenter Server and vSphere Update Manager require the database server to store its data, and each vCenter Server instance requires its own database. Also, it is recommended to use separate databases for vCenter Server and Update Manager.

vCenter can use DB2, Oracle, or MS SQL database. Microsoft SQL Server 2008 R2 Express can be used for smaller deployments—up to five hosts and up to 50 virtual machines. It will be installed during vCenter setup if you select the bundled database during installation. It's not supported for production environments however. Microsoft SQL Server 2005 or 2008 can be used for larger deployments.

For any supported databases, vCenter needs a 64-bit System DSN. If you are using the Microsoft SQL Server database on a different server, System DNS can be created by navigating to **Control Panel | Administrative Tools | Data Sources (ODBC)**. In the ODBC settings window, go to the **System DSN** tab. From there, you can either modify the existing ODBC connection or create a new one. To create a new connection, click on **Add**, select **SQL Native client**, and then click on **Finish**.

In the next step, enter the ODBC data source name, an optional description, and the SQL Server name. You may need to type the name in the dropbox if it's not listed there.

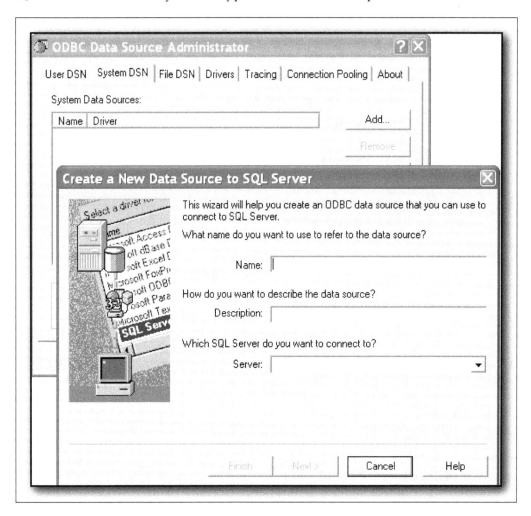

In the next step, choose either **Integrated Windows Authentication** or **SQL Server authentication** and enter the username and password if necessary. Select the database that will be used and then click on **Finish**. There is also an option to test the connection.

If you don't have a database ready yet, please refer to the section about setting up a database later in this chapter.

If the server name has been changed, make sure System DSN is configured to use the new name.

Once the vCenter Server database is in use, it's a good idea to perform standard database maintenance regularly. The suggested maintenance tasks are:

- Monitoring the growth of the logfile and compacting it as needed
- Scheduling regular backups of the database
- Backing up the database before any vCenter Server upgrades

Keep in mind that when you install vCenter Server, there are other components that will be installed as well. A list of the components that are installed by default can be found in the VMware documentation at `http://pubs.vmware.com/vsphere-51/index.jsp?topic=%2Fcom.vmware.vsphere.install.doc%2FGUID-78933728-7F02-43AF-ABD8-0BDCE10418A6.html`.

The vCenter Server that is installed is usually downloaded as a ZIP archive. Once it's downloaded and unzipped, run `autorun.exe` and select **vCenter Server**.

The next steps of the installation wizard are straightforward. You will be prompted to choose the installer language, accept the end user and license agreement, and enter your username, organization name, and license key.

The license key can be omitted in this step. In this case, vCenter Server will be in the evaluation mode that allows you to use the full feature set for a 60-day evaluation period. You will be able to enter the license key later and convert vCenter Server to the licensed mode.

In the next step, choose the type of database that you want to use:

- To use the bundled database, click on **Install a Microsoft SQL Server 2008 Express instance**. This option should be used only for small-scale deployments; up to five hosts and 50 virtual machines.
- To use an existing database, click on **Use an existing supported database** and select your database from the list of available DSNs. Enter the username and password for the DSN.

> A dialog box might appear warning you that the DSN points to an older version of a repository that must be upgraded. If you click on **Yes**, the installer upgrades the database schema making the database irreversibly incompatible with previous VirtualCenter versions.

In the next step, you'll need to set the login information for vCenter Server:

- For a non-bundled database, enter the administrator name and password that you use when you log in to the system where vCenter Server is being installed. This username and password will be needed to log in to vCenter Server after it's installed.

- If you are using the bundled SQL Server database, select **Use SYSTEM Account**.

In the next step, the **Fully Qualified Domain Name** field of the system that you are installing vCenter Server on is displayed. The installer checks that this FQDN is resolvable. A warning message will be displayed if FQDN is not resolvable. This is a requirement, so you may need to change the entry to a resolvable one. FQDN has to be entered in this step, not an IP address.

In the next step, you can either accept the default destination folders or click on **Change** to select another location.

Moving forward, select **Create a standalone VMware vCenter Server instance** or **Join Group**. When joining a Linked Mode group, you can enable vSphere Client to view, search, and manage data across multiple vCenter Server systems.

 This option is not available when upgrading VirtualCenter or the vCenter Server database schema. You will be able to join a Linked Mode group after the upgrade is complete.

If you join a group, enter the fully qualified domain name and LDAP port number of any remote vCenter Server system. The installer will allow entering IP address as well. However, to make sure that you don't run into any issues in future if the IP address changes, it is recommended to use FQDN.

For IPv6, it's better to use FQDN especially when a local or remote server is not in the IPv6 mode. If the local machine has an IPv4 address and the remote machine has an IPv6 address, make sure the local machine supports IPv4 and IPv6 mixed mode. The domain name server should also be able to resolve both IPv4 and IPv6 addresses if there are servers that use different addressing types in a single Linked Mode group.

In the next step, enter the port numbers that you want to use or accept the default port numbers.

Then, select the size of your vCenter Server inventory, which helps the installer to allocate memory for several Java services that are used by vCenter Server.

This setting determines the maximum JVM heap settings for VMware VirtualCenter Management Webservices (Tomcat), Inventory Service, and Profile-Driven Storage Service. It can also be changed after installation if the number of hosts in your environment changes.

Optionally, choose **Select this option to increase the number of ephemeral ports available** option in the **Ready to Install the Program** window. This option increases the number of available ephemeral ports. In case more than 2000 virtual machines are powered on simultaneously on different hosts managed by vCenter, this option prevents the pool of available ephemeral ports from being exhausted.

Click on **Install**; once installation is done, click on **Finish**.

After vCenter Server is installed, you may need to install additional modules. Some of them are listed as follows:

- **Update Manager**: It allows updating ESX/ESXi hosts as well as guest operating systems. For more details on the Update Manager module, see *Chapter 7, Events, Alarms, and Automated Actions*.

- **vSphere ESXi Dump Collector**: It allows configuring the ESXi server to dump memory to a network server instead of a local disk. It is installed and enabled by default in vCenter Server Appliance.

- **vSphere Syslog Collector**: It enables redirection of ESXi system logs to a remote server on the network.

- **vSphere Auto Deploy**: It helps to provision and customize physical hosts by loading the ESXi image directly into memory.

- **vSphere Authentication Proxy**: It enables ESXi hosts to join a domain without using Active Directory credentials. It eliminates the need to store Active Directory credentials in the host's configuration and therefore increases the security of PXE-booted hosts and hosts that are provisioned using Auto Deploy.

All the previous modules can be installed by selecting the appropriate option from the **Autorun** menu of the vCenter Server installer.

If there is a requirement for strong security, it's recommended to replace default vCenter Server certificates with certificates signed by a trusted **Certificate Authority** (**CA**). If you don't have a certificate yet, you will need to create a **certificate signing request** (**CSR**), submit it to CA, and get a certificate. This can be done with OpenSSL on any Windows or Linux machine. In most cases, OpenSSL needs to be installed on the server.

Once you receive the certificate, you will need to export it as a `.pfx` file, which combines the certificate and private key. This can be accomplished using the following command:

```
openssl pkcs12 -export -in <name>.crt -inkey <name>.key -name <name>
-passout pass:testpassword -out <name>.pfx
```

The `.crt` file contains the certificate and the `.key` file contains the private key.

If you have a certificate that you can use with vCenter, it's likely a `.pfx` file already, and you will need to split it into the certificate and private key as shown in the following lines of code :

```
openssl.exe pkcs12 -in <name>.pfx -nocerts -out <name>.pem
openssl.exe pkcs12 -in <name>.pfx -clcerts -nokeys -out <name>.pem
```

Eventually, you will have three files: `.crt`, `.key`, and `.pfx`. For vCenter Server 5.0 and later, you must also copy the certificate files to the `vSphere Web Client` directory and to the `Inventory Service` directory. Therefore, these files will need to be placed in the following folders:

- For Windows 2008, the default locations are:
    - `C:\Program Data\VMware\VMware VirtualCenter\SSL`
    - `C:\Program Files\VMware\Infrastructure\Inventory Service\SSL`
    - `C:\Program Files\VMware\Infrastructure\vSphere Web Client\DMServer\config\ssl`

- For Windows 2003, the default locations are:
    - `C:\Documents and Settings\All Users\Application Data\ VMware\VMware VirtualCenter\SSL`
    - `C:\Documents and Settings\All Users\Application Data\ VMware\Infrastructure\Inventory Service\SSL`
    - `C:\Documents and Settings\All Users\VMware\ Infrastructure\vSphere Web Client\DMServer\config\ssl`

Linked Mode groups

A Linked Mode group is a group of vCenter servers. It allows administrators to connect to one of them and manage inventories from all vCenter Servers in the group. vCenter Server can be joined to a group either during or after installation. It can also be joined to multiple Linked Mode groups.

There are a few considerations administrators should be aware of before configuring Linked groups:

- Groups with different versions of vCenter Server are not supported. Therefore, earlier versions of vCenter have to be upgraded before joining a group that has vCenter Server Version 5.

- If you are upgrading vCenter Server that is a part of a Linked Mode group, it will be removed from the group.

- A vCenter user has to have appropriate permissions on the other servers to be able to use them.

- The first vCenter Server of a group has to be installed in the standalone mode. Subsequent servers can be joined to the first one to form a group.

- vCenter Servers that are members of a Linked group should also be members of a domain. The domain user should be added as an administrator. However, servers don't need to use the same domain user.

- If you are joining vCenter Server to a group during installation and entering the IP address of the other server from the group, the IP address will be converted to FQDN. However, it is recommended to use FQDN to avoid any issues that can happen if the IP address is changed.

The following prerequisites should be met for each vCenter Server that needs to be joined to a Linked group:

- A Linked Mode group cannot contain different versions of vCenter Server. Therefore, if you are joining with an older version of vCenter Server, it should be upgraded. You will not be able to join vCenter Server to a group during the upgrade process; it has to be upgraded first and then joined. Also, do not join a Version 5.0 vCenter Server to servers running on earlier versions.

- vCenter Server must be in the evaluation mode or licensed as a Standard edition. vCenter Server Foundation and vCenter Server Essentials editions do not support Linked Mode groups.

- Make sure DNS is operational since it is essential for Linked Mode replication to work.

- If vCenter Servers are members of different domains, there must be a two-way trust relationship between these domains. In other words, if you are joining vCenter Server to a group, its domain must trust the other domains on which vCenter Server instances are installed.

- The user under whom you are running the vCenter Server installer must be a domain user who is an administrator on both the machines: the target vCenter Server machine as well as the one that is joining the group.

- All servers must show the correct time and need to have network time synchronization set up and operating correctly. The vCenter Server installer checks that the machine clocks' times are no more than five minutes apart.

If you are joining vCenter Server to a group after installation, go to **Start | All Programs | VMware** and run vCenter Server Linked Mode Configuration. Follow the wizard prompts.

Select the **Modify linked mode configuration** option, and in the next step, click on **join this vCenter Server instance to an existing linked mode group or another instance** and then click on **Next**.

In the next step, you will be prompted to enter the server name and LDAP port number of a remote vCenter Server instance that is a member of the group.

vCenter Server installer may detect a role conflict. In this case, you will be prompted to choose how to resolve the conflict. There will be two options to choose from:

- **Yes, let VMware vCenter Server resolve the conflicts for me**: The role on the system that is joining the group will be renamed to `vcenter_namerole_name`, where `vcenter_name` is the name of the vCenter Server system that is joining the Linked Mode group and `role_name` is the name of the original role.
- **No, I'll resolve the conflicts myself**: You will need to resolve conflicts manually by renaming the conflicting role.

vCenter Server needs to be restarted after joining a group.

To remove vCenter Server from a Linked Mode group, perform the following steps:

1. Navigate to **Start | All Programs | VMware**.
2. Run **vCenter Server Linked Mode Configuration**.
3. Click on **Modify linked mode configuration**.
4. On the next step, click on **Isolate this vCenter Server instance from linked mode group** and then click on **Next**.
5. Once you click on **Continue** followed by **Finish** and reboot vCenter Server, it will no longer be a part of the group.

Configuring a database for vCenter Server

In case you choose not to use the bundled database option for vCenter Server deployment, there are certain requirements and steps that need to be done to set up a database.

Using Microsoft SQL Server is the most common practice, and further on in this section, we will be assuming this database is used. More information on other supported databases—IBM DB2 and Oracle—can be found in the VMware vCenter Server documentation.

Microsoft SQL Server 2008 R2 Express can be used only as a bundled option for deployments with up to five hosts and 50 virtual machines. If you choose to use Microsoft SQL Server 2005 or Microsoft SQL Server 2008, make sure the machine has a valid ODBC DSN entry.

The first step is to create a database and user. This can be accomplished from Microsoft SQL Server Management Studio using the following script from /<installation directory>/vpx/dbschema/DB_and_schema_creation_scripts_MSSQL.txt:

```
use [master]
go
CREATE DATABASE [VCDB] ON PRIMARY
(NAME = N'vcdb', FILENAME = N'C:\VCDB.mdf', SIZE = 2000KB,
  FILEGROWTH = 10% )
LOG ON
(NAME = N'vcdb_log', FILENAME = N'C:\VCDB.ldf', SIZE = 1000KB,
  FILEGROWTH = 10%)
COLLATE SQL_Latin1_General_CP1_CI_AS
go
use VCDB
go
sp_addlogin @loginame=[vpxuser], @passwd=N'vpxuser!0',
  @defdb='VCDB', @deflanguage='us_english'
go
ALTER LOGIN [vpxuser] WITH CHECK_POLICY = OFF
go
CREATE USER [vpxuser] for LOGIN [vpxuser]
go
use MSDB
go
CREATE USER [vpxuser] for LOGIN [vpxuser]
go
```

Once the database and user have been created, the user needs to be assigned the db_owner role for the database.

The next step is to configure the ODBC connection. As described earlier, this can be done by navigating to **Control Panel | Administrative Tools | Data Sources (ODBC)**.

For vCenter statistics to function properly, the remote SQL server needs TCP/IP to be enabled for the database. To accomplish this, perform the following steps:

1. Navigate to **Start | All Programs | Microsoft SQL Server | Configuration Tool** and click on **SQL Server Configuration Manager**.

2. Navigate to **SQL Server Network Configuration | Protocols for Instance name**.

3. Enable the **TCP/IP** option.

4. Click on **TCP/IP Properties**.

5. In the **Protocol** tab, make the following entries:
   - **Enabled**: Yes
   - **Listen All**: Yes
   - **Keep Alive**: 30000

6. In the **IP Addresses** tab, make the following selections:
   - **Active**: Yes
   - **TCP Dynamic Ports**: 0

7. Restart the SQL Server service by navigating to **SQL Server Configuration Manager | SQL Server Services**.

8. Start the SQL Server Browser service by navigating to **SQL Server Configuration Manager | SQL Server Services**.

Accessing vCenter with vSphere Client

Once vCenter Server is installed, you can go to http://<Your vCenter server IP address or FQDN name> and click on **Download vSphere Client**. vSphere Client installation is straightforward. Make sure the user you are working under has local administrator rights on the machine and the system has an Internet connection.

Run vSphere Client by navigating to **Start | Programs | VMware | VMware vSphere Client** and type vCenter Server's or the host's address; if you are connecting directly to a host, enter the username and password.

You can ignore the security warning that appears. If you are not able to connect, make sure that the VMware VirtualCenter Management Webservices service on the server is running.

Accessing vCenter with web client

vSphere 5 also offers vSphere Web Client, which is an application that provides a browser-based alternative to the traditional vSphere Client. With vSphere Web Client, administrators can use a web browser to connect to vSphere or directly to the ESXi host through a vCenter Server.

In Version 5.1 and later of vSphere, web client becomes a core administrative interface for your virtual environment and comes with additional features not available in vSphere Client, which are listed as follows:

- For vSphere 5.1 and 5.5, hardware Versions 9 and 10 for virtual machines can be chosen only in web client
- Web client in vSphere 5.5 supports drag-and-drop actions for different objects, which gives administrators the ability to perform bulk operations easily
- vSphere 5.5 Web Client also supports filters for the list of displayed objects and recent items that improve navigation through vSphere objects

To install and start vSphere Web Client, you will need the vCenter installer. Launch `autorun.exe`, select the **VMware vSphere® Web Client (Server)** option, and then click on **Install**. Follow the wizard to finish installation. Once it's completed, register one or more vCenter servers on the vSphere Web Client Administration application page in the browser. You will need to use the address in IPv6 format if your vCenter uses an IPv6 address or enter FQDN, which is preferable.

vSphere Client hardware requirements are:

- At least one 500 MHz CPU. 1 GHz processor is recommended
- 500 MB of memory. 1 GB is recommended.
- At least 1 GB of disk space, which includes the space needed for installing the following products:
    ◦ Microsoft .NET 2.0 SP2
    ◦ Microsoft .NET 3.0 SP2
    ◦ Microsoft .NET 3.5 SP1
    ◦ Microsoft Visual J#
    ◦ vSphere Client
- A gigabit network connection is recommended.

vSphere Client requires Microsoft .NET Framework 3.5 SP1. If it is not installed, it will be deployed by the vSphere Client installer.

The operating systems supported by vSphere Client are Windows clients starting from Windows XP Service Pack 2 and Windows servers starting from Windows Server 2003 Service Pack 2.

The vSphere Web Client hardware requirements are:

- At least 2 GB of memory
- At least one 2 GHz processor with four cores

The following browsers are supported by vSphere Web Client 5:

- Microsoft Internet Explorer 7 and 8
- Mozilla Firefox 3.6

vSphere Web Client 5.1 also supports:

- Microsoft Internet Explorer 9
- Mozilla Firefox versions later than 3.6
- Google Chrome 14 or later

The operating systems supported by vSphere Web Client are:

- Microsoft Windows Server 2003 Standard, Enterprise, or Datacenter SP2 64-bit
- Microsoft Windows Server 2003 Standard, Enterprise, or Datacenter R2 SP2 64-bit
- Microsoft Windows Server 2008 Standard, Enterprise, or Datacenter SP2 64-bit
- Microsoft Windows Server 2008 Standard, Enterprise, or Datacenter R2 SP1 64-bit

vSphere Web Client also requires Adobe Flash Player Version 10.1.0 or later to be installed with the appropriate plugin for your browser.

Summary

vCenter is a tool for the centralized management of the vSphere suite. It allows the management of multiple ESX/ESXi servers and VMs through a single-console application.

The VMware software stack consists of three layers: virtualization, management, and interface layers.

vCenter Server comes in two editions: Standard and Foundation. Foundation is designed for small- and middle-sized environments and is able to manage up to three hosts. Standard edition is for large vSphere deployments.

vCenter deployment consists of the following tasks:

- Setting up vCenter Server databases.
- Installing vCenter Server and vCenter Server support tools. Then connect to vCenter Server from the vSphere Client or the vSphere Web Client.
- As an optional step, creating a Linked Mode group or joining vCenter Server to a Linked Mode group.

Before starting vCenter deployment, you need to make sure that all prerequisites and requirements are met.

There are two approaches to the deployment of vCenter Server: it can be deployed on a virtual server or on a physical server.

Virtual machines are easier to manage; so, in other words, you get all the advantages related to virtualization while deploying vCenter on a virtual server.

On the other hand, running virtualized vCenter has certain concerns.

A Linked Mode group is a group of vCenter servers. It allows administrators to connect to one of them and manage inventories from all vCenter Servers in the group.

2
Managing ESXi Hosts

This chapter focuses on different tasks related to host management in vCenter. We will discuss options available for storage, support, and redundancy.

Networking concepts incorporated in vSphere will be a large part of the discussion.

We will also talk about options available for the support of hosts with different processors.

The last part of this chapter is devoted to host profiles; a feature that can greatly simplify host management.

In this chapter, we will cover:

- Adding and removing existing hosts
- Host storage adapters and storage configuration—Fibre Channel, Internet SCSI, **network-attached storage (NAS)**
- Storage **logical unit number (LUNs)** and datastores
- Storage multipathing and failover
- Storage Thin Provisioning
- Network adapters and network configuration
- Virtual switch concept—vSphere Standard and Distributed Switch
- Setting up networking with redundancy
- Managing hosts with different CPUs
- Host profiles—profile workflow, managing profiles, and checking compliance

Adding and removing existing hosts

Once ESXi is installed on a server, connected to your network, and configured, it can be added to vCenter Server so that you can manage it. A host can be added under datacenter, folder, or cluster object. If a host already contains virtual machines, they will be added to the inventory together with the host.

Before adding a host:

- Make sure you have the permission to create a host object
- Make sure that datacenter, folder, or cluster object exist in the inventory
- Make sure you have a username and password with administrative privileges on this host
- Make sure the host is able to communicate with vCenter Server
- Make sure the NFS mounts on the host are active, if applicable

To add a host, select the appropriate object (datacenter, cluster, or folder) in the inventory and navigate to **File** | **New** | **Add host**. You will be prompted to enter the host's IP address and administrative credentials. Optionally, you can choose to enable lockdown mode, which will disable remote access to the host for the administrator account once the host is connected to vCenter.

You can assign a license key to the host if needed. Finally, select an existing resource pool or choose to create a new one in the **Choose Resource Pool** step if you are adding a host to a cluster, or select the location where virtual machines running on the host will be placed. Have a look at the following screenshot.

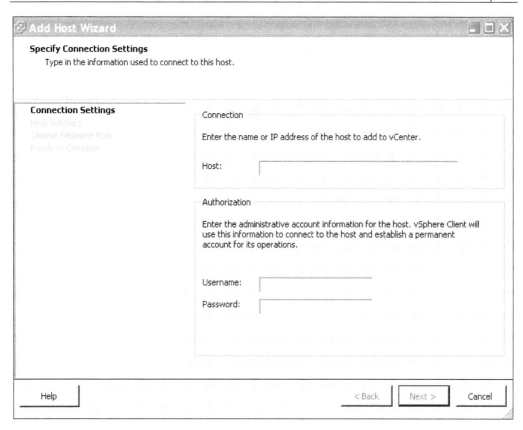

When a host is removed from vCenter, it's removed from the inventory and is not monitored by vCenter anymore. Virtual machines that are on this host will not be managed and monitored by vCenter either. Historical data related to this host, however, remains in the vCenter Server database. Removing a host from vCenter doesn't delete virtual machines that are running on this host. If this host is using a shared datastore to keep virtual disks and other data, it will still be able to use the datastore.

The following screenshot shows the process of removing a host:

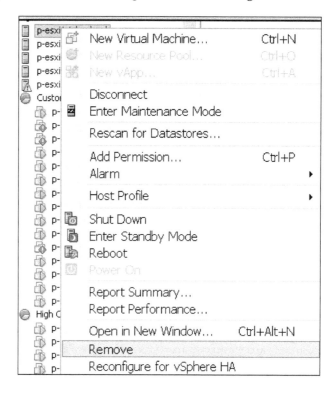

In other words, removing a host from vCenter removes vCenter's access to this host.

To remove a host, right-click on it and select **Remove**. You will need to put it in the maintenance mode if it's a part of the vCenter cluster.

Hosts that are already managed by vCenter Server can be disconnected and reconnected. This is different from adding and removing hosts. Disconnecting a host doesn't remove it from an inventory. When a host is disconnected, vCenter's monitoring activity is stopped. To disconnect or reconnect a host, right-click on it in the inventory and select **Disconnect** or **Connect**. One of these options will be available depending on the host's current state.

Hosts can also be added or removed from a cluster. When a host is not in the cluster, its resources are not a part of the cluster's pool anymore. A host has to be in the maintenance mode before it can be removed from the cluster. If you choose to migrate virtual machines off this host, they will remain in the cluster. If you choose to turn them off and leave them on this host, they will be removed from the cluster together with the host. To remove a host that's in maintenance mode from the cluster, simply drag-and-drop it to a new location.

Storage

ESXi abstracts physical storage from virtual machines by providing host-level storage virtualization. This additional virtualization level gives more flexibility and makes it possible to have storage-related features that are hard to implement with traditional physical servers.

For example, vSphere 5 introduced storage-related features such as:

- **Storage vMotion**: This allows migrating virtual machines between available storages without any downtime

- **Storage Thin Provisioning**: This improves space utilization by allocating available storage capacity between VMs dynamically

- **Storage DRS**: This provides load balancing between available storages based on I/O latency and storage capacity

- **VMFS5**: This is a high-performance filesystem optimized for VMs, and many more

Host storage adapters and storage configuration

The same way physical servers use disk controllers to access attached physical disks, VMs need virtual disc controllers to be able to use virtual disks. The following virtual SCSI controllers exist: BusLogic Parallel, LSI Logic Parallel, LSI Logic SAS, and VMware Paravirtual controllers. From the virtual machine point of view, each virtual disk looks like an SCSI drive attached via the SCSI controller. Each virtual disk is a file stored either on vSphere **Virtual Machine File System** (**VMFS**) datastore, or on NFS datastore. It can also be stored on a raw disk.

The LSI Parallel storage adapter is the most common choice for modern guest operating systems as it performs well and is compatible with many systems. LSI SAS is supported on few operating systems, however, it's faster than LSI Parallel.

The BusLogic Parallel adapter is supported by default on older operating systems (for example, Windows 2000), and is now considered as a legacy adapter. There are very minor differences between BusLogic and LSI Parallel adapters, mostly related to different physical adapters being used.

The **VMware Paravirtual SCSI (PVSCSI)** adapter is considered to be a high performance virtual adapter, which is available for a specific list of guest operating systems. For virtual machines that have high I/O usage, this type of adapter significantly improves performance by increasing the overall storage throughput while reducing CPU utilization. More information on virtual storage adapters, differences between them, and recommendations on when to use different types of adapters can be found in *Chapter 3, Virtual Machine Management*, under the *Creating a new VM* section.

There are different classes of physical adapters supported by ESXi. These include SCSI, iSCSI, RAID, Fibre Channel, Fibre Channel over Ethernet (FCoE), and Ethernet. The adapters are directly accessed by ESXi using VMkernel device drivers.

Sometimes, depending on the storage type being used, appropriate storage adapters may need to be enabled and configured on the host. This can be done from the **Storage Adapters** view in the **Configuration** tab. Storage devices can be viewed under **Devices**, and if you click on paths, you'll be able to view the paths the adapter uses.

There are two types of physical storage: local and networked.

Local storage is usually either internal hard drives installed in the server, or external storage systems connected to the server directly. Protocols that can be used here include SAS or SATA. ESXi doesn't support IDE/ATA or USB drives for a virtual machine store.

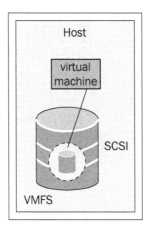

VMFS datastore can be created on such local storage to keep VM disk files. It is not recommended, however, to use local storage for critical environments. First of all, it doesn't provide any redundancy. Also, such storage cannot be shared in case it needs to be used by other hosts.

Networked storage is usually external storage systems used by ESXi to store VM files. Usually, these devices are connected to hosts via the storage network—SAN. In most cases, they are shared between a few hosts.

There are three technologies supported, which will be discussed in detail.

Fibre Channel (FC)

This SAN uses **Fibre Channel Protocol** (**FCP**) for SCSI traffic between hosts and storage devices.

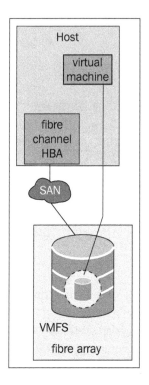

To enable your hosts to connect to FC SAN, Fibre Channel **Host Bus Adapters** (**HBAs**) must be installed on these hosts. In most cases, especially if you need to connect few hosts to the same storage, you'll need to use Fibre Channel switches.

You can also connect Fibre Channel devices via the Ethernet network using **Fibre Channel over Ethernet** (**FCoE**) adapters.

Internet SCSI (iSCSI)

Internet SCSI (**iSCSI**) encapsulates SCSI traffic in the TCP/IP protocol so that it can be transferred through a standard Ethernet network without using any specialized network, such as FC, for this purpose.

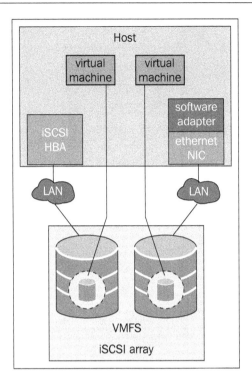

With iSCSI, hosts are initiators that communicate to iSCSI targets. To connect to storage, hosts can use the following devices:

- **iSCSI physical adapters**: These are specialized third-party adapters that are able to offload iSCSI processing tasks off the server.

- **Software iSCSI**: It is a VMkernel software-based initiator. With software iSCSI, hosts need only a regular network adapter.

Network-attached storage (NAS)

With this technology, virtual machine files are stored on remote file servers and are accessed by hosts over the TCP/IP network. ESXi has a built-in NFS client that uses Version 3 of the **Network File System** (**NFS**) protocol for communication with the NFS servers.

All that is required is a standard network adapter.

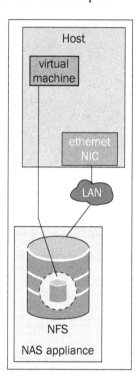

The storage options supported by ESXi are summarized in the following article in the VMware documentation, which is available at `http://pubs.vmware.com/ vsphere-50/index.jsp#com.vmware.vsphere.storage.doc_50/GUID-1FB1AD88- 3E49-4062-8DE5-8246A1DDF3E3.html`.

Networked storage is a recommended way to design your vSphere environment. The benefits of using SAN with ESXi are as follows:

- You can configure multiple paths to storage for redundancy purposes
- You can share your storage between few hosts
- You can use the vMotion feature to perform a live migration of running VMs
- VMware **High Availability** (**HA**) can be used to restart VMs on a different host in case of host failure
- VMware **Fault Tolerance** (**FT**) can help avoid any interruption in service for critical VMs by keeping two copies of such VMs on two different hosts
- With VMware **Distributed Resource Scheduler** (**DRS**), you can perform load balancing between hosts by migrating VMs transparently

All these benefits give you the flexibility to perform maintenance on your vSphere environment with little or no downtime.

Storage LUNs and datastores

In VMware terminology, target means a single storage unit that can be accessed by a host. LUN or device is a logical volume that can be used by a host, in other words, it's a space on the target. Therefore, a target may contain one or more LUNs.

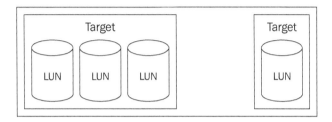

Storage devices connected to a host can be viewed under the **Storage** view in the **Configuration** tab. Click on **Devices** to get a list of available LUNs. Select a specific device from the list to view additional details.

To view devices for a specific adapter, select **Storage Adapters** and click on **Devices**. This is available in the **Hardware** section under the **Configuration** tab.

The following article lists the storage device information available when you review storage devices: `http://pubs.vmware.com/vsphere-50/index.jsp#com.vmware.vsphere.storage.doc_50/GUID-03C15BB7-991E-46FD-948E-83B98743BEC8.html`

It is important to remember that ESXi is not able to access the same LUN via two different protocols, such as iSCSI and FC. If you are designing a new environment or just need to add more storage to existing vSphere, you need to know how to make the right choice when it comes to supported storage technologies.

There are a few things to consider, which are listed as follows:

- **Price**: Generally, FC is more expensive. You need special adapters, cables, and very often, switches, while with iSCSI, you can use regular network adapters and cables.

- **Speed**: FC can run at 1 Gbps, 2 Gbps, 4 Gbps, 8 Gbps, 10 Gbps, and 20 Gbps speeds. Switches and other devices that work at 2 Gbps, 4 Gbps, and 8 Gbps speeds are usually backward compatible with their slower speeds. However, 10 Gbps and 20 Gbps devices are not compatible because they use a different mechanism for frame encoding.

vSphere 5.1 supports FC speeds up to 16 Gbps.

- **Performance**: FCP, the protocol used in FC networks, is optimized for storage traffic, whereas TCP/IP, which is used by iSCSI, is not. Therefore, iSCSI comes second to FC/FCP performance-wise. A small difference in few milliseconds of additional latency because of protocol encapsulation overhead makes a huge difference in environments with high I/O loads. Some experts say that iSCSI is unfit for use in enterprises.

 iSCSI also creates additional load on the CPU unless you use hardware iSCSI HBAs, which unload a server's processor by creating, sending, and interpreting storage commands.

- **Manageability**: Managing FC requires specific knowledge and experience. For example, FC zoning uses World Wide Node and port naming, which are similar to MAC addresses used by Ethernet. They are usually long hexadecimal values that may be difficult to manage.

 Many administrators find iSCSI much easier to deploy. At the same time, it's easier to deploy it incorrectly. Failure to use dedicated network interfaces to ensure support for switching features, such as flow control and jumbo framing, and for implementing multipath I/O can result in performance decrease.

FC, in its turn, can be more difficult to manage in environments that are geographically distributed. Interconnectivity over long distances can be expensive. For example, if you need to configure replication to a secondary SAN at a remote site, expensive **Fibre Channel over IP** (**FCIP**) gateways need to be purchased.

Also, you may need to use different storage technologies depending on the vSphere features you are going to use. The VMware documentation lists vSphere features supported by each storage technology which is available at `http://pubs.vmware. com/vsphere-50/index.jsp#com.vmware. vsphere.storage.doc_50/GUID-1FB1AD88-3E49-4062-8DE5-8246A1DDF3E3.html`.

Datastores are logical containers similar to filesystems that hide differences of each storage device from virtual machines. There are two ways to add a datastore in vSphere Client:

- They can be created on one of the available storage devices.

- They can also be discovered when a new host is added to the inventory. Once a host is added, vSphere Client displays all datastores that are accessible by the host.

Depending on the SAN technology that is used in your environment, datastores can have either VMFS or NFS filesystem formats.

Once you create datastores, they can be organized into folders and can also be assigned permissions and alarms. Grouping them into folders allows assigning same permissions and alarms to multiple datastores at the same time. These tasks can be completed in vCenter Client.

Connected datastores and information related to them are available in the **Datastores** and **Datastore Clusters** views. From these views, you can also create datastores and edit or remove existing ones.

The datastore details that can be seen under the **Datastores** and **Datastore Clusters** views are listed in VMware documentation available at `http://pubs.vmware.com/vsphere-50/index.jsp#com.vmware.vsphere.storage.doc_50/GUID-5AA74377-8A60-41B8-B767-B900E2BC0FBD.html`.

Datastore properties can be viewed from the **Datastores** view in the **Storage** section under the **Configuration** tab.

It is important to remember that each LUN should contain only one VMFS datastore. At the same time, each LUN must be configured with the right RAID level. It should also have other appropriate storage characteristics depending on virtual machines running from this LUN, and applications that are running inside these VMs.

When you work on LUN design for new storage, consider the following:

- With larger LUNs, you have more flexibility in creating virtual machines, resizing virtual disks, and creating snapshots
- With larger LUNs, there are also fewer VMFS datastores to manage
- With smaller LUNs, you get better performance as there will be less contention on a single volume
- With larger volumes, you also get more flexibility as you are able to set multipathing policy and shares per LUN, as well as have different RAID arrays for different applications

While using larger LUNs, you will need to consider I/O requirements for VMs running on a LUN. Depending on how much I/O load the existing storage can handle, you may need to reduce the number of VMs running on a single LUN for performance reasons, especially if these VMs are high I/O consumers.

When multiple virtual machines are using the same LUN, you may need to prioritize them so that VMs that need more I/Os have more disk access. This can be accomplished with disk shares. A share is a relative value expressed as **Low**, **Normal**, **High**, and **Custom**. It is set per virtual disk and compared with the total value of all shares for all VMs on the host.

Go to **Edit virtual machine settings**, switch to the **Resources** tab and select **Disk**. From there, you can double-click on the **Shares** column for any disk and choose the required value from the drop-down list, as shown in the following screenshot:

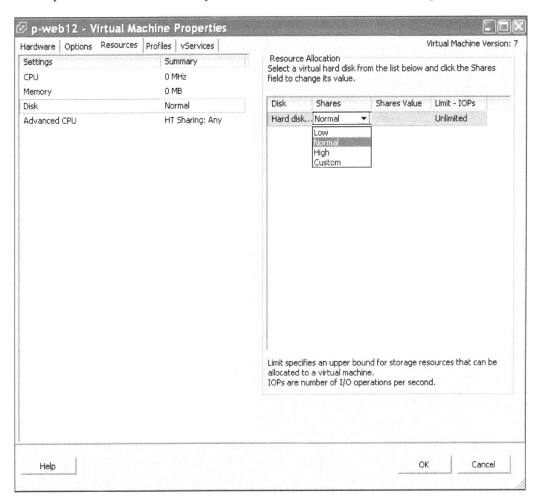

Disk shares are relevant only within a specific host. Therefore, if you move a VM to another host, the shares assigned before will have no effect.

Storage multipathing and failover

With ESXi, it's possible to use more than one physical path for data transfer between a host and external storage. This technique is called multipathing and allows administrators to maintain a constant connection between hosts and storage to ensure uptime in case of a failure.

Multiple paths to storage can also be used for load balancing purposes so that when all available paths are operational, I/O loads can be distributed between them, which reduces or eliminates potential bottlenecks.

When a host or SAN component such as an adapter, switch, or cable fails, ESXi switches to another working physical path. This process is called path failover.

Failover configuration with Fibre Channel usually involves two or more HBAs for each host and two or more FC switches. FBAs on the same host should be connected to different switches.

A typical configuration of Fibre Channel SAN with failover is shown in the following figure:

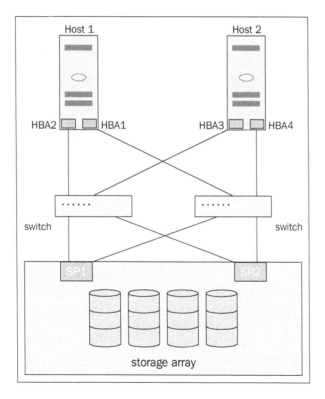

In case of HBA1 or FC switch failure, HBA2 takes over and provides a connection for Host1. This process of switching between HBAs is called the HBA failover. Similarly, if SP1 fails, SP2 takes over and provides storage connection to both hosts.

With iSCSI SANs, there are two failover options possible.

The so-called host-based failover is similar to the FC failover setup. Hosts use multiple iSCSI HBAs or multiple network cards connected to different IP switches.

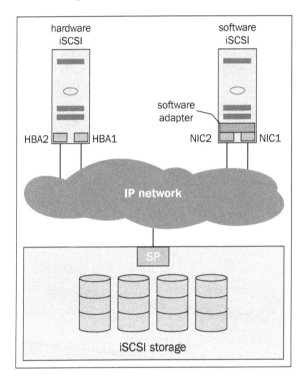

iSCSI adapters have to be either hardware- or software-based. ESXi doesn't support multipathing with combinations of different kinds of adapters.

Some iSCSI storage devices manage their ports and paths by themselves transparently for ESXi servers. In this case, there is usually a single virtual address that is used by hosts to communicate with storage. Therefore, hosts are not able to recognize that multiple ports exist on the storage. When hosts initially connect using a virtual address, the storage system makes a decision on which port will be used for this connection. If the storage decides to use a port different from the one where the initial request came in, it sends a reconnection request to the host. iSCSI initiators on the host switch to a different port following this reconnection request.

Storage uses this technique mostly for load balancing purposes. When the host loses the connection, it attempts to reconnect again using a virtual port address and usually gets quickly redirected to an active port.

From time to time, storage may request iSCSI initiators to reconnect so that it can switch them to another port, which allows using multiple paths in the most effective way.

The following figure illustrates the process of port redirection, performed by the storage system in this case:

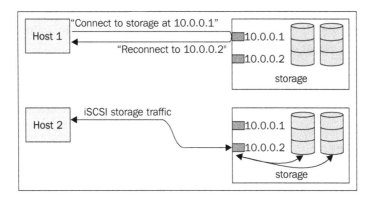

When the physical port on the storage to which the virtual address is assigned becomes unavailable, the virtual address is reassigned to another port. The following figure depicts this situation:

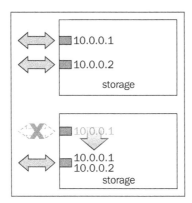

When the first port that has the address **10.0.0.1** assigned becomes unavailable, the storage system then reassigns this address to another available port. The second port starts responding to both addresses.

With array-based failover, all paths are active-active. You can have multiple paths to storage only if there are multiple ports on ESXi hosts.

When path failover happens, it usually takes 30 to 60 seconds for SAN to stabilize its configuration because of topology changes. Therefore, the virtual machine I/O can also be delayed leading to the virtual machine's failure. To avoid the failure, it may be necessary to increase the disk-timeout value.

On Windows, it can be done in the `HKEY_LOCAL_MACHINE/SYSTEM/CurrentControlSet/services/Disk` registry.

Open the **TimeOutValue** key by double-clicking on it and set its value to `0x3c` in the hexadecimal format, or to `60` in decimal.

In general, I/O delay in case of path failover takes more time on active-passive arrays and less time on active-active arrays. VMware, however, recommends increasing the timeout to 60 seconds, which is a longer delay, to be on the safe side.

Storage Thin Provisioning

Thin provisioning is a method of allocating space on a flexible basis. With this approach, you allocate what is currently needed and allow it to increase on demand when required up to a certain limit.

Thin provisioning can be compared with a traditional model called thick provisioning, where the maximum allowed amount of storage is provided right away, in advance, taking into account possible future needs. The obvious downside to the traditional approach is that lot of space is wasted as it remains unused for a long time, causing storage to be underutilized.

The Storage Thin Provisioning option is available at two levels: the whole storage array and virtual disk. Virtual disk thin provisioning will be discussed in more detail later in *Chapter 3, Virtual Machine Management*, under the *Creating a new VM* section.

Thin provisioning is a dangerous technique. With proper monitoring and management, however, it can be beneficial. The main reason of using it is that its so-called storage over-subscription is reported to hosts when the storage capacity is more than what is actually available.

In most cases, you use storage-specific tools to create thin-provisioned LUN. It is important to set a soft threshold limit and assign an alert so that it's triggered once this soft limit is reached.

In vSphere Client, a VMFS datastore can be created that uses thin-provisioned LUN. When LUN is thin provisioned, the VMFS datastore is able to see only the virtual size of the LUN. For example, if an array reports 2 TB of storage while there is only 1 TB of physical storage available, VMFS sees LUN size as 2 TB.

This is vital to monitor storage usage when you use over-subscription to make sure that you don't run out of space. As your datastore uses more space and reaches the specified threshold, an alarm is triggered and you get an alert. At this point, you can use one of the two possible options:

- Increase physical space on the storage
- Move some virtual machines off the datastore before LUN runs out of its capacity

If the alert is ignored and you run out of free space, an out-of-space condition is reported to the host by the storage array. The host in its turn pauses the virtual machines and the out-of-space alarm is generated. Once it happens, you have to deal with the out-of-space condition. There are a few things that can be done in this situation. More details can be found in *Chapter 3*, *Virtual Machine Management*, in the *Snapshots* section. In most cases, however, the fastest way to resolve this would be to get more space on storage.

Networking

A virtual network provides two types of services to hosts and virtual machines:

- Virtual machine communication to a physical network and between each other
- VMkernel services, such as NFS, iSCSI, and vMotion, and their connection to a physical network

Network adapters and network configuration

To view or configure networking as well as network adapters, select a host from the inventory, and go to the **Configuration** tab. Select **Networking** from the left-hand side of the screen, and choose the type of networking to view: **vSphere Standard Switch** or **vSphere Distributed Switch**, as shown in the following screenshot:

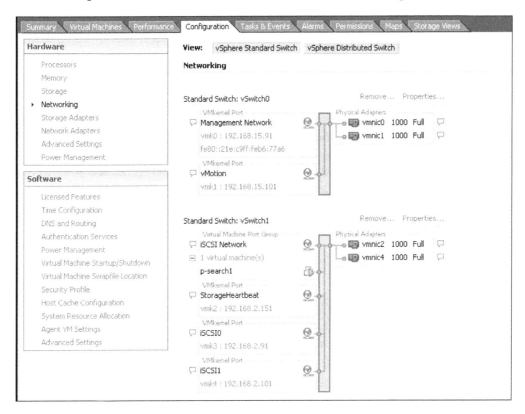

Information about physical adapters available on a host can be accessed from the **Network Adapters** view under the **Configuration** tab. The following table shows the available adapter parameters:

Option	Description
Device	Name of the network adapter
Speed	Actual speed and duplex of the network adapter
Configured	Configured speed and duplex of the network adapter
Switch	vSphere Standard Switch or vSphere Distributed Switch that the network adapter is associated with
Observed IP ranges	IP addresses that the network adapter is likely to have access to
Wake on LAN supported	Network adapter ability to support Wake on the LAN

Virtual switch concept

There are two types of virtual switches available: **vSphere Standard Switch** and **vSphere Distributed Switch**.

vSphere Standard Switch

vSphere Standard Switch is a virtual device that works similar to physical switches. It handles network traffic at the host level. vSphere Standard Switch routes traffic between virtual machines and is used to link to external networks by connecting to physical switches through physical adapters available on a host. It is the same as connecting two physical switches together to expand your network.

vSphere Client can be used to add networking based on the categories that reflect the types of network services and are listed as follows:

- Virtual machines
- VMkernel

Standard switches can be used to:

- Combine bandwidth of multiple network adapters
- Balance communication traffic among them
- Handle physical NIC failover

The default number of logical ports on a standard switch is 120. These ports can be used to connect VM's virtual adapters or uplink standard switch to other switches. Logical ports are members of a single port group. There can be one or more port groups on a standard switch.

VMs connected to the same standard switch are able to access each other. Traffic between them is routed locally. If standard switch is uplinked to an external network, virtual machines connected to it are also able to access this external network.

Port groups combine multiple ports under the same configuration. Each port group is labeled, and each label is unique for the current host. Labels help to make VM configuration portable across hosts. Labels are case sensitive and must match for vMotion to work.

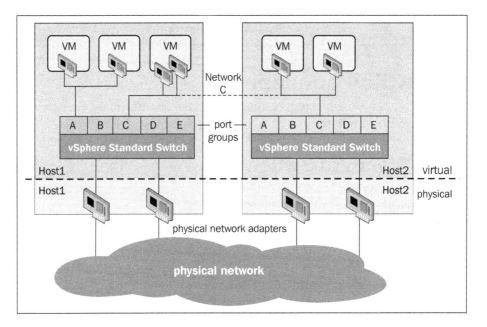

If two port groups are connected to the same physical network, they are given the same label and all hosts, virtual or physical, are able to receive broadcasts from each other. Therefore, a group label creates a single broadcast domain.

The broadcast domain is a logical part of a computer network where all nodes can reach each other by a broadcast at the data link layer. In Ethernet networks, each node checks the destination address when it receives data and ignores the data if the destination address is not the node's MAC (physical) address. If a node (sender) needs to send data to another node (receiver) but doesn't know the receiver node's MAC address, it sends a broadcast message asking the receiver node to reply with its MAC address. Such broadcast messages will be received by all nodes in the same broadcast domain, and if the receiver node is available, it will reply. Therefore, if two nodes are not in the same broadcast domain, they will not be able to communicate with each other.

Port group also has an optional field for VLAN ID. VLANs are used in physical networks to create separate broadcast domains. Therefore, you will need to use this field to restrict the port group traffic to the logical Ethernet segment within your physical network.

In vCenter, you can use the **Add Network Wizard** option to create a virtual network, standard switch, as well as a network label. To accomplish that, select a host, go to the **Configuration** tab, and then click on **Networking** to the left of the window. Choose **vSphere Standard Switch** view and then click on **Add Networking**.

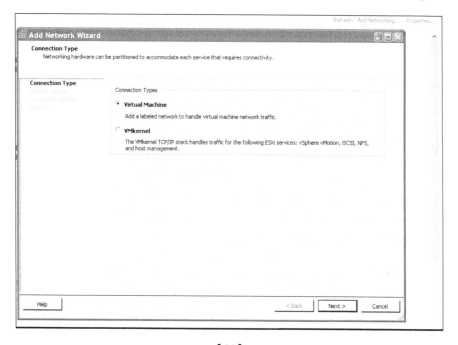

You can accept **Virtual Machine**, which is the default connection type. In the next step, choose **Create vSphere standard switch** or one of the existing switches and associated physical adapters for this port group, as shown in the following screenshot:

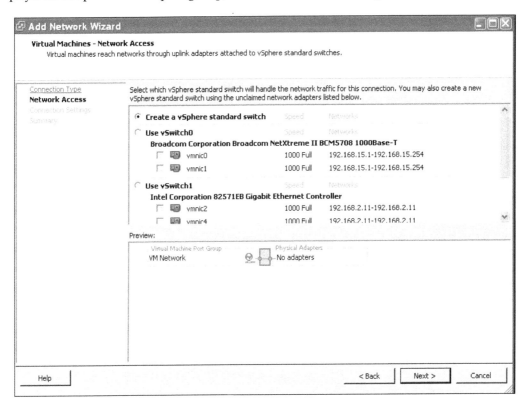

In the **Port Group Properties** group, enter a label and VLAN ID (optional).

If you need to migrate virtual machines between hosts, make sure that hosts are in the same broadcast domain as well.

Once the standard switch is configured, from its properties you will be able to do the following:

- Change the number of available ports. To do this, from the **Ports** tab **choose standard** switch item, then click on **Edit** and go to the **General** tab.

- Change the speed of the uplink adapter. This can be done by navigating to the **Network Adapters** tab. Under this tab, select network adapter and then click on **Edit** to change speed from the drop-down menu.

- Add uplink adapters.: To do this, under the **Network Adapters** tab, click on **Add**. Select one or more adapters from the list and optionally change their order.

Changes to the port number will not take effect until the system is restarted.

There is a special network interface that provides network connectivity for hosts and handles VMware vMotion, IP storage, and Fault Tolerance services. This interface is called VMkernel. VMkernel provides networking support for each of the services it handles in the following ways:

- iSCSI as a VM datastore and also for connecting ISO files, which are seen by VMs as CD-ROMs
- NFS as a VM datastore and also for connecting ISO files, which are seen by VMs as CD-ROMs
- Migration using vMotion
- Fault Tolerance logging
- vMotion interface port binding

VMkernel networking can be set up from the **Networking configuration** section under the **Configuration** tab. Click on **Add Networking** and choose **VMkernel**. As with port group configuration, in the following steps, you will need to choose the existing standard switch or create a new one by typing the network label and optionally entering the VLAN ID.

Optionally, you may choose port group for vMotion, Fault Tolerance, and management traffic.

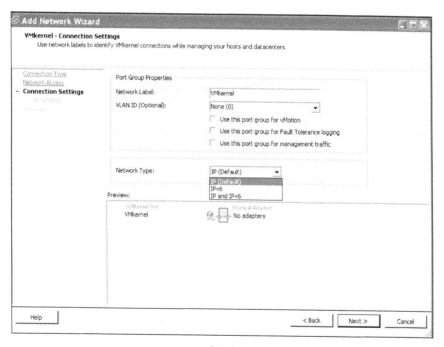

In the further steps, you will need to select how to obtain IP settings. If IPv6 is enabled on the host, you will be prompted for IPv6 settings as well.

vSphere Distributed Switch

vSphere Distributed Switch works as a single switch for all hosts associated with it. When it's used, virtual machines are able to maintain their network configuration while migrating from one host to another.

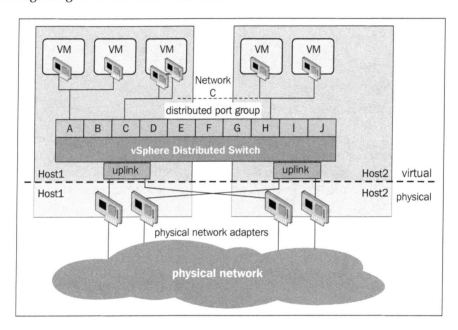

As in case of the standard switch, the distributed switch forwards traffic between VMs and connects them to external networks via existing physical adapters.

Distributed switches can also have distributed port groups assigned to them. They are identified by network labels and VLAN IDs, same as a regular port group. The network label for a distributed port group, however, is unique in the current datacenter, which allows having network configuration that spans across all hosts in the datacenter.

Setting up networking with redundancy

To ensure uptime and allow maintenance that is transparent for end users, it is recommended to plan and set up networking with redundancy. When uplinking hosts to an external network, you will need at least two uplink network adapters for each external network to provide redundancy. They need to be connected to two different physical network switches so that your network equipment doesn't become a single point of failure.

The same concept applies if a host is connected to a SAN with Fibre Channel and/or iSCSI, or to NFS volumes via the network. You will need to use at least two adapters for each type of storage you are connecting to.

If you use iSCSI or NFS, for performance reasons, it's also recommended to separate your storage data traffic from network traffic.

If you have more than one host in your environment and want hosts to communicate among each other, it's considered a best practice to have management traffic separate from network and storage traffic. Therefore, for a simple vSphere environment with two or more hosts, you will need at least four physical network adapters on each host if you use Fibre Channel to connect to storage, or you will need at least six physical network adapters on each host if you use iSCSI or NFS.

Once you use more than one network adapter for each network, you need to determine the way in which network traffic is distributed between adapters, and what happens in the event of an adapter failure. This can be accomplished by determining load balancing and the failover policy.

Failover and load balancing for vSphere Standard Switch can be configured from the **Ports** tab in standard switch properties. Choose standard switch item, and then click on **Properties**. Go to the **NIC Teaming** tab, as shown in the following screenshot:

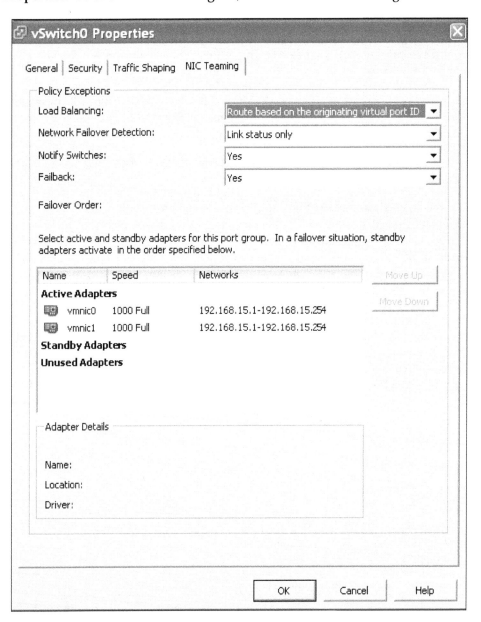

For the **Load Balancing:** drop-down, you can choose one of the following options:

- **Route based on the originating virtual port ID**: Uplink will be selected based on the virtual port on the standard switch where the traffic entered.

- **Route based on IP hash**: Uplink will be selected based on a hash of the source and destination IP addresses of each packet. If a packet is a non-IP packet, values from offsets are used to calculate the hash.

- **Route based on source MAC hash**: Uplink will be selected based on a hash of the source MAC address.

- **Use explicit failover order**: With this option chosen, always the highest order uplink from the list of Active adapters will be used.

- **Route based on physical NIC Load**: This option is available with the Virtual distributed switch that provides **Load Based Teaming** (**LBT**). LBT will balance VMs based on the amount of traffic passed through NICs.

In the **Network Failover Detection** list, choose an option from the following for failover detection:

- **Beacon probing**: In addition to link status information from NICs, it sends and listens for beacon probes on all network adapters in the team and uses this information as well to determine link failures. This option detects more failures than the **Link status only** option.

- **Link status only**: It relies on the link status as it's detected by the network adapter. With this option, you'll be able to detect failures such as disconnected cables or powered off physical switches. Issues such as configuration errors, physical switch ports blocked by spanning tree protocols, misconfigured VLAN IDs on ports, or disconnected cables on the other side of a physical switch will not be detected.

Select **Yes** or **No** for the **Notify Switches** drop-down to decide if switches should be notified in case of failover. If set to **Yes**, a notification will be sent to the network so that physical switches update their lookup tables in case:

- NIC is connected to a standard switch
- NIC's traffic is routed through a different physical NIC because of a failover event

Yes is recommended in most cases to reduce latency during failover or vMotion migration. This option should be set to **No** when virtual machines connected to the switch use Microsoft **Network Load Balancing** (**NLB**) in the unicast mode.

Then choose **Yes** or **No** to disable or enable failback. When this option is set to **Yes**, the physical adapter will return to the active mode right after its recovery, replacing the standby adapter. If it's set to **No**, the failed adapter will stay inactive until it's needed.

Set the failover order to determine work load distribution for adapters. The available options are as follows:

- **Active Adapters**: These adapters will be used while the network adapter connectivity is active
- **Standby Adapters**: These adapters will be used in case one of the active adapters is not connected anymore
- **Unused Adapters**: These adapters will not be used

The same options can also be configured for standard port groups as well as for distributed port groups separately from the standard switch.

When failover or failback occurs, MAC addresses assigned to virtual machines appear on another switch port, which in some cases may break the standard switch connectivity. To avoid this, it's recommended to put a physical switch connected to your virtual switch in the portfast or portfast trunk mode.

> **Spanning Tree Protocol** (STP) is the protocol used on most modern switching equipment to prevent network loops. When STP is enabled and a link on a switch port goes up, STP calculation happens. This allows the switch to decide if this port should be put into the forwarding mode, that is, become operational, or into blocking state, or become disabled to prevent a network loop. This calculation may take 30 to 50 seconds and while it's happening, no user data will be allowed to pass through this port. To allow immediate transition of the port into the forwarding state, enable the STP PortFast feature. While portfast allows the switch port to become operational right away, STP calculation still occurs, and if there is a network loop, STP will eventually block this port.

EVC mode

Before vCenter Server allows migration of running or suspended VM from one host to another, it performs a number of compatibility checks to make sure that this virtual machine will be able to resume or keep running on the new host.

One of the requirements is CPU compatibility, that is, the processor on the target host should be able to provide the same set of features to the VM after migration. This CPU feature set is determined based on the following items:

- Host CPU family and model
- CPU features that are available based on the settings in BIOS
- The ESX/ESXi version running on the host
- The virtual machine's virtual hardware version
- The virtual machine's guest operating system

The reason for the last requirement is that when a virtual machine is booting up, operating systems perform a check of the CPU type with the CPUID instruction. The response tells the OS which features and instructions are available with the current CPU. The OS in turn tells applications which functionality is available.

Typically, newer versions of processors have additional features that were not available before. More recent CPUs may also have a different set of instructions.

If you move a VM to a host with an older processor, which doesn't have features and instructions that are currently used by an application, the application is likely to crash. This sometimes will also be the case for older processors within the same CPU family. vCenter Server protects users from this situation by checking CPU compatibility on the other host.

Keep in mind that CPU compatibility check will be performed only on powered-on virtual machines.

It's important to mention that a mismatch between two hosts' CPUs will block VM migration only if it has access to a feature that the target host doesn't provide. User-level features and instructions used by a VM include SSE3, SSSE3, SSE4.1, SSE4.2, and AES. Kernel-level features — privileged instructions that may be used by a virtual machine — include AMD **No eXecute** (**NX**) and **Intel eXecute Disable** (**XD**) security features.

The requirement for host CPUs to be the same or similar for vMotion to work can be a problem for certain environments. For example, there may be a requirement to expand a cluster that's already running few hosts that were bought together some time ago and are exactly the same. Very often, after a certain period of time, servers with exactly the same processors may not be available anymore. Often manufacturers start selling the same server models with more recent processors or discontinue older server models completely. At the same time, if there are already a few servers in your cluster, it may not be cost-effective to replace all of them when the environment needs to be expanded.

VMware's solution to this issue is the **Enhanced vMotion Compatibility (EVC)** feature, which was introduced in ESX 3.5 Update 2. The main idea behind EVC is that certain CPU features can be hidden from guests by placing the host in an EVC cluster. In other words, EVC makes sure that all hosts from a cluster present the same CPU features to virtual machines while actual CPUs on hosts may be different. Of course, the eventual set of features available for VMs will be defined by the host with the least amount of available CPU features, or, in other words, by the oldest processor.

Another way to hide CPU features is to use the CPU compatibility mask for a virtual machine. This is not recommended, however, primarily because of administration overhead. A CPU mask has to be set per virtual machine, and besides it has to be set manually, which increases the chances for error. EVC, on the other hand, is configured per host and VMware is constantly working towards supporting a wider range of processors so that administrators who use the EVC feature don't need to worry about following frequent industry changes.

Managing hosts with different CPUs

To enable EVC on a cluster, hosts and members of the cluster must meet the following requirements:

- All CPUs must support EVC and must also be either Intel or AMD
- ESX/ESXi 3.5 Update 2 or later is required on all hosts
- All hosts must be managed by vCenter
- All VMs will need to be turned off

Hosts that are being added later must meet these requirements as well.

VMware documentation also gives detailed information on processor types supported by VMware EVC. It is available at `http://pubs.vmware.com/ vsphere-50/index.jsp#com.vmware.vsphere.vcenterhost.doc_50/GUID-FEC87C0B-7276-4152-8EAA-915305E64FED.html`.

Once all requirements are met, you can create an EVC cluster. There are two ways to do this:

- Create an empty cluster, enable EVC, and move hosts into the cluster
- Enable EVC on an existing cluster

Creating an empty cluster is the choice recommended by VMware, as it causes minimal disruption to an existing infrastructure. At the same time, if there is an existing cluster with different settings in place and features enabled, it may be better to enable EVC on it.

It is important to remember that no matter which way is chosen, all virtual machines need to be powered off, and in certain cases, it will be required to update VMware tools when they are powered back on.

The EVC mode can be enabled from the cluster settings. Right-click on a cluster and then select **Edit Settings**. Select **VMware EVC** in the left panel and click on **Change** to edit the EVC settings. From the **VMware EVC Mode** menu, select the baseline CPU feature that is going to be used, and then click on **OK**.

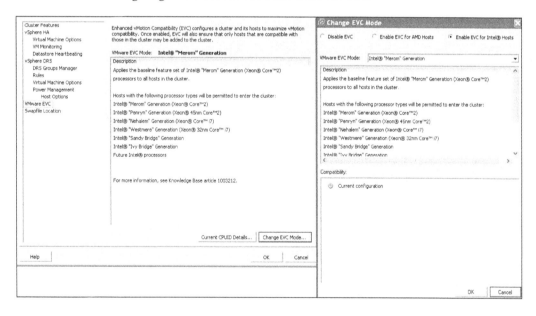

The same things mentioned previously apply if the EVC mode needs to be changed. It's possible to either lower or raise the EVC mode. To lower the EVC mode, you will need to shut down all virtual machines. To raise the EVC mode, however, it's not necessary to do this. It's important to keep in mind that virtual machines will not have access to new features until they are powered off and powered back on. Suspending or rebooting virtual machines will not be sufficient in this case.

The reason for this requirement is that the EVC mode for a virtual machine is determined when it's powered on. To see the EVC modes of running virtual machines, go to the **Virtual Machines** tab in the cluster or host inventory. You will be able to see the virtual machine EVC mode in the **EVC Mode** column. If this column is not displayed, right-click on column titles and select **EVC Mode**.

Host Profiles

With Host Profiles, administrators can better manage host configurations especially for larger environments with many ESX or ESXi servers. Host profiles eliminate manual per-host configuration and help to maintain consistency across your environment.

Host Profiles are supported only in vSphere 4 or later.

Host Profiles is a feature that needs to be licensed. It comes with the Enterprise Plus license. Therefore, if there are any issues with it, checking if you are using the correct license is going to be the first troubleshooting step.

If a host has been deployed with vSphere Auto Deploy, its configuration is captured in Host Profile. The profile in most cases is sufficient to store the whole configuration. In certain cases however, when a host that was provisioned with Auto Deploy boots, the user will be prompted for input. In this case, administrators can use the answer file.

Profile workflow

Tasks related to host profiles are usually performed in a certain workflow order.

- At least one host in your vSphere environment must be configured properly.
- Choose a host that will be used as a reference host. Set it up and configure it. A reference host is the host that will be used to create a profile.
- Using reference host, create a profile.
- Attach a host or cluster to the profile.
- Check if hosts are compliant to the reference host's profile. If a host is compliant, it means that it's configured correctly.

• Apply the host profile to any other hosts or clusters that need to be configured the same way.

Managing profiles

Existing host profiles can be found by navigating to **View | Management | Host Profiles**. This is the main view for managing profiles as well. The **Hosts and Clusters** view can be used to perform many tasks such as creating new profiles, attaching entities, or applying profiles.

Click on **Create Profile** to start **Create Profile wizard**. You will be prompted for the name and description as well as reference host for the new profile, as shown in the following screenshot:

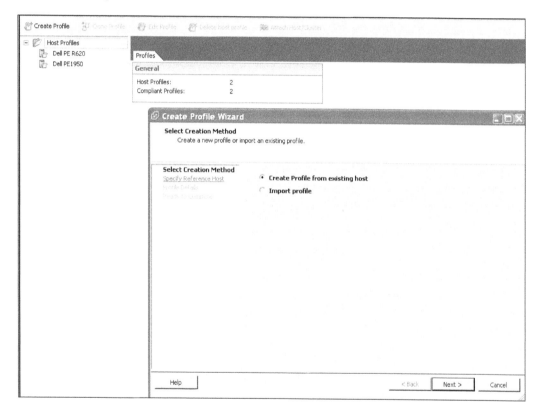

A new profile can also be created from the **Hosts and Clusters** view. Select a reference host, right-click on it, choose **Host Profile**, and then choose **Create Profile** from **Host options**. You will be prompted for the name and description. Once a new profile is created, it will appear under the host's **Summary** tab.

Existing profiles can also be exported by right-clicking on a profile and selecting **Export Profile**. You will need to choose location and name for the file. It will be saved to a `.vpf` file, which is the VMware profile file format. When you export a profile, for security reasons, passwords are not saved. You will be prompted to re-enter them once you import the profile and apply it to a host.

To import the host profile back, click on **Create Profile** and select an option to import a profile in **Create Profile wizard**. You will be prompted for the `.vpf` file, name, and description, as well as the reference host.

You can click on **Edit Host profile** to change the profile's name and description, edit policy, or enable/disable policy compliance check.

A policy describes the way in which configuration settings should be applied. Host profiles consist of several subprofiles grouped to represent different configuration instances. Subprofiles include policies and compliance checks which describe different configurations relevant to the profile. Policies consist of options with parameters. Parameters are keys with values.

More details on available subprofile configuration options can be found in the VMware documentation at `http://pubs.vmware.com/vsphere-50/index.jsp#com.vmware.vsphere.hostprofiles.doc_50/GUID-DA01F834-A8E3-4CE0-9E45-088387F438EB.html`.

Saving a profile is considered a vCenter task. Therefore, when you save a profile that has been changed, you will see this operation in the **Recent Tasks** list. If a profile is applied to a host before the task is completed, an old profile version will be applied.

The **Enable/Disable Compliance Check** option defines if this profile will be considered during compliance check. It's enabled by default.

Once the profile has been created and configured, it can be applied to other hosts that need to have the same configuration. This is done in two steps. First, you need to associate a host to a profile by attaching the host to the profile. After that, you attach the profile to a host to bring the host to a desired state.

You can attach either a host or a cluster to a profile. This can be accomplished using:

- The Host Profiles main view
- The Host context menu
- The Cluster's context menu
- The Cluster's **Profile Compliance** tab

From the **Host Profiles** view, select the profile, click on **Attach Host/Cluster**, select the host or cluster from the list, and click on **Attach**.

If you need to use the host's or cluster's view, right-click on the host or cluster and select **Host Profile** and then **Manage Profile**.

Profile application can also be either at the host or cluster level using:

- The Host Profiles main view
- The Host context menu
- The Cluster's **Profile Compliance** tab

In the **Hosts Profiles** view, go to the **Hosts and Clusters** tab. Check the list of attached hosts shown and click on **Apply Profile**. You may be prompted for additional parameters needed to apply the profile.

From the **Host and Clusters** view, right-click on a host or cluster, navigate to **Host Profile | Apply Profile**. Again, you may be prompted for additional parameters.

Checking compliance

There is a possibility that a host or cluster configuration can be changed after a profile has been applied. Compliance check helps to ensure that the host or cluster is still configured correctly. It's recommended to do a compliance check on a regular basis.

From the **Host Profiles** view, select a host or cluster in the **Host and Clusters** tab and click on **Check Compliance**.

From the **Host and Clusters** view, right-click on the host, choose the Host Profiles, and then click on **Check Compliance** to check the host's compliance.

To check the cluster's compliance, you will need to select the cluster, go to the **Profile Compliance** tab and choose **Check Compliance Now**. Depending on what kind of profile is attached to the cluster, vCenter will check only hosts compliance if it's a host profile, or compliance with specific settings such as DRS, HA, DPM, and so on, if the profile contains these settings.

Cluster specific settings can be checked for compliance even if the host profile is not attached to the cluster.

Summary

Once ESXi is installed on a server, connected to your network, and configured, it can be added to vCenter Server so that you can manage it.

ESXi abstracts physical storage from virtual machines by providing host-level storage virtualization. There are two types of physical storage: local and networked.

In VMware terminology, target means a single storage unit that can be accessed by a host. LUN or device is a logical volume that can be used by a host; in other words, it's a space on the target. Therefore, a target may contain one or more LUNs. Datastores are logical containers similar to filesystems that hide differences of each storage device from virtual machines.

With ESXi, it's possible to use more than one physical path for data transfer between a host and an external storage. This technique is called multipathing, and it allows administrators to maintain a constant connection between hosts and storage to ensure uptime in case of a failure.

Thin provisioning is a method of allocating space on a flexible basis. With this approach, you allocate the space that is currently needed and allow it to increase on demand when needed up to a certain limit. Thin provisioning is a dangerous technique. Virtual network provides two types of services to hosts and virtual machines. They are virtual machine communication to a physical network and between each other and VMkernel services such as NFS, iSCSI, and vMotion and their connection to physical network.

There are two types of virtual switches available: vSphere Standard Switch and vSphere Distributed Switch. A vSphere Standard Switch is a virtual device that works similar to physical switches. A vSphere Distributed Switch works as a single switch for all hosts associated with it.

To ensure uptime and allow maintenance that is transparent for end users, it is recommended to plan and set up networking with redundancy.

EVC allows certain CPU features to be hidden from guests by placing the host in an EVC cluster, and makes sure that all hosts from a cluster present the same CPU features to virtual machines while actual CPUs on hosts may be different. This allows bypassing the requirement for host CPUs to be the same or similar for vMotion to work, which can be a problem for certain environments.

3

Virtual Machine Management

This chapter focuses on managing virtual machines in vCenter. We will discuss the process of creating new VMs and cloning existing VMs as well as working with templates.

We will also talk about time synchronization challenges for the VM's operating system. Finally, we will discuss VM snapshots, why they can be helpful and also dangerous, and how to use them properly.

In this chapter, we will cover:

- Creating a new **virtual machine** (**VM**)
- Installing VMware Tools
- Time synchronization
- Cloning existing VMs
- Deploying a VM from a template and template best practices
- Importing/exporting OVF templates
- Snapshots

Creating a new VM

A virtual machine in VMware is a set of files stored on supported storage devices. Any virtual machine uses physical resources of a host and includes virtual devices that provide the same functionality as with physical hardware. Each set of files is stored in a separate folder with the same name as the virtual machine. When you rename a virtual machine, the folder name and filenames don't change. Therefore, if you are renaming a VM and want to keep the names on the storage consistent, it needs to be cloned or vmotioned to another storage if this feature is available to you.

The most important virtual machine files are listed in the VMware documentation at `http://pubs.vmware.com/vsphere-50/index.jsp#com.vmware.vsphere.vm_admin.doc_50/GUID-CEFF6D89-8C19-4143-8C26-4B6D6734D2CB.html`.

New VM wizard

To create a new virtual machine, you use the **Create New Virtual Machine** wizard that can be opened in vSphere client by right-clicking on any host, cluster, or datacenter object and choosing **New Virtual Machine...**.

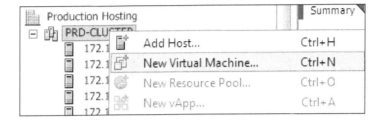

When one of these objects is selected, the same option is also available from the **File** menu under the **New** suboption as shown in the following screenshot:

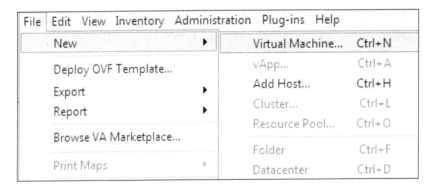

The new virtual machine is not created until you click on the **Finish** button in the last step. Therefore, if you cancel the wizard without completing all tasks, you'll need to start over. **Create New Virtual Machine** wizard steps are straightforward. It asks you to name the future virtual machine, choose the storage and host it will be running on, and choose network settings, CPU, and memory allocation.

Virtual hardware

The most important step is selecting the hardware version.

 This step is available only if the **Custom** configuration option has been chosen on the first step.

The following screenshot shows the first step with the **Custom** configuration option:

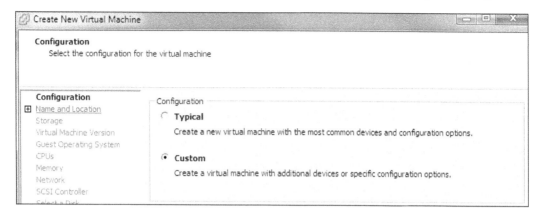

vSphere 5 comes with hardware Version 8 that supports Windows 8 and Windows Server 2012 guest operating systems. vSphere 5.1 with hardware Version 9 supports Ubuntu 13.04, Debian 6, Free BSD 8.3/9, and MAC OS 10.8. vSphere 5.5 with hardware Version 10 supports Debian 7 and free BSD 8.4/9.1.

 Hardware Versions 9 and 10 can be chosen only in the VMware Web Client interface.

Therefore, the hardware version you choose defines the list of available guest operating systems, as shown in the following screenshot, and if you are going to deploy one of the newer operating systems from Microsoft, choose hardware Version 8 or later:

At the same time, if you are going to move this VM to an older version of ESX, you may need to leave it at one of the previous versions.

For more information on differences between hardware versions, refer to the section on importing the OVF template described later in this chapter.

Virtual CPUs (vCPUs)

In the next step, the wizard asks you to choose how many virtual CPUs and how many cores per CPU this VM will be assigned. While the answer may seem obvious — the more vCPUs and cores a VM has, the faster it is — it's not always the case. There are at least two things to consider.

First of all, depending on the load in your environment and the applications that are running on a VM, there is a point when additional vCPUs start to worsen the performance.

In the nonvirtual world, the more CPUs and cores per CPU a server has, the more powerful it is. When it comes to a virtual environment, the host's processors are shared not only between virtual machines that are running on the host, but also between VMs and the host operating system.

In older versions of ESX, when the symmetric multiprocessor (SMP) feature was introduced, scheduler — a VMkernel service responsible for managing access to CPU resources — was designed such that all assigned vCPUs should be available at the same time in order for a VM to use its CPU. In other words, the same number of CPUs and cores assigned to a VM have to be idle on the host before this VM can use them.

Starting from ESX Version 3, VMware introduced so-called relaxed co-scheduling. This approach doesn't require all CPUs and cores to be available and allows only a subset of a VM's vCPUs to be scheduled simultaneously.

While this is a great improvement, availability of CPU resources for the host OS as well as CPU load have to be considered:

- SPM scheduler is less efficient than uniprocessor scheduler. This can be easily confirmed with benchmarking tools.
- Even if an additional CPU is not used, the ESX kernel requires more resources to support it, such as memory to maintain data structures and CPU resources to virtualize idle systems. According to VMware, the kernel requires 1 to 2 percent of a single CPU core to support idle vCPU.
- The resources required to deliver timer interrupts increase quadratically with the number of vCPUs.

Therefore, when in doubt, start with a single CPU and add more only if you are sure that the software running on a VM is capable of taking advantage of multiple processors.

If you are only planning to use the virtual infrastructure, it is a good idea to investigate application workloads and requirements in advance. This way, you will know the baseline and will be able to configure VMs correctly from the beginning.

Also, there are tools available that can be used to monitor performance so that administrators can actively respond to any workload change. One such tool is the vCenterOperation Management suite.

When an incorrect CPU assignment is suspected to cause poor VM performance, check the %**CSTP** value for this VM. %CSTP represents the amount of time a VM with multiple CPUs is waiting to be scheduled on multiple hosts' cores. To see this value, log in to the ESX console directly or through SSH and run the `esxtop` utility. It will list running VMs and their performance metrics; one of them is %CSTP. If it's close to 100 or higher, consider lowering the vCPU count.

The second consideration is that depending on guest operating systems and the applications that are running on a VM, there may be some licensing restrictions that will prevent the OS or application to use or even recognize additional CPUs.

A good example is Windows Server 2003 or 2008 Standard edition. Standard edition is licensed by sockets or physical processors and not by cores. According to Microsoft, you can have as many cores per socket as you want, as long as you use four or less CPUs.

Suppose you have an eight-socket ESX host and a VM with Windows Server 2003 Standard edition with four vCPUs assigned, and you would like to give it more CPU resources. If two more vCPUs are added to this VM, they will appear in Device Manager. However, Windows will not be able to use them because of licensing restrictions. It's possible to confirm this by opening **Windows Task Manager**. Under the **Performance** tab, there are only four CPUs listed while Device Manager has six as shown in the following screenshot:

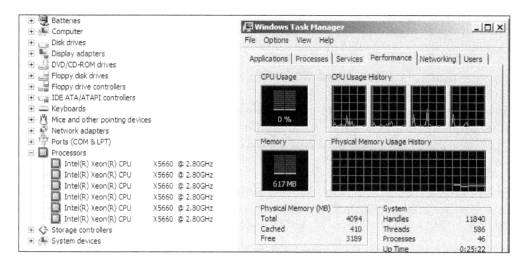

A workaround in this case is to change the `cpuid.coresPerSocket` parameter.

This parameter controls the number of cores per socket assigned to the VM. If there are six vCPUs with one core each assigned to a VM, the `cpuid.coresPerSocket` parameter set to 2 makes the VM think that it has three vCPUs with two cores each. It works like a multiplier; for example, if it's set to 2 for a VM with eight CPUs, this VM will get four two-core processors, and if it's set to 4, the VM will get two four-core CPUs.

The `cpuid.coresPerSocket` parameter can be adjusted either in the `.vmx` file directly or through vCenter in VM settings under **Options | Advanced | General | Configuration Parameters...** as shown in the following screenshot:

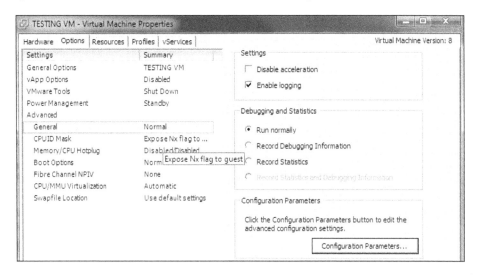

If this parameter is not listed there, click on **Add Row** to add it, as shown in the following screenshot:

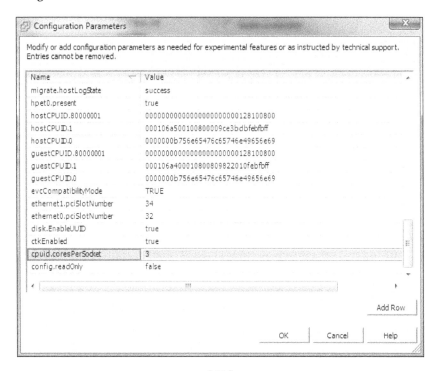

After the adjustment, all six CPUs become available as shown in the following screenshot:

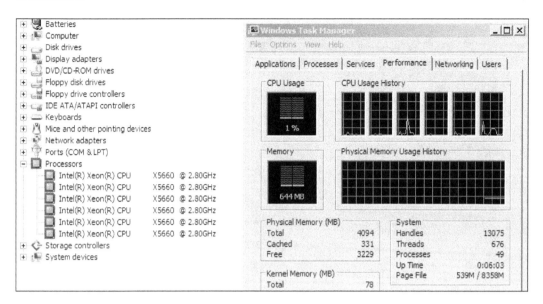

Therefore, the `cpuid.coresPerSocket` parameter allows you to choose how many virtual CPUs assigned to a VM will be presented to it as CPU cores.

The SCSI controller

In one of the following steps, you will be asked to choose a virtual storage adapter, as shown in the following screenshot:

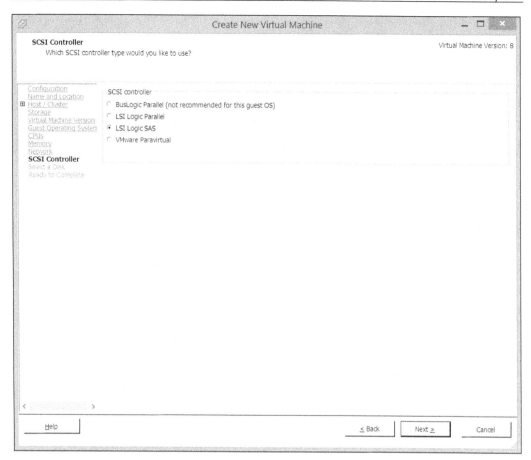

 This step is available only if the **Custom** configuration option has been chosen in the first step.

Depending on the hardware version and the operating system you've chosen in earlier steps, you may get a list that looks different. Also, depending on the guest operating system, vCenter makes a selection for you (in the preceding screenshot, **LSI Logic SAS**). This will be recommended by the VMware virtual storage adapter for the particular guest operating system that you chose earlier.

The BusLogic Parallel adapter is considered as a legacy adapter today. It's supported by default on older operating systems; for example, Windows 2000. There are no current updates or enhancements being made anymore. Therefore, for most operating systems that you will deploy, it will be marked in the list as not recommended for this guest OS.

LSI Logic Parallel (which is called just LSI Logic in older versions of vSphere) is the most commonly used option. It's the default option for Windows 2003, Windows Vista, and most Linux guest operating systems. The backend for BusLogic and LSI Logic Parallel is almost identical, with some minor differences depending on the hardware adapters used. There are performance tests that show almost the same I/O speed and CPU usage for both adapters. However, VMware recommends using the LSI Logic adapter. It has better performance and also works better with generic SCSI devices.

The main reason for having these two different controllers is the availability of drivers in different operating systems. Older operating systems support BusLogic by default, while newer systems have LSI Logic drivers included.

vSphere 4 introduced two new virtual storage adapters: LSI Logic SAS and VMware Paravirtual.

LSI Logic SAS is supported from hardware Version 7. It is the default adapter for Windows 2008, Windows 7 and 8, and Windows Server 2012. There is no huge improvement in performance with LSI Logic SAS as compared with LSI Logic Parallel, just that it's a little bit faster. There are also a few small things to consider while choosing between LSI Parallel and SAS, which are described as follows:

- The SAS adapter is more actively maintained by LSI; therefore, better bug fixes, updates, and OS support can be expected now and in the future
- The SAS adapter is needed by **Microsoft Cluster Server** (**MSCS**)
- The SAS adapter works better on Linux guests with SCSI hotplug disks, as there is no need to rescan an SCSI bus manually to find new devices

The VMware Paravirtual adapter (PVSCSI) is also supported on hardware Version 7 or later. It is a high-performance virtual storage adapter that is available, however, for only a specific list of guest operating systems. For virtual machines that have high I/O usage, these type of adapters provide significant performance improvement by increasing overall storage throughput while reducing CPU utilization.

On vSphere 4, prior to update, one PVSCSI could be used only on data volumes. With the release of U1, support for boot volumes has been added. The following guest operating systems support PVSCSI adapters:

- Windows Server 2003
- Windows Server 2008 and R2
- Windows Server 2012
- Windows 8
- Red Hat Linux 5

Performance tests show that cycles per I/O (CPIO) or CPU usage reduction can be anywhere between 10 to 30 percent with PVSCSI and Fibre Channel storage. With iSCSI storage, CPIO reduction can be up to 25 percent. The actual performance improvement depends on the I/O block size.

According to VMware, in high I/O environments with ESX 4, the PVSCSI adapter can provide a 12 percent increase in storage performance while consuming 18 percent less CPU space. These tests were performed in very high I/O situations, such as in 350,000 IOPS on VMFS volumes. According to the VMware knowledgebase article 1017652, PVSCSI performs better than LSI Logic for virtual machines that do more than 2,000 IOPS and issue less than four outstanding I/Os.

Therefore, it's not recommended to use PVSCSI for VMs that perform less than 2,000 IOPS. At the same time, if the PVSCSI adapter has already been chosen for a low I/O VM, it's not recommended to revert to LSI. Reverting takes time and effort, while the performance impact will be negligible as compared with LSI Logic's performance.

Another case when PVSCSI cannot be used is when MSCS is needed.

The following table summarizes the differences between the storage virtual adapters described earlier:

Virtual adapter	Guest OS with support by default	Use cases
BusLogic Parallel	Windows XP and earlier Windows Server 2000 and earlier	Rarely used, considered legacy
LSI Logic Parallel (LSI Logic)	Windows Vista Windows Server 2003 Linux	Most commonly used
LSI Logic SAS	Windows 7 and 8 Windows Server 2008 and 2012 Linux	MSCS
PVSCSI	N/A	High I/O usage (over 2,000 IOPS)

As mentioned earlier, guest operating systems don't have drivers for PVSCSI adapters by default. Therefore, if you choose to use this adapter, you will need to load the driver before a virtual disk can be recognized by the OS.

As you begin the operating system installation, you will notice there are no disks listed that can be used. As an example, we will use Windows Server 2008 R2.

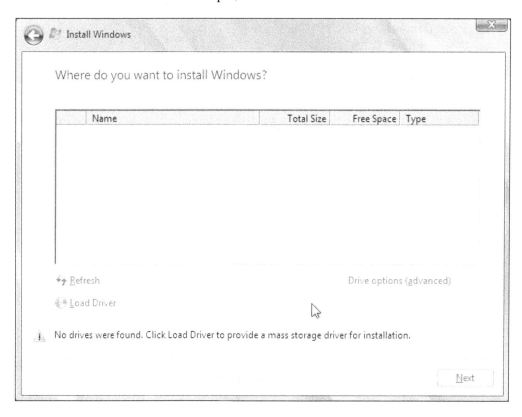

To load the appropriate driver, you will need to connect an image from the datastore to the VM's floppy drive. Click on the floppy drive image and choose **Connect to floppy image on a datastore...** as shown in the following screenshot:

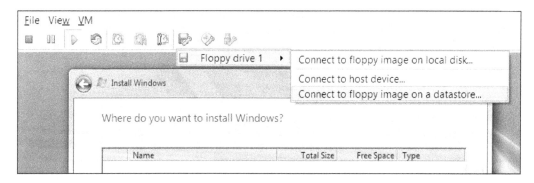

In the **Browse Datastores** dialog box, navigate to the **vmimages | floppies** folder. From there, choose an image according to the guest operating system you are trying to install, as shown in the following screenshot:

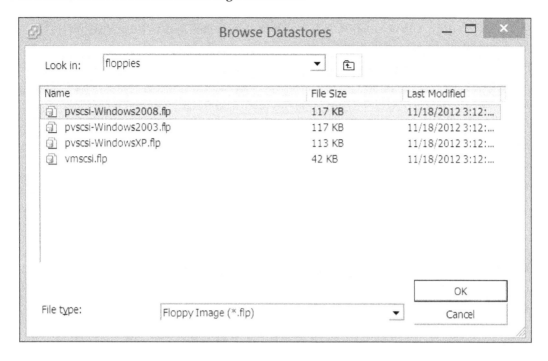

Once it's done, click on the **Load Driver** button on the Windows installation screen, click on browse and expand the floppy disk drive, and then choose the appropriate top level folder depending on the operating system. In our example, it will be the **amd64** folder. amd64 is a generic name for 64-bit systems. No matter which processors you use (Intel or AMD) for 64-bit operating systems, you will need to choose the folder called **amd64**.

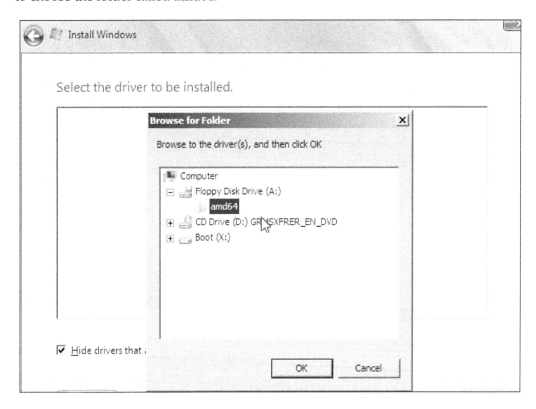

Once it's completed, you will see the virtual drive listed as shown in the following screenshot:

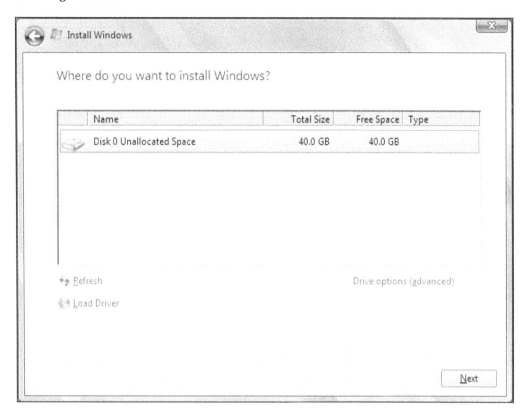

You will then be able to proceed with Windows installation as usual.

Virtual disks

Another step that needs to be described in more detail is virtual disk options.

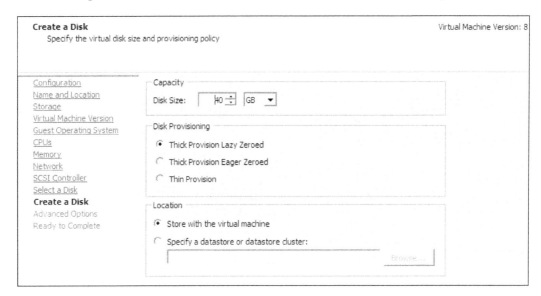

 In order to do this, the **Custom** configuration option should be chosen in the first step.

vCenter will offer a disk size based on your OS selection in previous steps. If you are planning to use this VM as a template or will migrate it to another environment later, it is better to accept the default virtual drive size and expand it when needed. Refer to the next section on expanding virtual drives.

The provisioning section has three options:

- **Thick Provision Lazy Zeroed**: By default, it creates a virtual disk as a thick disk. The space that is required for the disk is allocated right away during creation. If there is any data remaining on the physical device, it is not erased during disk creation; it will be overwritten later upon the first write request from the virtual machine. This option leaves the possibility to recover deleted files or restore old data on allocated space if it hasn't been overwritten by new data yet.

- **Thick Provision Eager Zeroed**: This creates a thick disk that supports clustering features such as Fault Tolerance. Any data remaining on the physical device will be zeroed out as part of the disk creation process. Usually, it takes much longer to create such disks as compared to other disk types.

- **Thin Provision**: This creates a disk that uses only as much space as it needs. If more space is needed, it will grow to the maximum capacity allocated to it. This option allows you to save space on storage. However, it may be dangerous if you are not controlling the available storage space or if the virtual disk starts growing fast. Please refer to the storage free space troubleshooting in the *Snapshots* section later in this chapter and the section on setting up storage usage alerts in *Chapter 7, Events, Alarms, and Automated Actions*.

From the VM settings dialog, a thin disk can be converted to a thick disk, but not the other way around. You can also change the disk format with Storage vMotion as you are prompted to choose the disk format during the migration. With Storage vMotion, you will be able to switch from the thin to thick format and the other way around.

The location section allows you to create a virtual disk on a different storage.

The advanced virtual disk options in the following step allow you to choose the way a disk is affected by snapshots:

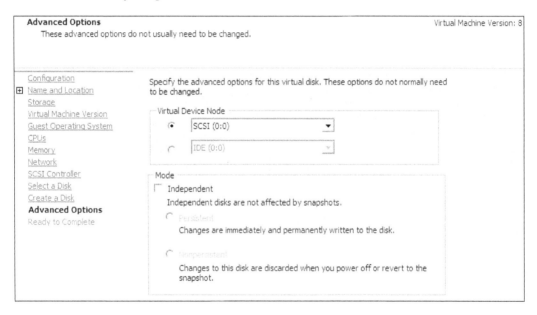

Independent (persistent) disks behave like regular drives on your physical computer and are not affected by snapshots. All of the data written to a disk in persistent mode is written permanently. Therefore, data stays on the disk even if the virtual machine is reverted to a snapshot.

Independent (nonpersistent) disks behave like read-only drives. Any changes are discarded as soon as a virtual machine is turned off, rebooted, or reverted to a snapshot. In the nonpersistent mode, the virtual machine is restarted with a virtual disk in the same state every time. Changes to the disk are written to and read from a `redo` logfile that is deleted when the VM is turned off, rebooted, or reverted to a snapshot.

Unless you are going to use an existing disk, it probably doesn't make much sense to choose the nonpersistent option at this point. Once an operating system is installed and configured, you'll be able to shut down the virtual machine and switch drives to the nonpersistent mode to preserve its state. One of the possible applications of nonpersistent disks is to simulate application installation or issue the revert VM image to the original state. Similar results can also be achieved with snapshots.

Once the virtual machine is created, you can boot it off a CD or an ISO image and deploy the operating system. The following options are available in vSphere client to connect devices or images to CD-ROM and is shown in the following screenshot:

Expanding a drive

When you need to expand a drive, the first step is to increase its size in VM settings, as shown in the following screenshot:

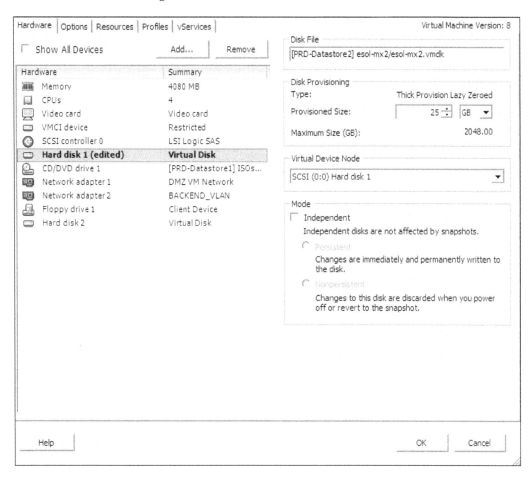

After it's done, the next step is to extend this drive inside the guest OS. In Windows Server 2008, Windows Vista, and later versions, any drives including system drives can be extended online while the virtual machine is running using the built-in **Disk Management** tool. Once in **Disk Management**, refresh the view to see additional unallocated space at the end of a partition, right-click on this partition, and choose **Extend Volume**.

Disks in Windows Server 2003 and Windows XP can be extended using the `diskpart` command-line tool. The following is an example of `diskpart` usage:

```
C:\Documents and Settings\administrator>diskpart
Microsoft DiskPartversion 5.2.3790.3959
Copyright (C) 1999-2001 Microsoft Corporation.

DISKPART> list volume
Volume ###  Ltr  Label        Fs     Type        Size     Status
Info
----------  ---  ----------   -----  ----------  -------  ---------
--------
Volume 0     E   Data         NTFS   Partition   12 GB    Healthy
Volume 1     D                       DVD-ROM      0 B     Healthy
Volume 2     C                NTFS   Partition   14 GB    Healthy
System

DISKPART> select volume 0
Volume 0 is the selected volume.

DISKPART> extend
DiskPart successfully extended the volume.

DISKPART> exit
Leaving DiskPart...

C:\Documents and Settings\administrator>
```

After running `diskpart`, I've listed the available volumes in the system. Volumes are listed with the corresponding drive letter, so it's hard to make a mistake. I've chosen a volume I need to extend and typed `extend`. If you choose a wrong volume that doesn't have any unallocated space later, `diskpart` will give you an error message, so the utility is quite safe.

In any case, it is highly recommended to have a full backup before doing any of these tasks.

Unfortunately, when it comes to extending system drives under Windows XP or Windows Server 2003, it can't be done with built-in tools while the system is running. One of the possible options will be to boot the VM from any live CD that has partitioning tools and extend the system drive from there. My personal preference is the GParted Live CD. Another option will be to connect the VM's system virtual drive to another VM and expand it with `diskpart` as the nonsystem drive. This approach requires additional VMs and seems to have more steps; however, it doesn't require any third-party software.

Booting a VM from CD-ROM

When you need to boot a VM from a CD-ROM or an ISO image, it may be frustrating to catch the moment when *Esc* has to be pressed in order to get to the **Boot Menu** option.

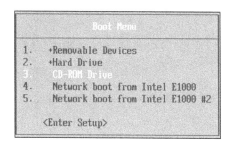

To increase this timeout, set the power on boot delay to 5,000 in VM settings under **Boot Options**. This will make the VM wait for you for 5 seconds to press *Esc* before it starts booting the OS from the virtual disk, as shown in the following screenshot:

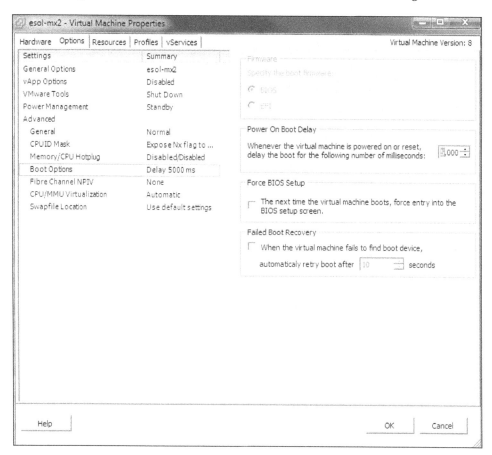

This setting can also be changed directly in the VM's `.vmx` file as follows:

```
bios.bootDelay = "5000"
```

If this line does not exist, it can be added at the end of the file.

Extending a drive in a Linux guest operating system

While running a Linux guest OS, in most cases, `ext3` volumes are used.

The following is a general sequence of commands to extend the logical `ext3` volume on CentOS or Red Hat virtual machines:

1. Turn on or reboot the virtual machine so that the system picks up changes to the virtual drive that was extended in VM settings.

2. Identify the device name. For a system drive, it is `/dev/sda` by default. Confirm the new size by running the following command:

    ```
    # fdisk -l
    ```

3. Create a new primary partition on this drive. You will need to specify the drive name using the results of the preceding step:

    ```
    # fdisk /dev/sda
    ```

4. Press *P* to print the partition table to identify the number of partitions. Often, there will be two of them: `sda1` and `sda2`.

5. Type `n` and press *Enter* to create a new primary partition.

6. Then, type `p` for primary.

7. Finally, type `3` for the partition number. This may be different depending on the output of the partition table.

Press *Enter* two times.

Type `w` and press *Enter*, which writes the changes to the partition table.

Run the following command to apply changes. Depending on your system, a restart may be needed.

```
# partprobe
```

To verify that the changes were applied to the partition table and that the new partition has an 83 type, run the following command:

```
# fdisk -l
```

To convert the new partition to a physical volume, you will need to run the following command:

```
# pvcreate /dev/sda3
```

 The pvdisplay command will help you determine which partition to convert.

Extend the physical volume by running the following command:

```
# vgextend VolGroup00 /dev/sda3
```

 The vgdisplay command will help you determine which volume group to extend.

Verify the amount of physical extents that are available to the volume group by running:

```
# vgdisplay VolGroup00 | grep "Free"
```

Extend the Logical Volume by running the following command where # is the amount of available free space in GB obtained from the previous command:

```
# lvextend -L+#G /dev/VolGroup00/LogVol00
```

 The uselvdisplay command finds out which Logical Volume to extend.

Finally, you can expand the ext3 filesystem online inside the Logical Volume by running the following command:

```
# ext2online /dev/VolGroup00/LogVol00
```

The following command can be used to verify that the / filesystem has the correct amount of new available free space:

```
# df -h /
```

For different Linux distributions, these commands may be different. For example, you may need to use resize2fs instead of ext2online.

VMware Tools

VMware Tools are meant to enhance the performance of virtual machines. Its installation is optional; however, certain tasks and features are not available without it being installed.

VMware Tools installs itself as a service and starts when the guest operating system boots.

Its main functions are as follows:

- Pass information between the guest OS and host and send heartbeats to the host indicating that the guest OS is running
- Execute scripts if the power state of a VM changes
- Synchronize the time of the guest OS with the time on the host
- Allow the mouse pointer to move freely outside the console window
- Fit screen resolutions of the guest to the size of the console window or to that of the client's resolution when in full-screen mode
- Help create a snapshot of the Windows guest

Many of the preceding features are accomplished with drivers that are installed together with the service. For example:

- The SVGA driver adjusts screen resolution and improves graphics performance
- The mouse driver allows the pointer to move freely, improves mouse performance, and is required for certain tools and programs such as Microsoft Terminal Services
- Most Windows virtual machines running in vSphere require audio drivers
- The `vmmemctl` driver is responsible for performing Memory Balooning, that is, returning unused memory from the VM to the host
- The VMXNet NIC driver replaces the VMware network card driver installed by default and improves network performance

For the full list of components and drivers, please refer to the section on MSI arguments for automated VMware Tools installation described later in this chapter.

The list of drivers that are installed together with VMware Tools will be different for different guest operating systems. There is also an option for custom installation where drivers and components can be chosen by a user.

In the vSphere Client inventory, if you select a virtual machine and go to the **Summary** tab, you can check if this virtual machine is running the latest version of VMware Tools. In the **General** section, it shows the tools' status as well as checks if their version is current or not.

In most cases, VMware Tools needs to be upgraded after:

- Upgrading hardware to a newer version
- Installing ESX updates
- Moving the virtual machine to a host running the newer version of ESX

Installing VMware Tools on a Windows guest

In vCenter, the VMware Tools installation can be initiated by right-clicking on a virtual machine from the **Guest** submenu.

The same option is also available from vCenter's main menu.

There are two options available for deploying VMware Tools:

- Interactive or manual installation or upgrade
- Automatic installation or upgrade

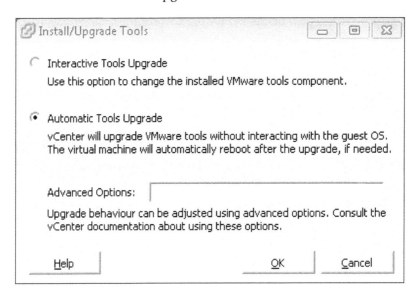

VMware Tools can be deployed on any Windows version that is supported by vSphere.

The interactive option connects a VMware Tools ISO image to the virtual machine's CD-ROM. If you are logged in to the console, in most cases, setup will start automatically. If it doesn't start automatically, you will need to run setup.exe from the CD drive. Go through the installation wizard steps, which are similar to any other software installation on Windows, where you are prompted to choose the installation type, the folder to install the software to, the components to add, and so on. Once the tools are deployed, you will be required to reboot the VM.

The automatic option deploys the tools silently. You don't need to be logged in. Once installation is finished, the virtual machine is automatically rebooted.

If you need to install VMware Tools on multiple Windows machines running on a specific host or cluster, the **Virtual Machines** tab can be used to select the virtual machines on which the installation or upgrade of VMware Tools is required. Choose multiple virtual machines by pressing *Ctrl* and then click on the **Install/Upgrade Tools** option and select **Automatic Installation**.

The **Advanced Option** field under **Automatic Installation** is for MSI arguments that we use for `setup.exe`. You can put arguments in this field the same way you type them after `setup.exe` while running it from the Windows command line.

The command-line arguments for the installation of VMware Tools are standard MSI arguments.

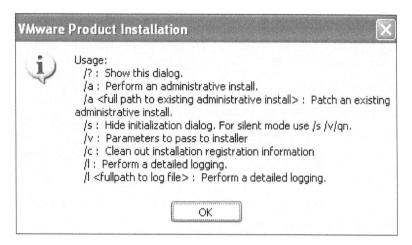

The `ADDLOCAL` and `REMOVE` options can be used to exclude some of the VMware Tools components. Valid values for available VMware Tools components are listed at `http://pubs.vmware.com/vsphere-50/index.jsp#com.vmware.vmtools.install.doc/GUID-E45C572D-6448-410F-BFA2-F729F2CDA8AC.html`.

It's important to remember that names are case-sensitive. Also, the components that are installed depend on the guest operating systems.

For example, the following command excludes the shared folders component:

```
setup.exe /S /v "/qn REBOOT=R ADDLOCAL=ALL REMOVE=Hgfs"
```

The preceding command also performs silent installation and doesn't reboot the guest once the installation is complete.

The following example is the same command but with the logging option added:

```
setup.exe /S /v "/qn /l*v ""%TEMP%\vmmsi.log"" REBOOT=R
  ADDLOCAL=ALL REMOVE=Hgfs"
```

Installing VMware Tools on a Linux guest

Unlike the installer for Windows guests, Linux installation can be completed using only the interactive option. This option connects the VMware Tools Linux ISO image file from the ESX server host to the VM's virtual CD-ROM device.

Once it's done, log in to the Linux console and execute the following command sequence:

Create a mount point—a folder where ISO images connected to the CD-ROM will be mounted—as follows:

```
# sudomkdir /mnt/cdrom
```

Mount the image using the following command:

```
# sudo mount /dev/cdrom /mnt/cdrom
```

Extract VMware Tools from the archive to the `/tmp` folder using the following command:

```
# tarxzvf /mnt/cdrom/VMwareTools-<x.x.x-xxxx>.tar.gz -C /tmp/
```

Open the folder where the tools have been extracted and start installation:

```
# cd /tmp/vmware-tools-distrib/
```

```
# sudo ./vmware-install.pl -d
```

> The `-d` switch assumes that you want to accept the defaults. If you do not use `-d`, supply your answers or press *Enter* to accept each default value.
>
> Depending on the Linux distribution you use, the command sequence may be different. The preceding commands have been tested on CentOS 5.x and should also work for Red Hat distributions.

Reboot the virtual machine. It's not necessary to reboot it right away; however, this needs to be done at some point after VMware Tools installation or upgrade.

```
# sudo reboot
```

Time synchronization

For long-term accuracy and consistency, both virtual and physical machines need to run the software that maintains the operating system's clock accuracy. The challenge with virtual machines is that because they share the host's physical hardware, they are not able to repeat the timing activity of physical machines with the same result.

Operating systems usually use one of two approaches to measure time: **tick counting** and **tickless timekeeping**.

Tick counting

The OS sets up the CPU to interrupt periodically at a known rate and then keeps count of these interrupts to determine how much time has passed.

Obviously, when it comes to virtual machines, it's hard to support this timekeeping approach. VMs share the host's CPU, and at the moment when the virtual CPU should generate a virtual timer interrupt, it simply may not be able to do this as it doesn't have physical CPU time. Therefore, VMs check for pending virtual timer interrupts only at certain points of time, such as when its host receives a physical timer interrupt, which in turn makes the guest OS time fall behind real time.

The more competition there is for the physical CPU, the more the delay in the VM's time as compared with real time. At the same time, depending on the CPU load, it may be possible to give a VM enough interrupts to keep its time current.

If an interrupt has been missed, the VM accumulates it in a backlog and starts delivering timer interrupts more frequently in order to catch up.

If a backlog of interrupts grows beyond 60 seconds, a VM resets the count to zero. This is the event where VMware Tools, if installed and configured for time synchronization, corrects clock reading on the VM. The VM then resumes, keeping track of the backlog and catching up.

Tickless timekeeping

With this approach, there is a hardware device that keeps track of time units passed after the system has booted. Operating systems simply read the current counter value when it's needed. Tickless timekeeping doesn't keep the CPU busy with handling interrupts and allows better granularity of time values. However, it works only on machines that have a suitable hardware counter which must be able to run at constant rates and are expected to be reasonably fast.

Virtual machines that use tickless timekeeping don't need to keep track of the interrupt backlog and start catching up once they fall behind. This saves CPU resources and allows the guest OS to have more accurate time.

However, a VM needs to know that the guest OS uses an approach to keep a track of time. If the guest OS hasn't set any virtual time devices to generate periodic interrupts, the VM will assume that it uses tickless timekeeping. Some operating systems program timer devices for periodic interrupts even if they use the tickless approach. In this case, this can be determined from the guest OS type. Alternatively, software can make a hypercall to inform the VM that it's tickless.

A hypercall is a system call from a guest system to its hypervisor below. It's usually a call that requests a service. Guests are required to have hypervisor-specific code in order to make such calls.

VM time synchronization

For VMware guest operating systems, there are two options available for time synchronization:

- An OS service such as W32Time in Windows or NTP in Linux
- VMware Tools

Both options have advantages and disadvantages.

VMware Tools synchronization is able to detect the virtual machine's catch-up and properly interact with it. If a time error is only by a known backlog, VMware Tools lets OS correct the time. Otherwise, it instructs the VM to set its backlog to zero and corrects the time. One of the advantages of using VMware Tools is that it doesn't require networking to be operational on a VM in order to be able to synchronize its time.

If guest time is ahead of real time for some reason, newer versions of VMware Tools cause it to run slower to catch up. However, older versions are not able to correct the guest time that is ahead.

All versions of VMware Tools make one-shot corrections which are able to change the time when it's ahead of the correct time. One-shot corrections happen even if the periodic synchronization feature is off for a VM.

Native software is generally able to correct guest time that is ahead or behind real time. In many cases, however, it's not able to make any corrections in the case of a large difference from real time. Native software is not able to detect a VM's built-in catch-up and therefore does not perform synchronization as well when it runs on physical hardware.

It's considered a best practice to use only one synchronization method.

To configure VMware Tools for time synchronization, simply select the following options under **Miscellaneous Options** in **VMware Tools Properties**:

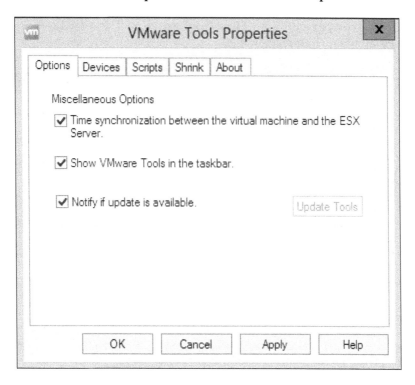

Alternatively, you can set `tools.syncTime = true` in the `.vms` configuration file.

If you use VMware Tools for time synchronization, it's important to make sure that the host OS has the correct time and synchronizes its time periodically with an external source. For ESX/ESXi 4.1 and ESXi 5.0 hosts, this can be done in the **Configuration** tab by navigating to **Time Configuration | Properties | Options | NTP settings** shown as follows:

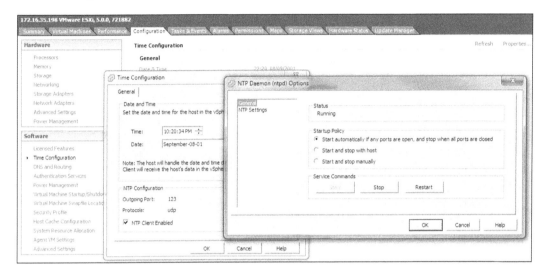

In the **General** settings, you can configure start, stop, and restart NTP Daemon. Under **NTP settings**, you can add or remove NTP servers.

In certain cases, for testing or because of old software that needs the OS to have a date before the year 2000, you may need to disable any time synchronization. This can be accomplished with the following lines in VM configuration:

```
tools.syncTime = FALSE
time.synchronize.continue = FALSE
time.synchronize.restore = FALSE
time.synchronize.resume.disk = FALSE
time.synchronize.shrink = FALSE
time.synchronize.tools.startup = FALSE
time.synchronize.resume.host = FALSE
```

Some older versions may need 0 instead of FALSE.

The following table explains the meaning of each parameter:

Parameter	Meaning
`tools.syncTime`	This parameter controls periodic clock synchronization
`time.synchronize.continue`	This parameter controls clock synchronization after snapshot creation
`time.synchronize.restore`	This parameter controls clock synchronization after reverting to a snapshot
`time.synchronize.resume.disk`	This parameter controls clock synchronization after a VM is resumed or migrated to another host
`time.synchronize.shrink`	This parameter controls clock synchronization after a virtual disk has been defragmented
`time.synchronize.tools.startup`	This parameter controls clock synchronization after the VMware Tools service has been started
`time.synchronize.resume.host`	This parameter controls clock synchronization after the host resumes from sleep

Cloning the existing VM

Cloning is the process of creating a copy of existing virtual machines. It saves time in installing operating systems and doing initial configuration; however, this may be dangerous. There are post-cloning tasks that have to be performed, and they are discussed in the next section.

Hot and cold cloning

To clone a virtual machine, right-click on a VM in the inventory and choose the **Clone...** option from the menu:

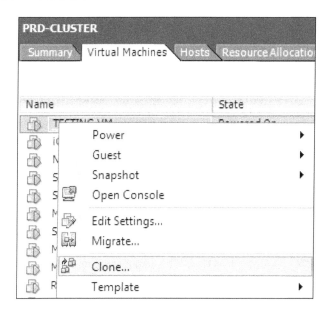

Follow the wizard prompts that will ask you to choose the name and location for the new virtual machine.

Cloning can be done while a VM is running or while it's off. There are two options, which are referred to as hot and cold cloning.

When you do hot cloning, vCenter creates a snapshot and then makes a copy of the snapshot that will become the new virtual machine. Therefore, if any data has been changed during cloning, the new virtual machine will be out-of-date as these changes have not been committed.

Cold cloning takes less time and less space as it doesn't require a snapshot.

In vCenter versions earlier than 2.5 Update 2, a virtual machine has to be turned off in order to clone it.

Postcloning tasks for Windows guests

When you clone VMs, it's important to be extra careful to not harm the existing environment. Two identical servers in your environment may cause different issues—IP address conflicts, name resolution conflicts, and so on.

The following should be considered before switching on a new virtual machine:

- Clones are assigned a new **Universally Unique Identifier** (**UUID**), which may affect user scripts and API calls to the virtual machine.

- Clones have new MAC addresses for all existing network adapters, which may affect software or licensing that is sensitive to MAC address changes.

- Guest operating systems for virtual machine clones will share computer names, SIDs, and static IP addresses with their source VM. Therefore, it may be a good idea to disable NICs before a new VM is switched on until the name, SIDs, and other settings are changed.

The official documentation recommends running `sysprep` on a Windows virtual machine before cloning. However, it's not always possible to do so, especially if you need to clone production servers. By experience, it should be enough to just run the NewSID utility from Mark Russinovich on new VMs after cloning. When Windows Server 2008 was released, Microsoft stopped supporting this utility; therefore, it may be hard to find this today. You don't need it for Windows Server 2008, Windows Vista, or later operating systems unless you are going to use Kerberos authentication.

However, it is a good idea to run it each time you clone a VM with an older version of Windows, especially if you are planning to join the new machine to the same domain.

After the cloning process is finished, make sure you disable the network adapter before powering the VM on, especially if its network adapter is in the same virtual network and has a static IP address assigned from the source machine.

Therefore, if you are planning to run NewSID on new VMs after cloning, it may be a good idea to copy the utility to the source machine before cloning so that you don't need to connect the new machine to your network with an old SID.

vCenter offers a good alternative to running NewSID manually. It's called guest customization, and it's available in one of the last steps if you are cloning virtual machines or deploying them from a template. Further information on using customizations can be found in the next section.

Deploying a VM from a template

The main reason for using templates is efficiency. While creating a template, you go through common tasks only once when you need to deploy multiple VMs that are the same. For all future VMs, you don't need to go through the same tasks every time you need a new virtual server.

Another reason for using templates is that they allow the elimination of human errors. Often there is a need to have two or more identical servers in a production environment. Going through the same setup tasks for each server is not only labor intensive, but also highly error prone. A better way would be to create a template once and deploy each new VM from it. Have a look at the following figure:

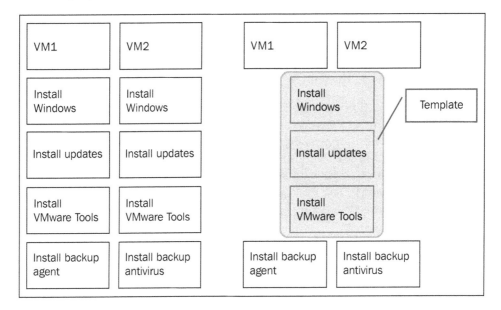

The more VMs you deploy using templates, the more time and effort you save.

Creating a template

To create a template, build a new VM and set up and configure only the things that will be common between future deployments. Make sure that the VM is named properly and the machine name in the OS is something temporary that will never be used in your environment. Also, once it's ready, make sure network adapters are not assigned any static IP addresses.

Once all tasks are done, shut down the VM and convert it to a template.

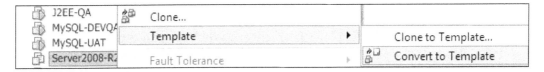

If you are planning to use this VM as well, you can choose the **Clone to template...** option instead. Templates should not be connected to a domain. Therefore, if you are planning to use this VM, make sure you clone it to a template before connecting it to the domain.

To be able to see templates in vCenter, you may need to switch to the **VMs and Templates** view as shown in the following screenshot:

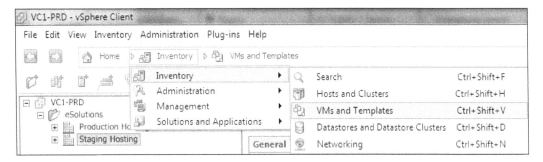

When you need to deploy a new virtual machine from a template, simply right-click on the template, choose **Deploy Virtual Machine from this Template...**, and go through the wizard that lets you select a new VM name, its location, and so on:

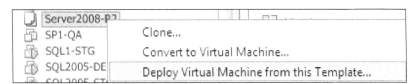

Postdeployment tasks

Everything mentioned in the section about cloning VMs (regarding post-cloning tasks) applies to new deployments from templates as well. Therefore, if you are creating a new template for Windows XP or Windows Server 2003, make sure you have a copy of the NewSID utility on the VM's virtual drive before converting it to a template, or make sure you run `sysprep` before connecting a new virtual machine to the existing environment.

As mentioned before, vCenter offers an alternative to running NewSID, that is, guest customization. Customizations allow you to do much more than just changing SID. They allow you to do the following:

- Change the Windows registration information
- Change the Windows computer name
- Change the administrator password

- Change IP, DNS, WINS, and other network configuration settings
- Join a VM to the Windows domain
- Change the Windows product key
- Change the time zone
- Run any custom scripts on first time login

Customization options are available in the last step of the **Deploy template** wizard:

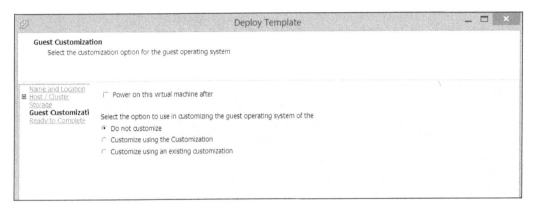

If you are running an older version of vCenter, for the last two options to be available, the server needs to have `sysprep` files for the operating system you need to customize the settings for. Therefore, if the two last options are greyed out, check if there are files for this OS under `C:\Documents and Settings\All Users\ Application Data\VMware\VMware VirtualCenter\sysprep` or `/etc/vmware/ vmware-vpx/sysprep/` if you are using vCenter Appliance.

If the necessary files are missing, you may need to download `sysprep` for this operating system from the Microsoft website. You will also need to place it in the appropriate folder; for example, for Windows Server 2003, the folder should be called `svr2003`, and for the 64-bit version, it is `svr2003-64`. Instead of downloading `sysprep` from Microsoft's website, you can extract `\SUPPORT\TOOLS\DEPLOY.CAB` from the OS installation disk to the appropriate folder.

If you choose the **Customize using the Customization** option, the customization wizard will open and you will be able to choose the options that are needed.

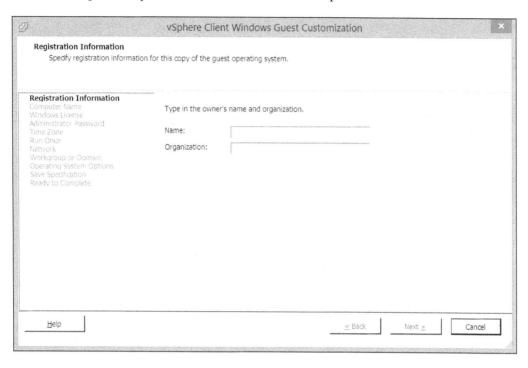

All of the steps and questions are straightforward. You can also create customizations with different options and reuse them for future deployments. If you already have existing customizations, choose the last option.

Customizations can be created in **Customization Specifications Manager** by accessing it from vCenter's **Home** page, as shown in the following screenshot:

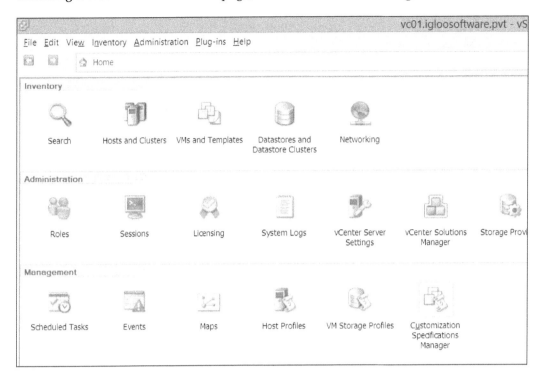

Once you click on **New**, you can go through the customization wizard and save your settings for future use. To have the SID replaced, make sure you choose the **Generate New Security ID (SID)** option:

Customization Specifications Manager allows you to edit existing customizations as well as copy, export, and import them.

There are certain requirements that have to be met in order to be able to customize the guest operating system, which are as follows:

- The virtual machine or template should have the current version of VMware Tools installed.

- The guest operating system being customized must be installed on a disk attached as SCSI node `0:0` in the virtual machine configuration.

- For Windows guest customization, the ESXi host that the virtual machine is running on must have Version 3.5 or later.

- Customization of Linux guest operating systems requires the installation of Perl in these systems.

- Guest operating systems that you are running must be supported for customization. Supported operating systems can be checked in the VMware compatibility guide at `VMware.com`.

Keeping templates up-to-date

As changes happen to existing virtual machines, either OS updates or configuration changes, you will probably want to keep your template updated as well so that there is no need to go through the same changes when new deployments need to be made from this template.

In order to make changes to a template, you will need to convert it to a virtual machine.

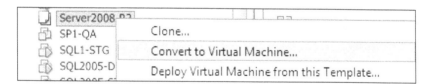

Then, power it on, make the changes, shut it down, and convert it back to a template:

Template best practices

As there may be many virtual machines deployed from one template, it is important to follow best practices while using templates, as any configuration mistake may be replicated multiple times before it's noticed.

Suggested best practices for using VM templates are:

- Keep your templates up-to-date with patches, antivirus definitions, and so on
- Use the template's notes field to store information and comments
- Install VMware Tools on the templates
- Use a temporary network connection to update templates
- Don't join templates to the domain
- Name templates appropriately
- Use vCenter folders to organize templates
- Tune up and harden the operating system as necessary (for example, disable unused Windows services)

Importing/exporting an OVF template

To export a virtual machine as an OVF template, select the VM and use the vCenter option from the **File** menu:

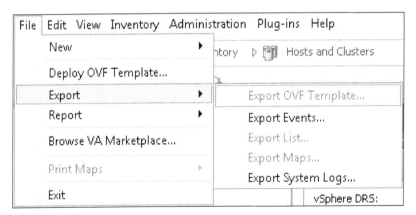

You will need to specify the template name and the folder where you want it saved. The virtual machine needs to be off before this option is available. Therefore, if you need to export the live production server, you can hot-clone it and then export the cloned VM to the template.

The OVF template is very convenient if you need to move virtual machines to a different location or a remote environment. Because OVF compresses VM files, the final template's size will be smaller than raw virtual disk files.

Importing the OVF template using the command line and GUI

Version 5 of vCenter has the option to import OVF templates from GUI:

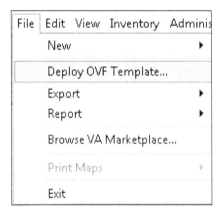

Once you select it, follow the wizard prompts to choose the host, storage, and other settings for a new virtual machine in your environment.

OVF templates can also be imported using the OVF Tool, which is a command-line utility. It can be downloaded from the VMware website. The following is an example of its usage:

```
ovftool.exe -ds=PRD-Datastore1 -nw=DMZ_LAN D:\temp\Backups\web1-
   prd\web1-prd.ovf vi://administrator@vc1-prd/Contoso/Production
     Hosting/host/"ESX1 & ESX2 3950"/
```

Where –ds specifies storage LUN, -nw specifies where the network VM's virtual adapter will be assigned to, and vi points to the location in vSphere where the template will be imported to.

Depending on your environment, the `vi` path may be different from what you can see in the vCenter hierarchy. In this case, you will get an error message that the path has not been found. To be able to build a correct path, you can remove all subfolders except for the first one. Once you press *Enter*, you should get an error message saying that the path is not complete with options available for the next subfolder. Add the next subfolder and so on until it points to the correct location as shown in the following lines of code:

```
ovftool.exe -ds=PRD-Datastore1 -nw=DMZ_LAN D:\temp\Backups\web1-prd\web1-
prd.ovf vi://administrator@vc1-prd

Opening OVF source: D:\temp\Backups\web1-prd\web1-prd.ovf

Please enter login information for target vi://vc1-prd/

Username: administrator

Password: ***************

Error: Found wrong kind of object (Folder)

Possible completions are:

Contoso/


ovftool.exe -ds=PRD-Datastore1 -nw=DMZ_LAN D:\temp\Backups\web1-prd\web1-
prd.ovf vi://administrator@vc1-prd/Contoso

Opening OVF source: D:\temp\Backups\web1-prd\web1-prd.ovf

Please enter login information for target vi://vc1-prd/

Username: administrator

Password: ***************

Error: Found wrong kind of object (Folder)

Possible completions are:

  Production Hosting/

  Staging Hosting/
```

Importing OVF templates into previous versions of vSphere

If you try to import OVF templates that were created in ESXi 5 into the older 4.1 server, it will fail with the following error message:

```
Unsupported hardware family
```

The solution is to replace `vmx-08` with `vmx-07` in the `.ovf` file.

To be able to successfully import templates after this change with OVF Tools, you'll need to use the `skipManifestCheck` parameter to skip validation of the OVF package manifest. Otherwise, you'll get an error saying that the template is corrupt.

The same approach works if you need to move a VM from ESXi 5.0 to ESXi4.1. Before you can turn it on, you need to replace Version 8 with Version 7 in the .vmx file (four to five occurrences).

Unless you use any special features of the vmx-08 hardware, this solution works fine.

The preceding error message happens because later versions of ESXi support new versions of virtual hardware with additional features when Version 4.1 doesn't. The full list of new features supported by hardware Versions 8, 9, and 10 is given in the following table:

Hardware Version 7 (vSphere 4.1)	Hardware Version 8 (vSphere 5.0)	Hardware Version 9 (vSphere 5.1)	Hardware Version 10 (vSphere 5.5)
255 GB RAM	1 TB RAM		4 TB RAM
	3D graphics for Windows Aero support	Improved 3D graphics support that allows you to run intensive graphics applications such as CAD but works only with NVidia GPUs.	Improved 3D graphics; works also with AMD-based and Intel-based cards.
USB 2.0	Support for USB 3.0 devices in virtual machines with Linux guest operating systems. USB 3.0 devices attached to the client computer running the vSphere Web Client or the vSphere Client can be connected to a virtual machine and accessed within it. USB 3.0 devices connected to the ESXi host are not supported at this time.		
Up to eight virtual CPUs (SMP)	Up to 32 virtual CPUs	Up to 64 virtual CPs	
Up to 2 TB virtual disks			Up to 64 TB virtual disks
EFI – No	EFI – Yes		
	Support for Windows 8, Server 2012, and Mac OS 10.6 and 10.7, both 32- and 64-bit guests.	Support for Ubuntu 13.04, Debian 6, Free BSD 8.3/9, and MAC OS 10.8, both 32- and 64-bit guests.	Support for Debian 7, Free BSD 8.4/9.1, both 32- and 64-bit guests.

Hardware Versions 9 and 10 can be selected only through web client. However, it is possible to upgrade the VM hardware to later versions in vCenter Client.

USB support

USB controllers can be added to a virtual machine to connect USB devices from an ESX host or client computer. They can be added from the **Edit Settings** dialog:

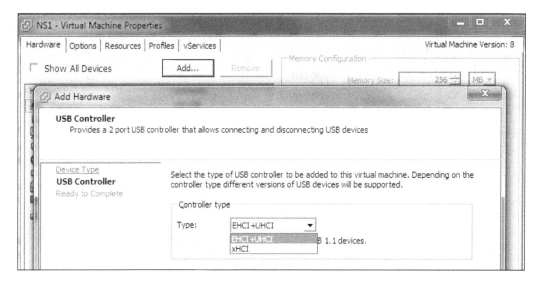

There are two types of controllers that can be added to a VM:

- **xHCI**: This is supported in hardware Version 8 for the Linux guest OS. It supports USB 3.0 as well as 2.0 and 1.1. Drivers for Windows OS are not yet available.

- **EHCI + UHCI**: This is supported in hardware Versions 7 and 8 and supports USB 2.0 and 1.1.

It's possible to add one controller of each type to a VM that supports them. Two controllers of the same type cannot be added to a single VM.

> If you connect USB devices from an ESX host, vSphere, DPM, and Fault Tolerance features will not be available.
>
> The VMware documentation says that if a host with connected USB devices resides in a DRS cluster with DPM enabled, you must disable DPM for that host. Otherwise, DPM might turn off the host with the device, which disconnects the device from the virtual machine.

For VMs that have USB devices connected from a host, DRS and vMotion are supported. You will also be able to move a VM from one host to another and keep existing USB connections from the old host. USB devices from the old host will be attached until this VM is turned off or suspended, and they cannot be reconnected while the VM is on another host. You will need to move this VM back to the original host in order to be able to reconnect USB devices.

To be able to successfully vMotion a VM with host USB devices attached, they need to be configured for vMotion:

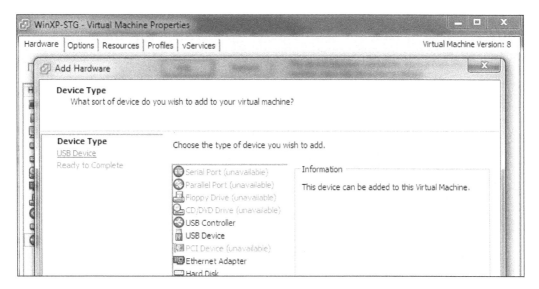

This should be done when the USB device is being attached:

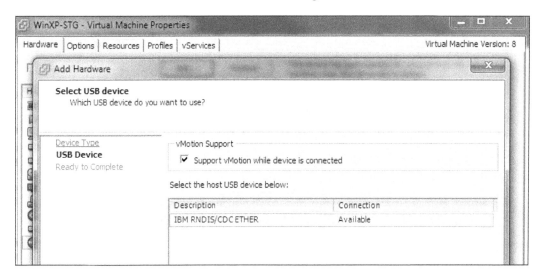

With USB devices connected from the client computer, HA and Fault Tolerance features will not be available to VMs, while DPM, DRS, and vMotion will work.

A summary of the features supported with connected USB devices is given in the following table:

Feature	Pass through from host	Pass through from client PC
vSphere Distributed Power Management (DPM)	No	Yes
vSphere Distributed Resource Scheduler (DRS)	Yes	Yes
vSphere HA	-	No
vSphere Fault Tolerance	No	No
vSPhere vMotion	Yes	Yes

A summary of USB support is given in the following table:

Controller type	Guest OS	Support	USB version	Pass through from host	Pass through from client PC
EHCI + UHCI	Linux	Yes	1.1, 2.0	Yes	Yes
	Windows	Yes	1.1, 2.0	Yes	Yes
	Mac OS	Yes (enabled by default)	1.1, 2.0	Yes	Yes
xHCI	Linux	Yes (kernel 2.6.35 or later)	1.1, 2.0, 3.0	Yes (only USB 1.1, 2.0)	Yes
	Windows	No	-	-	No
	Mac OS	No	-	-	No

Snapshots

Each time you make a snapshot, vCenter Server creates a new file, usually with **delta** in its name. It starts writing all the changes into this file, leaving the original .vmdk file (which represents a virtual machine's hard drive) untouched. Changes are written on the blocks' level, that is, even if you are moving a file from one folder to another (inside the guest OS), it's already considered as a change to VM and this change is added to the delta file.

This means that vCenter Server is just adding changes and increasing delta files. There is no limit for it to grow (it grows while there is free space on the storage) and a snapshot can become several times bigger than a VM's virtual disk itself.

If one more snapshot is made, the server creates another delta file and starts writing changes there.

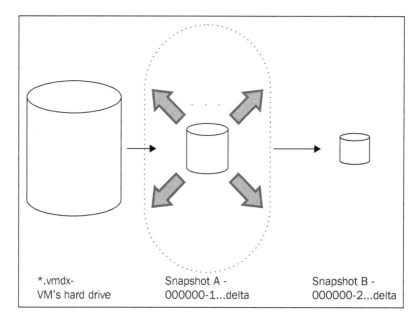

| *.vmdx- | Snapshot A - | Snapshot B - |
| VM's hard drive | 000000-1...delta | 000000-2...delta |

We are facing two potential problems here. The first one is that large delta files start causing performance issues. The second one is that growing delta files can use all the available space on the storage.

The size of the delta file becomes a problem, especially if the guest is a database server where there are small portions of data that are added and moved frequently.

All of the above means that snapshots are good if you want to test something and then revert to the previous state in case there are problems, but snapshots don't work well for backing up the state of the VM. And of course, snapshots should be deleted after testing as soon as possible.

When vSphere starts deleting a snapshot, it creates a temporary delta file, also called a helper, where it starts saving changes to the VM while it's consolidating the snapshot. Therefore, snapshot consolidation is equivalent to creating one more snapshot and merging the previous one to the main .vmdk file. Once the merging is done, it creates another delta file to merge the first one, and so on until the delta file is 64 KB, that is, the size of a block that can be merged at once.

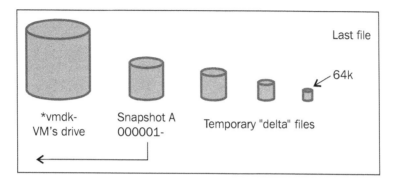

The size of this delta file depends on how long it takes to delete the previous snapshot as well as on how many changes are happening to the disk during the operation. Obviously, the slower your storage is and the more actively you use the VM, the larger the delta files will be.

Free space

If a snapshot hasn't been deleted and took up all the free space on the storage partition, the guest will shut down with the error that there is no more space for the .vmdk file to grow.

The logical step will be to try to delete one or more snapshots to free some space; however, that may not be the best approach in this situation.

vCenter will not be able to create a temporary delta because there is no free space on the storage anymore, and you will be stuck with pending tasks that cannot be canceled and which are taking up all the space that you are able to free right away.

As soon as there is no free space for this temporary delta file, you will probably get an error message as follows:

```
there is no more space for the redo log of -0000xx.vmdk.
```

You will be given the option to abort or retry.

If you choose **Abort**, the virtual machine is turned off, the snapshot is aborted, and a Consolidate Helper snapshot is created. The Snapshot Manager UI shows this Consolidate Helper snapshot. You can delete the Consolidate Helper snapshot after you have made some space available.

If you click on **Retry**, Snapshot Manager returns to the Consolidate Helper snapshot mode, unless you have made more disk space available.

You will see Consolidate Helper each time the snapshot removal fails for whatever reason, not because of free space alone.

So, if you didn't know that it was necessary to free space before trying to remove a snapshot, you have to free some space now and click on **Retry**. However, this option does not always work as it's described in the documentation. Sometimes you get a series of unpleasant surprises, starting from the situation when the server doesn't even try to remove a snapshot if free space is available and ending with unresponsive VMs and frozen VM processes on the server.

Unfortunately, it's hard to tell exactly how much free space will be necessary to successfully remove a snapshot as it depends on many factors. In slow environments, you may need to free at least the same space as the size of the snapshot you are removing or even more.

Seeking additional free space

What if it's not possible to free enough space for some reason?

There are still some things that can be done, which are described as follows:

- Power off other virtual machines residing on the same storage partition. This operation deallocates the swap file. A virtual machine's swap file is usually the same size as the allocated amount of RAM. This operation does not have to be done to the machine which is running off of the snapshot. If there are non-critical machines residing on the same partition, they can be powered off to free up storage for the commit operation.

- Add an extent to the existing partition. If there is a lack of disk space, the Add Extent wizard on your storage can be used to increase the amount of space available. The Add Extent operation is irreversible and creates a dependence of multiple LUNs for a single one.

- Clone the virtual machine to a partition or storage that has more space. For more details, refer to the cloning section earlier in this chapter. Cloning will consolidate all snapshots and create a single .vmdk file.

Another task is in progress

In case you are already stuck with the issues described earlier, do not turn on the guest VM until you are done with removing snapshots. If you try, it will only make the situation worse as you will get a hanged or an unresponsive client process. This means that the `vmware-mgmt` service is unable to get any responses from the client process and so it thinks that the task is still in progress (even if it finished a long time ago).

In this situation, you will not be able to do anything with the guest through the VMware client. It will be impossible to shut down the guest or reset it (as management services still thinks that another task is in progress), and if you shut down a running OS from the console or remote access, you will not be able to start it again. The guest will never go to the shutdown state because of the same error message described as follows:

```
There is another task in progress.
```

If you use an older version of vCenter and the snapshot you are trying to delete is big enough, you may get an "operation timed out" message. This happens because there is a default 15-minute timeout for operations in older versions of vCenter. You would get this message after 15 minutes regardless of the task status, and it doesn't mean that the operation was interrupted, failed, or aborted. Most likely, it's still running and will be finished successfully.

The only way to check if the task is still running or not is to make `ssh` connection to ESX server and go to a folder where the VM's files are located, which can be done as follows:

```
# cd /vmfs/volumes/
# ls -la
```

Check if there are any files with delta in their name or not. If not, this means the snapshot was deleted successfully. If there are still some delta files, the may be that you have other snapshots for this VM or the task is still running. Check if the size of the files and date/time are changing.

This behavior has been fixed in vCenter 5. It doesn't timeout anymore and shows true progress.

If you are running a vSphere version older than 4.0 Update 2, do not choose a **Delete all** option if there are several snapshots, especially if you are running out of free space on the storage. This operation requires more time and more free space. It's much better to delete snapshots one by one. It's much better to delete snapshots starting from the oldest one and remove a current snapshot when it's the only one left.

This has been changed in vSphere 4.0 U2; it deletes snapshots starting from the oldest one, illustrated in the following figure:

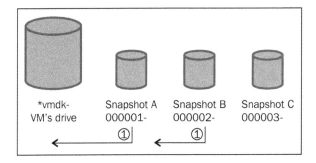

If you had more than one snapshot, this will free space before you need additional space to delete the previous snapshot. This means that if you have only one snapshot and are running out of space on the storage, it may be better to create a new snapshot and delete the old one first instead of deleting the existing snapshot right away.

Summary

A virtual machine in VMware is a set of files stored on a supported storage device. To create a new virtual machine, you can use the Create New Virtual Machine wizard. VMware Tools enhances the performance of a virtual machine. Its installation is optional; however, certain tasks and features are not available without it being installed. Virtual machine cloning can be done while a VM is running or while it's off— two options referred to as hot and cold cloning.

The main reason for using templates is efficiency. While creating a template, you go through common tasks only once when you need to deploy multiple VMs that are the same. So, for all future VMs, you don't need to go through the same tasks every time you need a new virtual server. Another reason for using templates is that they allow the elimination of human errors.

The OVF template is very convenient if you need to move a virtual machine to a different location or a remote environment. Because OVF compresses VM files, the final template's size will be smaller than raw virtual disk files.

Each time you make a snapshot, vCenter Server creates a new file, usually with delta in its name. It starts writing all the changes into this file, leaving the original .vmdk file (which represents a virtual machine's hard drive) untouched.

Availability Management

This chapter focuses on the features in vCenter that allow you to reduce downtime and ensure that your services are available for end users most of the time.

We will discuss the different aspects of vSphere's **High Availability** (**HA**) and **Fault Tolerance** (**FT**), including host and VM monitoring, datastore heartbeating, and **Distributed Resource Scheduler** (**DRS**).

In this chapter we will cover the following topics:

- Reducing planned and unplanned downtime
- Creating a vSphere HA cluster
- HA security, logging, and admission control
- Preparing hosts and configuring FT

Reducing planned and unplanned downtime

Whether we are talking about a highly available and critically productive environment or not, any planned or unexpected downtime means financial losses. Historically, solutions that could provide high availability and redundancy were costly and complex.

With the virtualization technologies available today, it becomes easier to provide higher levels of availability for environments where they are needed. With VMware products, and vSphere in particular, it's possible to do the following things:

- Have higher availability that is independent of hardware, operating systems, or applications

- Choose a planned downtime for many maintenance tasks, and shorten or eliminate them
- Provide automatic recovery in case of failure

Planned downtime

Planned downtime usually happens during hardware maintenance, firmware or operating system updates, and server migrations. To reduce the impact of planned downtime, IT administrators are forced to schedule small maintenance windows outside the working hours.

vSphere makes it possible to dramatically reduce the planned downtime. With vSphere, IT administrators can perform many maintenance tasks at any point in time as it allows downtime elimination for many common maintenance operations.

This is possible mainly because workloads in a vSphere can be dynamically moved between different physical servers and storage resources without any service interruption.

The main availability capabilities that are built into vSphere allow the use of HA and redundancy features, and are as follows:

- **Shared storage**: Storage resources such as Fibre Channel, iSCSI, **Storage Area Network (SAN)**, or **Network Access Storage (NAS)** help eliminate the single points of failure. SAN mirroring and replication features can be used to have fresh copies of the virtual disk at disaster recovery sites.
- **Network interface teaming**: This feature provides tolerance for individual network card failures.
- **Storage multipathing**: This helps to tolerate storage path failures.

vSphere vMotion® and Storage vMotion functionalities allow the migration of VMs between ESXi hosts and their underlying storage without service interruption, as shown in the following figure:

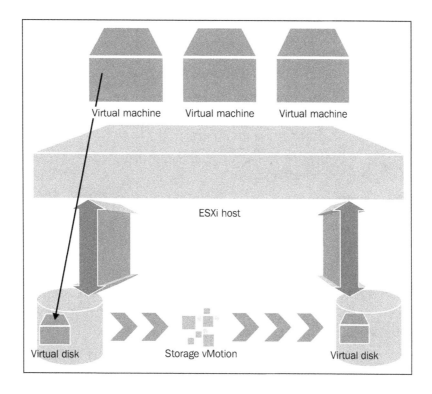

In other words, vMotion is the live migration of VMs between ESXi hosts, and Storage vMotion is the live migration of VMs between storage LUNs. In both cases, VM retains its network and disk connection. With vSphere 5.1 and the later versions, it's possible to combine vMotion with Storage vMotion into a single migration that simplifies administration. The entire process takes less than two seconds on a GB network.

vMotion keeps track of the ongoing memory transaction while memory and system states get copied to the target host. Once copying is done, vMotion suspends the source VM, copies the transactions that happened during the process to the target host, and resumes the VM on the target host. This way, vMotion ensures transaction integrity.

vSphere requirements for vMotion

vSphere requirements for vMotion are as follows:

- All the hosts must have the following features:
  - ° They should be correctly licensed for vMotion
  - ° Have access to the shared storage
  - ° Use a GB Ethernet adapter for vMotion, preferably a dedicated one
  - ° The VMkernel port group is configured for vMotion with the same name (the name is case sensitive)
  - ° Have access to the same subnets
  - ° Must be members of all the vSphere distributed switches that VMs use for networking
  - ° Use jumbo frames for best vMotion performance

- All the virtual machines that need to be vMotioned must have the following features:
  - ° Shouldn't use raw disks if migration between storage LUNs is needed
  - ° Shouldn't use devices that are not available on the destination host (for example, a CD drive or USB devices not enabled for vMotion)
  - ° Should be located on a shared storage resource
  - ° Shouldn't use devices connected from the client computer

Migration with vMotion

Migration with vMotion happens in three stages:

- vCenter server verifies that the existing VM is in a stable state and that the CPU on the target host is compatible with the CPU this VM is currently using
- vCenter migrates VM state information such as memory, registers, and network connections to the target host
- The virtual machine resumes its activities on the new host

VMs with snapshots can be vMotioned regardless of their power state as long as their files stay on the same storage. Obviously, this storage has to be accessible for both the source and destination hosts.

If migration involves moving configuration files or virtual disks, the following additional requirements apply:

- Both the source and destination hosts must be of ESX or ESXi version 3.5 or later

- All the VM files should be kept in a single directory on a shared storage resource

To vMotion a VM in vCenter, right-click on a VM and choose **Migrate...** as shown in the following screenshot:

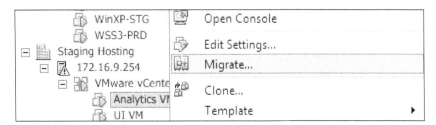

This opens a migration wizard where you can select whether it's going to migrate between hosts or storage or both. The **Change host** option is the standard vMotion, and **Change datastore** is the Storage vMotion. As you can see, the **Change both host and datastore** option is not available because this VM is currently running. As mentioned earlier, vSphere 5.1 and later support vMotion and Storage vMotion in one transaction.

In the next steps, you are able to choose the destination as well as the priority for this migration. Multiple VMs can be migrated at the same time if you make multiple selections in the **Virtual Machines** tab for the host or the cluster.

VM vMotion is widely used to perform host maintenance such as upgrading the ESX operating system, memory, or any other configuration changes. When maintenance is needed on a host, all the VMs can be migrated to other hosts and this host can be switched into the maintenance mode. This can be accomplished by right-clicking on the host and selecting **Enter Maintenance Mode**.

Unplanned downtime

Environments, especially critical ones, need to be protected from any unplanned downtime caused by possible hardware or application failures. vSphere has important capabilities that can address this challenge and help to eliminate unplanned downtime.

These vSphere capabilities are transparent to the guest operating system and any applications running inside the VMs; they are also a part of the virtual infrastructure. The following features can be configured for VMs in order to reduce the cost and complexity of HA. More detail on these features will be given in the following sections of this chapter.

High availability (HA)

vSphere's HA is a feature that allows a group of hosts connected together to provide high levels of availability for VMs running on these hosts. It protects VMs and their applications in the following ways:

- In case of ESX server failure, it restarts VMs on the other hosts that are members of the cluster
- In case of guest OS failure, it resets the VM
- If application failure is detected, it can reset a VM

With vSphere HA, there is no need to install any additional software in a VM. After vSphere HA is configured, all the new VMs will be protected automatically.

The HA option can be combined with vSphere DRS to protect against failures and to provide load balancing across the hosts within a cluster (see the *DRS* section in *Chapter 6, Resource Management*, for more details).

The advantages of HA over traditional failover solutions are listed in the VMware article at http://pubs.vmware.com/vsphere-51/index. jsp?topic=%2Fcom.vmware.vsphere.avail.doc%2FGUID-CB46CEC4-87CD-4704- A9AC-058281CFD8F8.html.

Creating a vSphere HA cluster

Before HA can be enabled, a cluster itself needs to be created. To create a new cluster, right-click on the datacenter object in the **Hosts and Clusters** view and select **New Cluster...** as shown in the following screenshot:

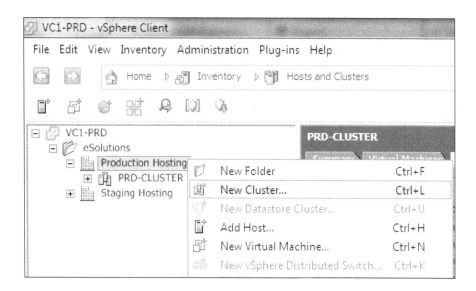

The following prerequisites have to be considered before setting up a HA cluster:

- All the hosts must be licensed for vSphere HA.

ESX/ESXi 3.5 hosts are supported for vSphere HA with the following patches installed; these fix an issue involving file locks:

ESX 3.5: `patch ESX350-201012401-SG` and prerequisites

ESXi 3.5: `patch ESXe350-201012401-I-BG` and prerequisites

- At least two hosts must exist in the cluster.
- All the hosts' IP addresses need to be assigned statically or configured via DHCP with static reservations to ensure address consistency across host reboots.
- At least one network should exist that is shared by all the hosts, that is, a management network. It is best practice to have at least two (see *Chapter 2, Managing ESXi Hosts*, for more details about setting up the host's networking).
- To ensure VMs can run on any host, all the hosts should also share the same datastores and virtual networks.

- All the VMs must be stored on shared, and not local, storage.
- VMware tools must be installed for VM monitoring to work.
- Host certificate checking should be enabled.

Once all of the requirements have been met, vSphere HA can be enabled in vCenter under the cluster settings dialog. In the following screenshot, it appears as **PRD-CLUSTER Settings**:

Once HA is enabled, all the cluster hosts that are running and are not in maintenance mode become a part of HA.

HA settings

The following HA settings can also be changed at the same time:

- Host monitoring status is enabled by default
- Admission control is enabled by default
- Virtual machine options (restart priority is **Medium** by default and isolation response by default is set to **Leave** powered on)
- VM monitoring is disabled by default
- Datastore heartbeating is selected by vCenter by default

More details on each of these settings can be found in the following sections of this chapter.

Host monitoring status

When a HA cluster is created, an agent is uploaded to all the hosts and configured to communicate with other agents within the cluster. One of the hosts becomes the master host, and the rest become slave hosts. There is an election process to choose the master host, and the host that mounts more datastores has an advantage in this election. In cases where we have a tie, the host with the lexically-highest **Managed Object ID (MOID)** is chosen.

> MOID, also called MoRef ID, is a value generated by vCenter for each object: host, datastore, VM, and so on. It is guaranteed to be unique across the infrastructure managed by this particular vCenter server.
>
> When it comes to the election process for choosing the master host, a host with ID 99 will have higher priority than a host with ID 100.

If a master host fails or becomes unavailable, a new election process is initiated.

Slave hosts monitor whether the VMs are running locally and report to the master host.

In its turn, the master host communicates with vCenter and monitors other hosts for failures. Its main responsibilities are listed as follows:

- Monitoring the state of the slave hosts and in case of failure, identifying which VMs must be restarted
- Monitoring the state of all the protected VMs and restarting them in case of failure
- Managing a list of hosts and protected VMs
- Communicating with vCenter and reporting the cluster's health state

Host availability monitoring is done through a network heartbeat exchange, which happens every second by default. In cases where we lose network heartbeats with a host, before declaring it as failed, the master host checks whether this host communicates with any of the existing datastores using datastore heartbeats and responds to pings sent to its management IP address or not.

The master host detects the following types of host failure:

Type of failure	Network heartbeats	ICMP ping	Datastore heartbeats
Lost connectivity to the master host	-	+	+
Network isolation	-	-	+
Failure	-	-	-

If host failure is detected, the host's VMs will be restarted on other hosts.

Host network isolation happens when a host is running but doesn't see any traffic from vSphere HA agents, which means that it's disconnected from the management network. Isolation is handled as a special case of failure in VMware HA. If a host becomes network isolated, the master host continues to monitor this host and the VMs running on it. Depending on the isolation settings chosen for individual VMs, some of them may be restarted on another host.

The master host has to communicate with vCenter, therefore, it can't be in the isolation mode. Once that happens, a new master host will be elected.

When network isolation happens, certain hosts are not able to communicate with vCenter, which may result in configuration changes not having effect on certain parts of the infrastructure. If a network infrastructure is configured correctly and has redundant network paths, isolation should happen rarely.

Datastore heartbeating

Datastore heartbeating was introduced in vSphere 5. In the previous versions of vSphere, once a host became unreachable through the management network, HA always initiated VM restart, even if the VMs were still running. This, of course, created unnecessary downtime and additional stress to the host. Datastore heartbeating allows HA to make a distinction between hosts that are isolated or partitioned and hosts that have failed, which adds more stability to the way HA works.

vCenter server selects a list of datastores for heartbeat verification to maximize the number of hosts that can be verified. It uses a selection algorithm designed to select datastores that are connected to the highest number of hosts. This algorithm attempts to choose datastores that are hosted on different storage arrays or NFS servers. It also prefers VMFS-formatted LUNs over NFS-hosted datastores.

vCenter selects datastores for heartbeating in the following scenarios:

- When HA is enabled
- If a new datastore is added
- If the accessibility to a datastore changes

By default, two datastores are selected. This is the minimum amount of datastores needed. It can be changed using the `das.heartbeatDsPerHost` parameter under **Advanced Settings** for up to five datastores. The **PRD-CLUSTER Settings** dialog box can be used to verify or change the datastores selected for heartbeating, as shown in the following screenshot:

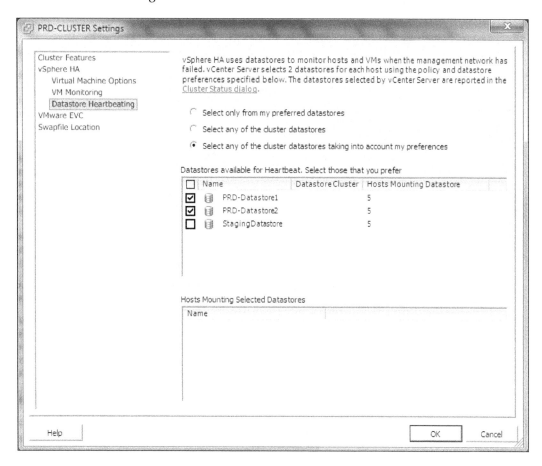

It is recommended, however, to let vCenter choose the datastores. Only the datastores that are mounted to more than one host are available in the list.

Datastore heartbeating leverages the existing VMFS filesystem locking mechanism. There is a so-called heartbeat region that exists on each datastore and is updated as long as the lock on a file exists. A host updates the datastore's heartbeat region if it has at least one file opened on this volume. HA creates a file for datastore heartbeating purposes only to make sure there is at least one file opened on a volume. Each host creates its own file and HA to be able to determine whether an unresponsive host still has connection to a datastore, and simply checks whether the heartbeat region has been updated or not.

By default, an isolation response is triggered after 5 seconds for the master host and after approximately 30 seconds if the host was a slave in vSphere 5. This time difference occurs because of the fact that if the host was a slave, it would need to go through the election process to determine whether there are any other hosts that exist, or whether the master host is simply down. This election starts within 10 seconds after the slave host has lost its heartbeats. If there is no response for 15 seconds, the HA agent on this host elects itself as the master. The isolation response time can be increased using the `das.config.fdm.isolationPolicyDelaySec` parameter under **Advanced Settings**. This is, however, not recommended as it increases the downtime when a problem occurs.

If a host becomes a master in a cluster with more than one host and has no slaves, it continuously starts checking whether it's in the isolation mode or not. It keeps doing so until it becomes a master with slaves or connects to a master as a slave. At this point, the host will ping its isolation address to determine whether the management network is available again. By default, the isolation address is a gateway configured for the management network. This option can be changed using the `das.isolationaddress[X]` parameter under **Advanced Settings**. [X] takes values from 1 to 10 and allows configuration of multiple isolation addresses. Additionally, the `das.usedefaultisolationaddress` parameter can be used to indicate whether the default gateway address should be used as an isolation address or not. This parameter should be set to `False` if the default gateway is not configured to respond to the ICMP ping packets.

Generally, it's recommended to have one isolation address for each management network. If this network uses redundant paths, the isolation address should always be available under normal circumstances.

In certain cases, a host may be isolated, that is, not accessible via the management network but still able to receive election traffic. This host is called partitioned. Have a look at the following figure to gain more insight about this:

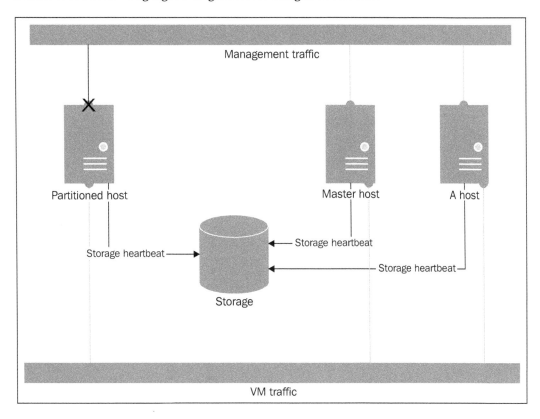

When multiple hosts are isolated but can still communicate with each other, it's called a network partition. This can happen for various reasons; one of them is when a cluster spans multiple sites over a metropolitan area network. This is called the stretched cluster configuration.

When a cluster partition occurs, one subset of hosts is able to communicate with the master while the other is not. Depending on the isolation response selected for VMs, they may be left running or restarted. When a network partition happens, the master election process is initiated within the subset of hosts that loses its connection to the master. This is done to make sure that the host failure or isolation results in appropriate action on the VMs. Therefore, a cluster will have multiple masters; each one in a different partition as long as the partition exists. Once the partition is resolved, the masters are able to communicate with each other and discover the multiplicity of master hosts. Each time this happens, one of them becomes a slave.

The hosts' HA state is reported by vCenter through the **Summary** tab for each host as shown in the following screenshot:

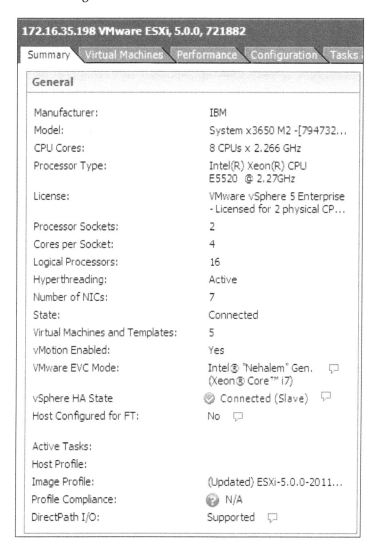

This is done under the **Hosts** tab for cluster objects as shown in the following screenshot:

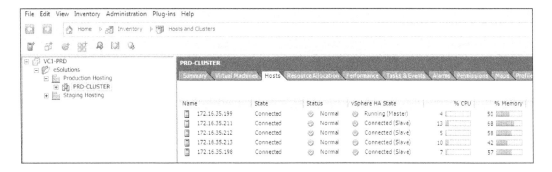

Running (Master) indicates that HA is enabled and the host is a master host.

Connected (Slave) means that HA is enabled and the host is a slave host.

Only the running VMs are protected by HA. Therefore, the master host monitors the VM's state and once it changes from powered off to powered on, the master adds this VM to the list of protected machines.

Virtual machine options

Each VM's HA behavior can be adjusted under vSphere HA settings or in the **Virtual Machine Options** option found in the **PRD-CLUSTER Settings** page as shown in the following screenshot:

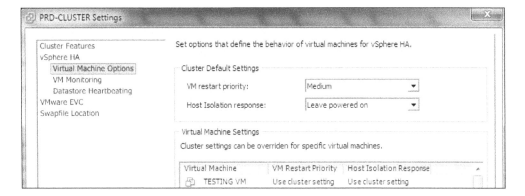

Restart priority

The restart priority setting determines which VMs will be restarted first after the host failure. The default setting is **Medium**. Depending on the applications running on a VM, it may need to be restarted before other VMs, for example, if it's a database, a DNS, or a DHCP server. It may be restarted after others if it's not a critical VM.

If you select **Disabled**, this VM will never be restarted if there is a host failure. In other words, HA will be disabled for this VM.

Isolation response

The isolation response setting defines HA actions against a VM if its host loses connection to the management network but is still running. The default setting is **Leave powered on**. To be able to understand why this setting is important, imagine the situation where a host loses connection to the management network and at the same time or shortly afterwards, to the storage network as well—a so-called split-brain situation.

In vSphere, only one host can have access to a VM at a time. For this purpose, the .vmdk file is locked and there is an additional .lck file present in the same folder where .vmdk file is stored. As HA is enabled, VMs will fail over to another host, however, their original instances will keep running on the old host. Once this host comes out of isolation, we will end up with two copies of VMs. Therefore, the isolated host will not have access to the .vmdk file as it's locked. In vCenter, however, this VM will look as if it is flipping between two hosts.

With the default settings, the original host is not able to reacquire the disk locks and will be querying the VM. HA will send a reply instead which allows the host to power off the second running copy.

If the **Power Off** option is selected for a VM under the isolation response settings, this VM will be immediately stopped when isolation occurs. This can cause inconsistency with the filesystem on a virtual drive. However, the advantage of this is that VM restart on another host will happen more quickly, thus reducing the downtime.

The **Shut down** option attempts to gracefully shut down a VM. By default, HA waits for 5 minutes for this to happen. When this time is over, if the VM is not off yet, it will be powered off. This timeout is controlled by the das.isolationshutdowntimeout parameter under the **Advanced Settings** option. VM must have VMware tools installed to be able to shut down gracefully. Otherwise, the shutdown option is equivalent to power off.

VM monitoring

Under **VM Monitoring**, the monitoring settings of individual applications can be adjusted as shown in the following screenshot:

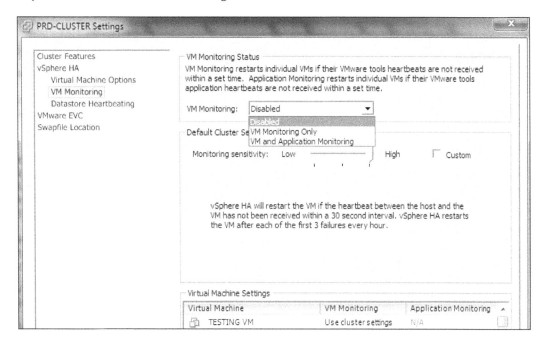

The default setting is **Disabled**. However, **VM and Application Monitoring** can be enabled so that if the VM heartbeat (VMware tool's heartbeat) or its application heartbeat is lost, the VM is restarted. To avoid false positives, the VM monitoring service also monitors VM's I/O activity. If a heartbeat is lost and there was no I/O activity (by default during the last 2 minutes), VM is considered as unresponsive. This feature allows you to power cycle nonresponsive VMs.

 I/O interval can be changed under the advanced attribute settings (for more details, check the HA Advanced attributes table later in this section).

Monitoring sensitivity can be adjusted as well. Sensitivity means the time interval between the loss of heartbeats and restarting of the VM. The available options are listed in the table from the VMware documentation article available at `http://pubs.vmware.com/vsphere-50/index.jsp?topic=%2Fcom.vmware.vsphere.avail.doc_50%2FGUID-62B80D7A-C764-40CB-AE59-752DA6AD78E7.html`.

To avoid repeating VM resets by default, they will be restarted only three times during the reset period. This can be changed in the **Custom** mode as shown in the following screenshot:

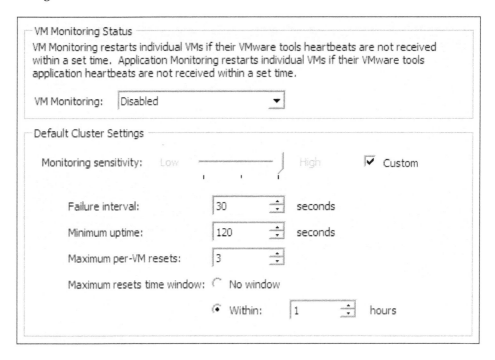

In order to be able to monitor applications within a VM, they need to support VMware application monitoring. Alternatively, you can download the appropriate SDK and set up customized heartbeats for the application that needs to be monitored.

Under **Advanced Options**, the following vSphere HA behaviors can be set. Some of them have already been mentioned in sections of this chapter.

The following screenshot shows the **Advanced Options (vSphere HA)** window where advanced HA options can be added and set to specific values:

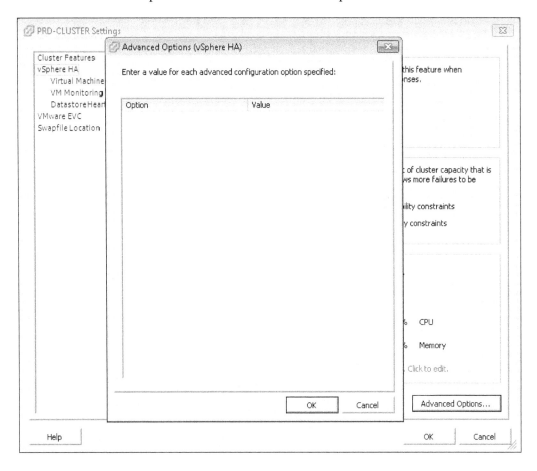

vSphere HA advanced options are listed in the article from VMware documentation available at `http://pubs.vmware.com/vsphere-50/index.jsp?topic=%2Fcom.vmware.vsphere.avail.doc_50%2FGUID-E0161CB5-BD3F-425F-A7E0-BF83B005FECA.html`. This mentioned article also lists the options that are not supported in vCenter 5. You will get an error message if you try to add one of them. Also, the options will be deleted after being upgraded from the previous versions.

Admission control

Admission control ensures there are sufficient resources available to provide failover protection as and when VM resource reservations are kept.

Admission control is available for the following:

- Hosts
- Resource pools
- vSphere HA

Admission control can only be disabled for vSphere HA. The following screenshot shows **PRD-CLUSTER Settings** with the option to disable admission control:

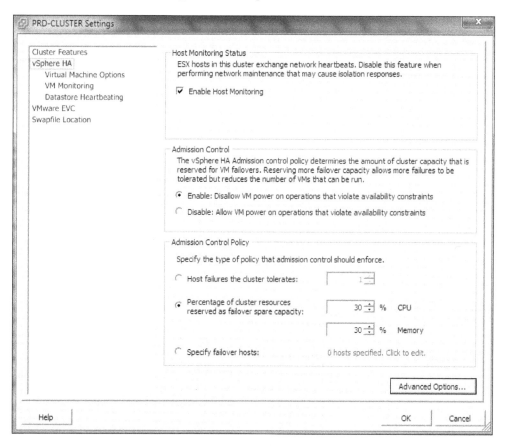

Examples of actions that may not be permitted because of insufficient resources are as follows:

- Power on a VM
- Migrate a VM to another host, cluster, or resource pool
- Increase CPU or memory reservation for a VM

Admission control policies

There are three possible types of admission control policies available for HA configuration that are as follows:

- **Host failure cluster tolerates**: When this option is chosen, HA ensures that a specified number of hosts can fail, but sufficient resources will still be available to accommodate all the VMs from these hosts. The decision to either allow or deny an operation is based on the following calculations:

  - **Slot size**: A hypothetical VM that has the largest amount of memory and CPU that is assigned to an existing VM in the environment. For example, for the following VMs, the slot size will be 4 GHz and 6 GB:

VM	CPU	RAM
VM1	4 GHz	2 GB
VM2	2 GHz	4 GB
VM3	1 GHz	6 GB

  - **Host capacity**: It gives the number of slots each host can hold based on the resources available for VMs; not the total host memory and CPU. For example, for the previous slot size, the host capacity will be as given in the following table:

Host	CPU	RAM	Slots
Host1	4 GHz	128 GB	1
Host2	24 GHz	6 GB	1
Host3	8 GHz	14 GB	2

○ **Cluster failover capacity**: This gives the number of hosts that can fail before there aren't enough slots left to accommodate all the VMs. For example, for previous hosts with 1 host failure policy, the failover capacity is 2 slots. In case of Host3 failure (host with larger capacity), the cluster is left with only two slots. But if the current failover capacity is less than the allowed limit, admission control disallows the operation. For example, if we are running two VMs and need to power the third one, it will be denied as the cluster capacity is two and it may not be able to accommodate three VMs.

This option is probably not the best one for an environment that has VMs with significantly more of resources assigned than the rest of the VMs.

The **Host failure cluster tolerates** option can be used when all cluster hosts are sized pretty much equally. Otherwise, if you use this option, then excessive capacity is reserved such that the cluster tolerates the largest host failure. When this option is used, VM reservations should be kept similar across the cluster as well. Because vCenter uses the slot sizes model to calculate capacity, and the slot size is based on the largest reservation, having VMs with a large reservation will again result in additional unnecessary capacity being reserved.

• **Percentage of cluster resources**: With this policy enabled, HA ensures that a specified percentage of resources are reserved for failover across all the hosts. It also checks that there are at least two hosts available. The calculation happens as follows:

○ The total resource requirement for all the running VMs is calculated. For example, for three VMs in the previous table, the total requirement will be 7 GHz and 12 GB.

○ The total available host resources are calculated. For the previous example, the total is 34 GHz and 148 GB.

○ The current CPU and memory failover capacity for the cluster is calculated as follows:

CPU: $(1-7/34)*100\%=79\%$

RAM: $(1-12/148)*100\%=92\%$

○ If the current CPU and memory capacity is less than allowed, the operation is denied.

With such different hosts from the example, the CPU and RAM capacity should be configured carefully to avoid a situation when, for example, the host with most amount of RAM fails and the other hosts are not able to accommodate all the VMs because of memory resources. Therefore, RAM should be configured at 87 percent based on the two smallest hosts (#2 and #3) and not 30% based on the number of hosts in the environment:

[1-(6+14)/148]*100%=87%

In other words, if the host with 128 GB fails, we need to make sure that the total resources needed by the VMs are less than the sum of 6 GB and 14 GB, which is only 13 percent of the total cluster's 148 GB. Therefore, we need to make sure that in all instances, the VMs use only 13 percent of the RAM or that the cluster has 87 percent of RAM that is free.

- **Specified failover hosts**: With this policy enabled, HA keeps the chosen failover hosts reserved, doesn't allow the powering on or migrating of any VMs to this host, and restarts VMs on this host only when failure occurs. If for some reason, it's not possible to use a designated failover host to restart the VMs, HA will restart them on other available hosts.

It is recommended to use the **Percentage of cluster resources reserved** option in most cases. This option offers more flexibility in terms of host and VM sizing than other options.

HA security and logging

vSphere HA configuration files for each host are stored on the host's local storage and are protected by the filesystem permissions. These files are only available to the root user.

For security reasons, ESXi 5 hosts log HA activity only to syslog. Therefore, logs are placed at a location where syslog is configured to keep them. Log entries related to HA are prepended with `fdm`, which stands for fault domain manager. This is what the vSphere HA ESX service is called.

Older versions of ESXi write HA activity to `fdm` logfiles in `/var/log/vmware/fdm` stored on the local disk. There is also an option to enable syslog logging on these hosts. Older ESX hosts are able to save HA activity only in the `fdm` local logfile in `/var/log/vmware/`.

HA agent logging configuration also depends on the ESX host version. For ESXi 5 hosts, the logging options that can be configured via the **Advanced Options** tab under HA are listed in the article under the logging section available at `http://kb.vmware.com/selfservice/microsites/search.do?language=en_US&cmd=displayKC&externalId=2033250`.

The `das.config.log.maxFileNum` option causes ESXi 5 hosts to maintain two copies of the logfiles: one is a file created by the Version 5 logging mechanism, and the other one is maintained by the pre-5.0 logging mechanism. After any of these options are changed, HA needs to be reconfigured.

The following table provides log capacity recommendations according to VMware for environments of different sizes based on the requirement to keep one week of history:

Size	Minimum log capacity per host in MB
40 VMs in total with 8 VMs per host	4
375 VMs in total with 25 VMs per host	35
1,280 VMs in total with 40 VMs per host	120
3,000 VMs in total with 512 VMs per host	300

These are just recommendations; additional capacity may be needed depending on the environment. Increasing the log capacity involves specifying the number of rotations together with the file size as well as making sure there is enough space on the storage resource where the logfiles are kept.

The vCenter server uses the `vpxuser` account to connect to the HA agents. When HA is enabled for the first time, vCenter creates this account with a random password and makes sure the password is changed periodically. The time period for a password change is controlled by the `VirtualCenter.VimPasswordExpirationInDays` parameter that can be set under the **Advanced Settings** option in vCenter.

All communication between vCenter and HA agents, as well as agent-to-agent traffic, is secured with SSL. Therefore, for vSphere HA, it's necessary that each host has verified SSL certificates. New certificates require HA to be reconfigured. It will also be reconfigured automatically if a host has been disconnected before the certificate is replaced. For more information about installing and using host certificates, please see *Chapter 5, Security Management*.

SSL certificates are also used to verify election messages so if there is a rogue agent running, it will only be able to affect the host it's running on. This issue, if it occurs, is reported to the administrator.

HA uses TCP/8182 and UDP/8182 ports for communication between agents. These ports are opened and closed automatically by the host's firewall. This helps to ensure that these ports are open only when they are needed.

Using HA with DRS

When vSphere HA restarts VMs on a different host after a failure, the main priority is the immediate availability of VMs. Based on CPU and memory reservations, HA determines which host to use to power the VMs on. This decision is based, of course, on the available capacity of the host. It's quite possible that after all the VMs have been restarted, some hosts become highly loaded while others are relatively lightly loaded.

DRS is the load balancing and failover solution that can be enabled in vCenter for better host resource management. More details about DRS and a description of its capabilities and features can be found in *Chapter 6, Resource Management*.

vSphere HA, together with DRS, is able to deliver automatic failover and load balancing solutions, which may result in a more balanced cluster. However, there are a few things to consider when it comes to using both features together.

In a cluster with DRS, HA, and the admission control enabled; VMs may not be automatically evacuated from a host entering the maintenance mode. This occurs because of resources reserved for VMs that need to be restarted. In this case, the administrator needs to migrate these VMs manually.

Some VMs may not fail over because of resource constraints. This can happen in one of the following cases:

- HA admission control is disabled and DPM is enabled, which may result in insufficient capacity available to perform failover as some hosts may be in the standby mode and therefore, fewer hosts would be available.

- VM to host affinity rules limit hosts where certain VMs can be placed.

- Total resources are sufficient but fragmented across multiple hosts. In this case, these resources can't be used by the VMs for failover.

- DPM is in the manual mode that requires an administrator's confirmation before a host can be powered on from the standby mode.

- DRS is in the manual mode, and an administrator's confirmation may be needed so that the migration of VMs can be started.

What to expect when HA is enabled

HA only restarts a VM if there is a host failure. In other words, it will power on all the VMs that were running on a failed host placed on another member of the cluster. Therefore, even with HA enabled, there will still be a short downtime for VMs that are running on faulty hosts. In fast environments, however, VM reboot happens quickly. So if you are using some kind of monitoring system, it may not even trigger an alarm. Therefore, if a bunch of VMs have been rebooted unexpectedly, you know there was an issue with one of the hosts and can review the logs to find out what the issue was.

Of course, if you have set up vCenter notifications, you should get an alert (for more details about setting up alerts, see *Chapter 7, Events, Alarms, and Automated Actions*).

If you need VMs to be up all the time even if the host goes down, there is another feature that can be enabled called Fault Tolerance.

Fault Tolerance

It's fair to say that vSphere HA provides only a basic level of protection; in the event of a host failure, it restarts VMs. vSphere FT, however, provides a higher level of availability and protects VMs from host failure without any downtime, any loss of data, or connection interruptions.

FT can be enabled for any critical VMs. Continuous availability is provided by creating and maintaining a secondary VM that is an exact copy of the primary one. Primary and secondary machines exchange heartbeats. This allows them to monitor each other's status.

If a host where primary VM is running fails, the secondary VM is activated within a few seconds to replace the primary one, and a transparent failover occurs.

To ensure that both VMs are exactly the same, VMware uses the vLockstep technology. vLockstep executes identical sequences of x86 instructions on both the machines. The primary VM replays all the events taking place between the processor and virtual I/O devices back to the secondary VM. The secondary VM executes these events the same way as the primary VM does, while only the primary VM executes the actual workload. Therefore, failover from the primary VM to the secondary VM happens seamlessly without any loss of the existing network connections or in-progress transactions. The whole process is transparent, fully automated, and doesn't require the vCenter server to be available.

Obviously, primary and secondary VMs are not allowed to run on the same host. When primary VMs are powered on, an anti-affinity check takes place and the secondary VM gets moved to another host.

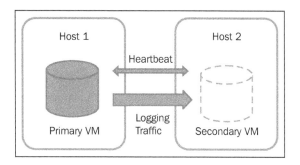

Logging traffic, by default, is unencrypted and contains all of the network and I/O data. This traffic can contain sensitive data such as passwords. Therefore, it's important to make sure that this network is secure to avoid, for example, man-in-the-middle attacks. Best practice is to make this network private.

Preparing hosts and VMs

Hosts and VMs need to be configured correctly before FT is enabled.

The following requirements should be considered:

- The cluster requirements for FT are as follows:
    - All the hosts share the same datastores and network.
    - The vSphere HA cluster has been created and enabled. For more details about creating a HA cluster, please see the previous section about vSphere HA.
    - FT logging and VMotion are configured (see the host requirements for details).

- Host certificate checking is enabled. Certificate checking can be enabled under the **SSL Settings** section in the **vCenter Server Settings** page as shown in the following screenshot:

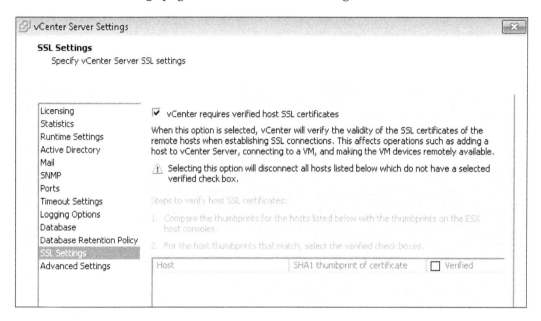

- At least two FT-certified hosts that have the same build number or are running the same FT version should be present. It's better, however, to use three hosts. If the primary VM fails on one of the hosts, the secondary VM becomes primary and creates a new secondary VM on the third host. The FT version can be checked on a host's **Summary** tab in vCenter.

 For hosts older than ESX/ESXi version 4.1, the **Summary** tab shows the host's build number instead. It is not recommended to combine ESX and ESXi hosts in an FT pair.

- The host requirements for FT are as follows:
  - **Hardware Virtualization** (**HV**) is enabled in the host's BIOS.
  - Host's CPUs are of the FT-compatible processor group. It is also recommended to use host processors that are compatible with one another. The list of supported CPUs can be found in the VMware knowledge base.
  - Hosts are licensed for FT.

° Hosts are certified for FT. This can also be verified in VMware's compatibility lists. To confirm the host's ability in supporting FT, you can also use vCenter's compliance checker in the following manner:

1. Select the cluster in the vCenter inventory and go to the **Profile Compliance** tab.

2. Click on **Check Compliance Now**, which will run the compliance tests.

3. To view the running tests, click on **Description**. The compliance status appears at the bottom of the screen. A host is labeled as either **Compliant** or **Noncompliant**.

 When a host is not compliant for FT, the reasons for this can be viewed on the **Summary** tab for each host in the vSphere Client. Click on the blue caption icon next to the **Host Configured for FT** field as shown in the following screenshot:

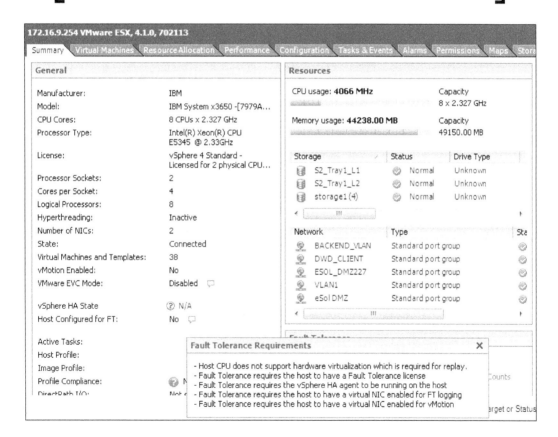

° Each host in a cluster must be configured with two different networking switches to support FT. Therefore, a minimum of two physical GB network adapters are required on each host so that it can support FT. VMware, however, recommends 10 GB adapters. vMotion and FT logging network cards must be connected to different subnets.

 IPv6 is not yet supported on FT logging NIC.

For more details on configuring virtual network switches, see *Chapter 2, Managing ESXi Hosts*.

• The VM requirements for FT are as follows:

° All the devices attached to VM are supported, and all the features it's using are compatible.

The following table gives a list of the features and devices that are not supported:

Incompatible feature	Corrective action
Snapshots	Remove all the snapshots to enable FT, or disable FT to create a snapshot
Storage vMotion	Turn off FT to migrate a VM to a different storage resource
Linked clones	Unfortunately, it's not possible to enable FT on a linked clone or to create a clone from a VM that has FT enabled on it
VM backup	Disable FT or use backup solutions that do not require snapshot creation

You will need additional products such as VMware View Composer to be able to create linked clones. Therefore, this type of clone is out of the scope of this book.

The article from the VMware documentation that lists the features and devices that are not compatible with FT is available at `http://pubs.vmware.com/vsphere-50/index.jsp?topic=%2Fcom.vmware.vsphere.avail.doc_50%2FGUID-05EA00B4-8142-4388-9439-F949C30ACA03.html`.

° VM files are thick provisioned. If you need to enable FT for a VM that uses thin provisioning, its `.vmdk` files must be converted. VM should be powered off to perform the conversion. For more details on the differences between thin- and thick-provisioned virtual drives, see the section about creating a new VM in *Chapter 3, Virtual Machine Management*.

° VM files are stored on the shared storage.

° VMs only have a single vCPU.

° VMs run on one of the following supported guest operating systems:

Supported Guest Operating Systems	Notes or Limitations
Windows 7	Requires VMware vSphere 4.0 Update 1 or greater
Windows Server 2003 (32 bit)	Requires Service Pack 2 or greater when the AMD Opteron Barcelona processor type is used
Windows XP (32 bit)	The AMD Opteron Barcelona processor type is not supported
Windows 2000	The AMD Opteron Barcelona processor type is not supported
Windows NT 4.0	The AMD Opteron Barcelona processor type is not supported
Solaris 10 (64 bit)	Requires Solaris U1 when the AMD Barcelona processor type is used
Solaris 10 (32 bit)	The AMD Opteron Barcelona processor type is not supported

Configuring FT

To enable FT on a VM, right-click on **Fault Tolerance** in vCenter and choose **Turn On Fault Tolerance** as shown in the following screenshot:

This VM will become the primary VM, and the secondary VM will be created on a different host.

Unfortunately, there is no option to turn on FT for multiple VMs. When multiple VMs are selected, the FT option is not available. FT has to be enabled on each VM separately.

When FT is on, vCenter removes the VM's memory limit and sets the memory reservation to be the same as the memory size of the VM. Therefore, the memory reservation size, limit, and shares on the VM can't be changed while FT is on.

The FT state for a particular VM can be viewed in vCenter under the **Summary** tab in the **Fault Tolerance** section for a primary VM. Under **Fault Tolerance Status**, there is an indication whether the VM is protected or not protected.

When the status is protected, it means that both the primary and secondary VMs are powered on and up and running. Not protected means that for some reason, the secondary VM is not running.

Possible reasons for a VM being in the unprotected status are listed in a table in the article available at `http://pubs.vmware.com/vsphere-51/index.jsp?topic=%2Fcom.vmware.vsphere.avail.doc%2FGUID-2E8A03D7-178E-45C6-9297-A965A9EDFA4E.html`.

Under the **Fault Tolerance** tab, you will also be able to see the location of the secondary VM, its CPU, and memory, as well as **vLockstep Interval** and **Log Bandwidth**.

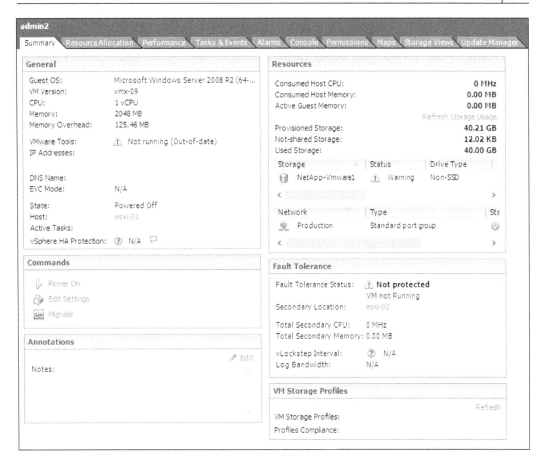

vLockstep Interval is a delay in seconds before changes in the primary VM are replicated to the secondary one. Typically, this delay is in fractions of a second. **Log Bandwidth** is the network capacity that is being used to transfer data with changes from the primary to secondary VM.

FT can be disabled from the same menu when you right-click on the VM. However, it can be disabled only from the primary VM. When FT is used together with HA, HA detects the use of FT and is able to ensure proper operation.

In cases where we have host isolation, where FT is enabled, isolation responses are not performed on VMs. Primary and secondary VMs are already communicating with each other. Therefore, they will either keep functioning if there is network connectivity or will fail over if there is no connectivity and/or the heartbeat is lost.

If a host partition occurs, HA will restart a secondary VM if the primary VM is running in the same partition as the master HA agent, or the secondary VM will not be restarted until partitioning is resolved.

Using FT with DRS

When FT is used together with DRS, the behavior will be different depending on the EVC settings. For more information about EVC, please see the section about managing hosts with different CPUs in *Chapter 2, Managing ESXi Hosts*.

If EVC is not enabled, fault tolerant VMs will have the DRS status set to disabled. In this case, the primary VM is turned on only on its registered host, the secondary VM is automatically placed, and neither of them are moved for FT purposes.

Enabled EVC allows fault-tolerant VMs to be placed and be included in the cluster's load balancing calculations. By default, DRS does not place more than four primary and secondary VMs on a single host. This limit can be changed in **Advanced Options** by adjusting the `das.maxftvmsperhost` parameter. When set to `0`, this option will be ignored by DRS.

When DRS is used with affinity rules, VM-to-VM rules apply only to primary VM, while VM-to-Host affinity rules apply to both primary and secondary VMs. The VM-to-VM rule set for the primary VM will apply to a secondary one after a failover, that is, after this secondary VM becomes primary.

Summary

Any downtime, either planned or unexpected, means financial losses. With the virtualization technologies available today, it becomes easier to provide higher levels of availability for environments where they are needed. vSphere HA is a feature that allows a group of hosts connected together to provide high levels of availability for VMs running on these hosts.

Admission control ensures that there are sufficient resources available for failover protection as and when VM resource reservations are kept. It is available for hosts, resource pools, and vSphere HA.

HA offers only a basic level of protection; in the event of a host failure, it restarts the VMs. vSphere FT provides a higher level of availability and protects VMs from host failure without any downtime, or any loss of data, transactions, or connections.

5
Security Management

In this chapter, we will discuss some aspects of security management of vCenter Server and ESXi hosts.

We will focus on users and groups, and see the logic behind them, as well as focusing on user authentication, roles, and permissions. Correct permissions assigned to the right users and groups are a basic starting point for the security of any system or application. At the same time, it's the key basis for further security improvements and enhancements.

In the second part of this chapter, we will explore the ESXi firewall, security certificates, and ESXi lockdown mode.

In this chapter, the following topics will be covered:

- User authentication
- Users and groups
- Roles and permissions
- ESXi firewall
- ESXi security certificates and encryption
- ESXi lockdown mode

User management

Proper user management is a vital component of a secure environment. To be able to manage vSphere in a secure manner, administrators are expected to know and understand the logic behind users, groups, as well as roles and permissions in vCenter and ESXi.

The following sections focus on items mentioned earlier and the authentication process in general.

Authentication

When vCenter Server connects to ESXi, it authenticates the host using **Pluggable Authentication Modules (PAM)**. PAM's configuration, including paths to authentication modules, is stored at /etc/pam.d/system-auth-generic. vCenter establishes a connection with the VMware Host Agent process. By default, the local password database is used for authentication.

vCenter Server users connect to the Host Agent process via TCP/80 and TCP/443 ports. The client sends the username and password to the host process. Host Agent process in turn passes these credentials to the PAM module that performs authentication.

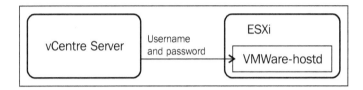

VMware ESX is a modified version of CentOS 5.0, therefore, ESX local users and groups' concept is very close to the Linux model. If you know the basics of Linux users and groups, it's a good start for understanding ESX. When it comes to vCenter, however, it uses Windows users and groups separately from ESX Linux, as local users, as well as uses a different approach for managing users, groups, and permissions.

vCenter's model is outlined in the following figure. Role, in this case, is what you are allowed to do. In vCenter, you give permissions to certain users by assigning users and groups to roles for different objects in an environment, including VMs, hosts, clusters, and so on. Roles generate permission at the vCenter object level, where they were created, and this information is stored in the vCenter database. More details about users, groups, roles, and permissions can be found later in this chapter.

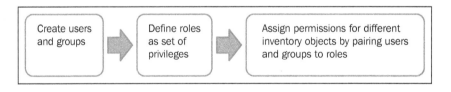

Users and groups

Users and groups are used to control access to vSphere.

There are two categories of users in vSphere:

- **vCenter users**: These users are authorized to access the environment through vCenter. These are either users of the Windows domain that this vCenter belongs to, or local Windows users on the host where vCenter Server is installed.

- **Direct access users**: They are the users who can log in to ESX hosts directly. These users are maintained locally on the ESX host and are separate from vCenter users.

Local ESX users can be created or modified under the **Local Users & Groups** tab. You will need to log in to the host directly using vSphere Client.

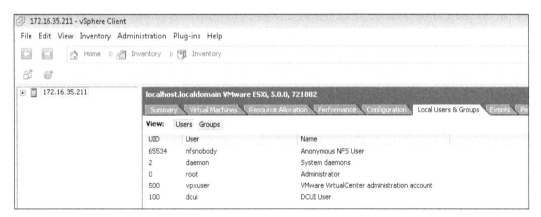

To create a new user, right-click anywhere in the **Users** table, then select **Add**, which will open the **Add New User** dialog box. Enter **User Name**, **Login**, and **Password** as well as choose the group membership, and grant shell access to enable access to ESX through the command shell. The dialog box is shown in the following screenshot:

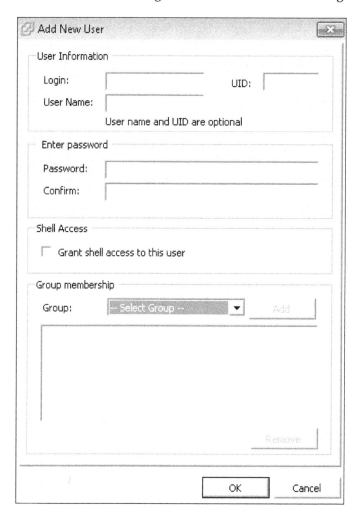

ESXi assigns the next available UID, therefore, specifying it is optional. The password you choose must comply with the following password requirements:

- At least eight characters long if it contains characters from only one or two character classes
- At least seven characters long if it contains characters from three character classes

- At least six characters long if it contains characters from all four character classes

User creation will fail with the following error if the chosen password is not compliant:

```
passwd: Authentication token manipulation error.
```

To modify or delete a user, simply right-click on the user in the list and click on **Edit** or **Remove**. If you remove users who are currently logged in, their host permissions will be kept until the host is restarted. Make sure you don't remove the root user.

Local users can also be sorted and exported to XML, HTML, CSV, or Microsoft Excel format, as shown in the following screenshot:

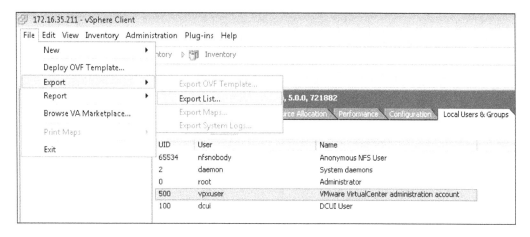

Local groups can be managed in a similar way from the **Groups** view.

You'll be able to add, remove, and edit groups as well as assign users to groups, as shown in the following screenshot:

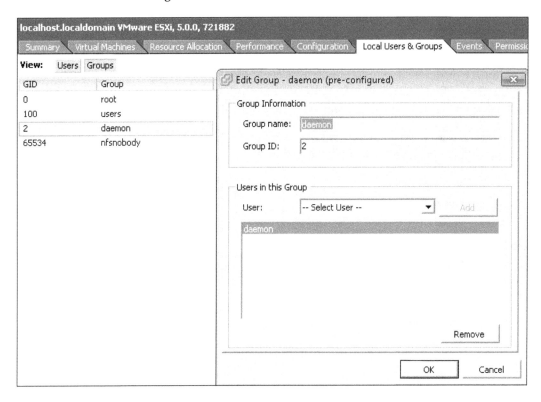

Of course, rather than creating users and groups on each host separately, it's more convenient and efficient to manage them centrally in **Active Directory** (**AD**).

It is recommended not to use the built-in Windows groups and distribution groups. Distribution groups are not yet enforced in vCenter.

To remove users from vCenter, they must be removed from the Active Directory users list. Permissions granted to these users will be lost.

If certain permissions were granted individually to users or granted by including a user in another group, removing the group—which this user is a member of—does not affect these permissions.

When changing a user's name in your Active Directory, keep in mind that the old name will become invalid in vCenter. The case is similar with group names; old names become invalid. This happens, however, only after vCenter is restarted.

A host can also be configured to use Active Directory users for authentication. To do this, the following conditions should be true:

- ESXi should use FQDN

- The host's time should be synchronized with the directory server, which can be done using NTP

- One of the AD controllers should be the user as the DNS server so that the ESX host can resolve names from this domain

Once these prerequisites have been checked, select a host in the inventory list in vCenter, navigate to **Configuration** | **Authentication Services**, and click on **Properties…**. Select **Active Directory** from the drop-down menu, type your domain name, and click on **Join Domain**, as shown in the following screenshot:

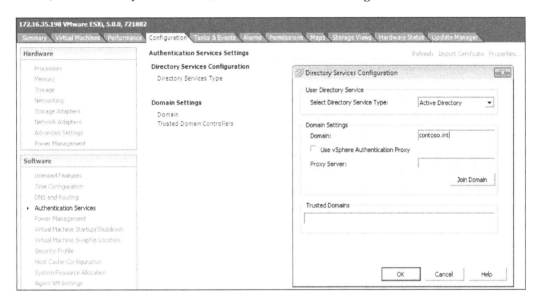

Roles and permissions

A role is a predefined set of privileges. When you assign a role to a user or a group, you assign a group of permissions for an object to this user or group. Therefore, one user can have different privileges for different objects. For example, a user can be assigned the administrator role to one resource pool and read-only privileges to another.

There are three main default roles in ESXi, and other roles inherit their privileges and contain additional privileges. Default ESXi roles cannot be edited and are called system roles. Other roles called "sample" are provided for convenience, as guidelines and suggestions, and can be modified or removed.

Default ESXi and vCenter roles are listed in the following article from the VMware documentation:

```
http://pubs.vmware.com/vsphere-50/index.jsp#com.vmware.vsphere.
security.doc_50/GUID-9A748247-BFCF-4A8C-816A-3DB404B612C4.html
```

When a new role is created, it gets the Read Only privileges plus three system-defined privileges, which are System.Anonymous, System.View, and System.Read. Therefore, custom roles created by the administrator by default don't inherit privileges from any built-in roles.

Roles on hosts, and in vCenter, are separate. With vCenter, you get additional roles to choose from. Roles created directly on a host are not accessible in vCenter; the administrator will need to connect to the host directly each time these roles need to be used. Therefore, using custom roles on the host is not recommended if you are running vCenter as this may add additional confusion and complexity. If you are running vCenter, use only vCenter custom roles.

Roles in vCenter can be managed under **Administration | Roles**, as shown in the following screenshot:

Administrators can add, remove, edit, or clone the existing roles. When you create a new role, you are asked to give it a name and choose one or more privileges that will be assigned to this role.

Any changes to roles or permissions take effect immediately with the exception of searches user log off. Even if a user is logged on, he or she will be affected by changes in roles.

Once a user or a group is assigned a role, this user or group has permissions to perform certain tasks according to the role's privileges. Therefore, roles are used to control the tasks that the users can perform on different objects. Permissions are assigned on a level of object's hierarchy, and an administrator can choose whether these permissions will be inherited by a child object or not.

Inheritance of permissions is also hierarchical. Please refer to the following figure for vSphere's hierarchy:

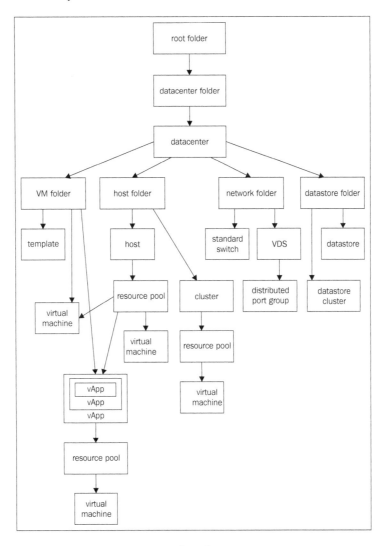

An object can have multiple permissions. For each group, however, you can assign one permission per object. Permissions applied to a child object overwrite the permissions inherited from the parent objects.

Object permissions are assigned under the **Permissions** tab, as shown in the following screenshot:

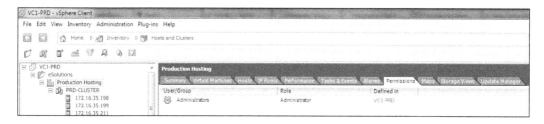

Once you right-click on the page and click on **Add Permission**, you'll get a dialog window from where certain roles can be assigned to one or more user or groups, as shown in the following screenshot:

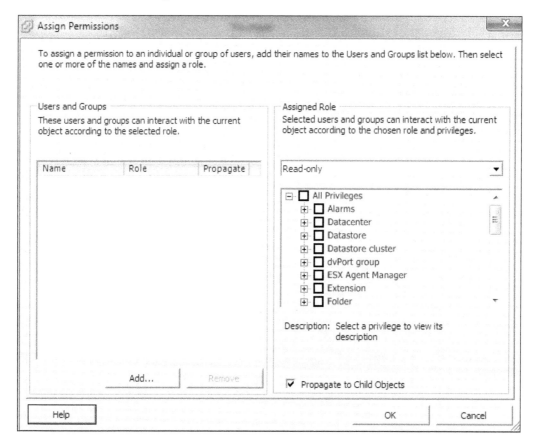

If this task is performed on a host directly, once you click on **Add**, you'll get a list of local ESX users to choose from, as shown in the screenshot that follows:

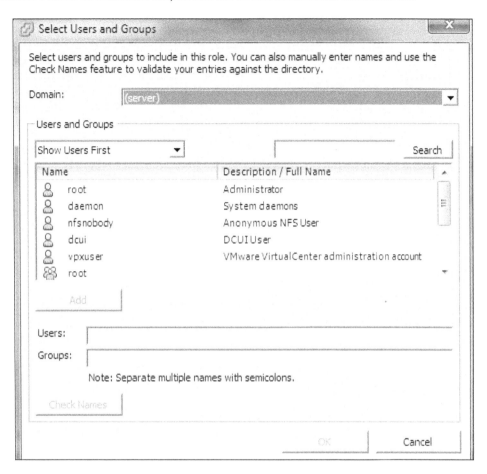

In vCenter, you'll get a list of users and groups that exist on the local Windows server that is running vCenter, and if vCenter is connected to the Active Directory domain, you'll get a list of available domain users.

Let's take a look at permissions of built-in users:

- **Root user**: Its activities are limited to the particular host. It's not recommended to remove this user or to use it in an Administrator role.

- **Vpxuser**:This is created once a host is added to vCenter. It has administrative privileges on its host and is used by vCenter to manage activities on the host. **Vpxuser** has all of the root privileges and can also schedule tasks, work with templates to move VMs, and make configuration changes to the host. Vpxuser cannot, however, create, edit, or delete users and groups on the host. It is not recommended to make any changes to this user.

- **Dcui user**: It has administrator rights and is used primarily for the lockdown mode configuration from **Direct Console User Interface** (DCUI). For more information about lockdown mode please see the next section in this chapter. It is not recommended to make any changes to this user.

vCenter validates users against the Active Directory at regular intervals, as well as each time the vCenter Server starts. If it's not able to find a user in the Active Directory by username, it assumes that this user has been deleted along with all of the permissions assigned to this user.

Settings for validation can be changed under **Administration** | **vCenter Server Settings**. Select **Active Directory** in navigation pane, enable or disable validation, or choose validation period in minutes.

Securing ESXi

There are other aspects of ESXi security besides users, groups, and roles. Many of them are related to network security, such as firewall and the SSL certificates, and the ability to access hosts remotely.

These network-related security features just mentioned will be discussed in the later sections of this chapter.

Using a firewall

The primary objective of a firewall is to control the network traffic by analyzing it and making a decision whether this traffic should be allowed or blocked.

When it comes to a virtual environment, firewalls can be implemented in the following components:

- **Physical machines**: A firewall can be used between physical machines, such as ESXi hosts and vCenter Server, if it's running on a physical server.

- **Virtual machines**: A firewall can be used between virtual machines connected to different network segments, such as internal and external networks.

- **Virtual and physical machines**: A firewall can also be used in between a virtual and a physical machine. For example, between a virtual web server and a physical workstation.

Two types of firewalls exist: software-based and hardware-based. Most modern operating systems have built-in software-based firewalls, and so does ESXi. It's built-in firewall, running on CentOS kernel of ESXi, is installed and enabled by default. The firewall can be configured through vCenter in **Security Profile** under the **Configuration** tab, as shown in the following screenshot:

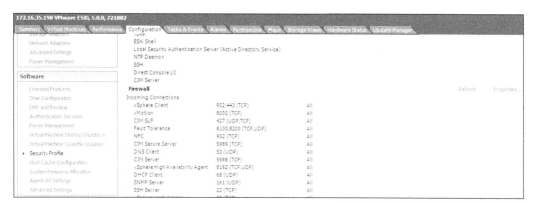

Once you go to **Properties...**, you will be able to allow or block certain TCP or UDP ports as well as enable or disable firewall, as shown in the following screenshot:

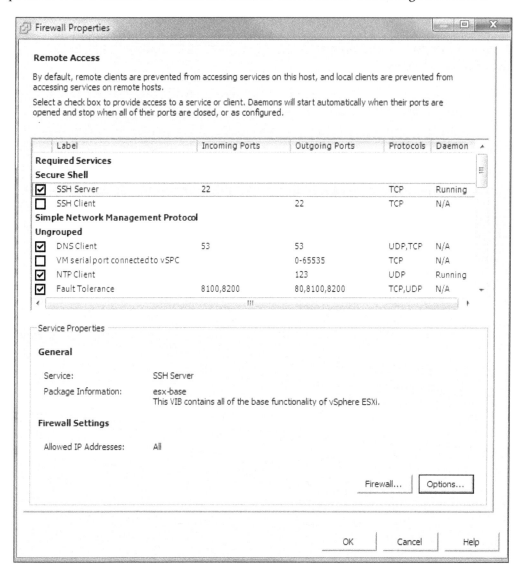

The ESXi firewall can also be disabled from the command line with the following commands:

```
esxcfg-firewall -allowOutgoing
esxcfg-firewall -allowIncoming
```

It can be re-enabled with the following commands:

```
esxcfg-firewall -BlockIncoming
esxcfg-firewall -BlockOutgoing
```

When you manage the ESXi hosts from vCenter, at least the following ports need to be open:

- **TCP/443**: Allows vCenter to access the host.
- **TCP/902**: Allows vCenter to access virtual machine consoles, and hosts can then access each other for migration and provisioning purposes.

  It is used to connect vCenter Server to the host through **vmware-authd**; that is, VMware Authorization Daemon. vmware-authd multiplexes data and passes it to the appropriate recipient for processing. The port for this connection can't be changed.

- **TCP/903**: Allows the vSphere clients to access VM consoles, so that the MKS transactions can happen (xinetd/vmware-authd-mks).

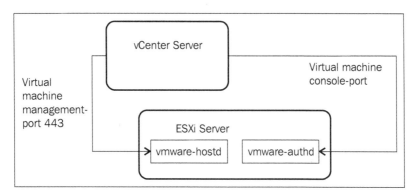

In the following table, you can find other TCP and UDP ports that may be needed for different services:

Port	Service	Direction
TCP/22	SSH	Incoming
UDP/53	DNS client	Outgoing and incoming
UDP/68	DHCP client	Outgoing and incoming
UDP/161	SNMP Server	Incoming
UDP/80	vSphere FT	Incoming
TCP/80	HTTP access	Outgoing and incoming
UDP/123	NTP Client	Outgoing
UDP/427	Service Location Protocol used by CIM client to find CIM servers	Outgoing and incoming
TCP/1234 TCP/1235	vSphere Replication	Outgoing
TCP/2049	NFS storage transactions	Outgoing and incoming
TCP/3260	iSCSI storage transactions	Outgoing
TCP/5900-5964	RFB protocol, used by management tools for example VNC)	Outgoing and incoming
TCP/5988	CIM transactions over HTTP	Incoming
TCP/5989	CIM XML transactions over HTTPS	Outgoing and incoming
TCP/8000	vMotion requests	Outgoing and incoming
UDP/8100 UDP/8200 TCP/8100 TCP/8200	vSphere FT traffic that's happening between hosts	Outgoing and incoming
UDP/8182 TCP/8182	vSphere HA traffic that's happening between hosts	Outgoing and incoming

To secure vCenter Server, you can use Windows firewall. Depending on the implementation, vSphere Clients may be accessing it through the hardware-based firewall. TCP port 443 needs to be open on vCenter Server so that clients can access vCenter.

Using security certificates and encryption

ESXi and vCenter support the X.509v3 certificates. By default, SSL is enabled and all traffic is encrypted. Certificates that are used by default are generated during the installation process; they are unique but self-signed, which means that they are not verifiable and are not signed by any well-known certification authority. These default certificates are vulnerable, and it is recommended to replace them with CA-signed certificates.

By default, on ESXi 5, certificates are located at `/etc/vmware/ssl`. On a vCenter Server running on Windows Server 2008, certificates can be found at `C:\Program Data\VMware\VMware VirtualCenter\SSL`. When vCenter is installed on Windows Server 2003, certificates are located at `C:\Documents and Settings\All Users\ Application Data\VMware\VMware VirtualCenter\SSL`. Any certificate will be represented by two files: `.crt` with the certificate itself, and `.key` with the private key.

The default certificate location for an ESXi host can be changed by modifying the `<privateKey>` and `<certificate>` tags at `/etc/vmware/hostd/config.xml`:

```
<ssl>
  <!-- The server private key file -->
  <privateKey>/etc/vmware/ssl/rui.key</privateKey>
  <!-- The server side certificate file -->
  <certificate>/etc/vmware/ssl/rui.crt</certificate>
</ssl>
```

Restart the `hostd` process to apply the preceding changes by using the following command:

```
# /etc/init.d/hostd restart
```

The default certificate needs to be recreated if the host name has been changed. To accomplish this, run the following commands from ESXi Shell:

```
# cd /etc/vmware/ssl
# mv rui.crt rui.crt.backup
# mv rui.key rui.key.backup
# /sbin/generate-certificates
```

To confirm that the new certificate has been generated, run the following command:

```
# ls -la
```

You should see new `rui.crt` and `rui.key` files listed.

You will need to restart the host. If you've entered the maintenance mode before generating the certificates, it will be enough to just restart the management agents from DCUI.

To replace default certificates with CA-signed SSLs, simply replace the `rui.crt` and `rui.key` files. New certificates can be uploaded from the command line using the following commands:

```
# vifs --server hostname --username username --
  put rui.crt /host/ssl_cert
```

```
# vifs --server hostname --username username --
  put rui.key /host/ssl_key
```

The host needs to be restarted each time new certificates are installed. Again, the host needs to be put into the maintenance mode first; it's enough to restart only the management agents from DCUI.

If **Verify Certificates** is enabled on the host, new certificates may cause vCenter to stop managing the host. In this case, the host must be reconnected using vSphere Client.

If you use SSH to access hosts, you can also use authorized keys to authenticate remote hosts. This approach provides authentication without a password. To accomplish this, you will need to upload the following keys (mentioned in the article) to the host; see the article available at http://pubs.vmware. com/vsphere-50/index.jsp?topic=%2Fcom.vmware.vsphere.security. doc_50%2FGUID-392ADDE9-FD3B-49A2-BF64-4ACBB60EB149.html.

As with the host certificates, all the keys listed earlier can be uploaded using the `vifs` command:

```
# vifs --server hostname --username username --
put filename /host/ssh_host_dsa_key_pub
```

But to do this, you'll need Root privileges.

There are two types of SSL timeouts that can be configured on the ESXi host:

- **Handshake Timeout for new connections:** Edit the `<handshakeTimeoutMs>` value at `/etc/vmware/hostd/config.xml`
- **Read Timeout for existing connections:** Edit the `<readTimeoutMs>` value at `/etc/vmware/hostd/config.xml`

Both values are specified in milliseconds; for example, the value `20000` corresponds to 20 seconds.

Restart the `hostd` process to apply any SSL timeout changes, using the following command:

```
# /etc/init.d/hostd restart
```

Be aware that, by default, connections that have been established do not expire.

If certain services are needed to be accessible through HTTP, you can change the **Web Proxy Service** settings at /etc/vmware/hostd/proxy.xml. The following code is an example of a typical service configuration in a proxy.xml file:

```
<e id="1">
  <_type>vim.ProxyService.LocalServiceSpec</_type>
  <accessMode>httpAndHttps</accessMode>
  <port>8309</port>
  <serverNamespace>/client/clients.xml</serverNamespace>
</e>
```

If you edit this file, make sure the following conditions are met:

* The IDs are unique within the HTTP area
* The <_type> tag contains a service name
* The <port> tag includes the TCP port the service is listening on
* The <serverNamespace> tag contains the namespace for the server that provides this service

The <accessmode> tag defines the form of communication allowed for a particular service. Acceptable values for this tag include the following:

* httpOnly: By using this value, the service will be accessible only over the HTTP protocol
* httpsOnly: When this value is used, the service will be accessible only over the HTTPS protocol
* httpsWithRedirect: If this value is used, the service will be accessible only over the HTTPS protocol; any HTTP requests will be redirected to the secure connection
* httpAndHttps: The service will be accessible over HTTP and HTTPS when this value is used

You will need to restart the hostd process to apply these changes, which can be done using the following command:

```
# /etc/init.d/hostd restart
```

Enabling lockdown mode

As an additional security measure, you can use the lockdown mode. When this mode is enabled, only vpxuser can authenticate against a host, which means that all operations on the ESXi host can be performed only through vCenter. In other words, you will not be able to log in directly to the console. Therefore, you will not be able to run any CLI commands, as well as use scripts or any other external software, to read or change any settings on this host. A root user will still be able to log in directly to the console, however, not to the shell.

It is recommended to enable or disable the lockdown mode through vCenter. It can also be accomplished through DCUI, wherein all existing permissions for users and groups will be lost.

A lockdown mode can only be enabled for hosts that are connected to vCenter. Once it's enabled, users who are currently logged in remain connected and can still run commands. However, they will not be able to disable the lockdown mode. Users with administrator privileges will be able to disable the lockdown mode through vCenter, or using DCUI, root users will be able to disable the lockdown mode.

The services that will be available for different types of users when a host is in a lockdown mode are listed in the VMware documentation article available at:

```
http://pubs.vmware.com/vsphere-50/index.jsp?topic=%2Fcom.vmware.
vsphere.security.doc_50%2FGUID-F8F105F7-CF93-46DF-9319-F8991839D265.
html
```

The possible lockdown mode configurations are listed in the article available at:

```
pubs.vmware.com/vsphere-4-esxi-installable-vcenter/index.jsp?topic=/
com.vmware.vsphere.esxi_server_config.doc_41/esx_server_config/
security_deployments_and_recommendations/c_lockdown_use_cases.html
```

 If access to vCenter is lost and a host is in the Total Lockdown Mode, ESXi will have to be reinstalled in order to restore access to this host.

The lockdown mode can be enabled in vCenter from **Security profile** under the **Configuration** tab, as shown in the following screenshot:

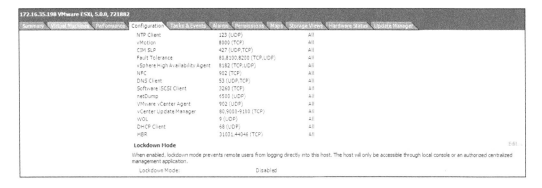

Click on **Edit...** and check **Enable Lockdown Mode**.

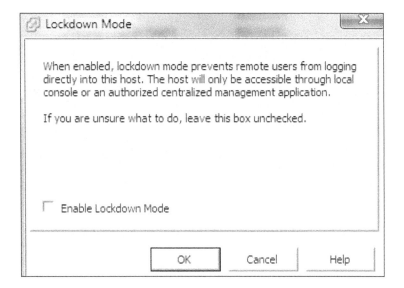

To enable the lockdown mode from DCUI, press *F2* and log in with the username and password. Then, scroll down to the **Configure Lockdown Mode** option and press *Enter*. As mentioned earlier in this chapter, existing permissions for users and groups will be lost once the lockdown mode is enabled.

Apart from vCenter and Direct Console, there is another way to access ESXi host—ESXi Shell, which is also known as Tech Support Mode. It can be accessed locally from the console or remotely through SSH. By default, shell access is disabled.

It can be enabled either from DCUI or through vCenter.

- From DCUI, press *F2*, go to the **System Customization** menu, select **Troubleshooting**, and hit *Enter*. From this menu, you can enable the ESXi Shell and SSH as well as choose the Shell timeout in minutes. After timeout, the Shell disables so that other users can't use it; however, the current user stays logged in.

- From vCenter, go to **Configuration | Security profile** and click on **Options** under the **Services** section. Select the **ESXi Shell** service from the list, choose a startup option, and then click on **Start** to enable the service.

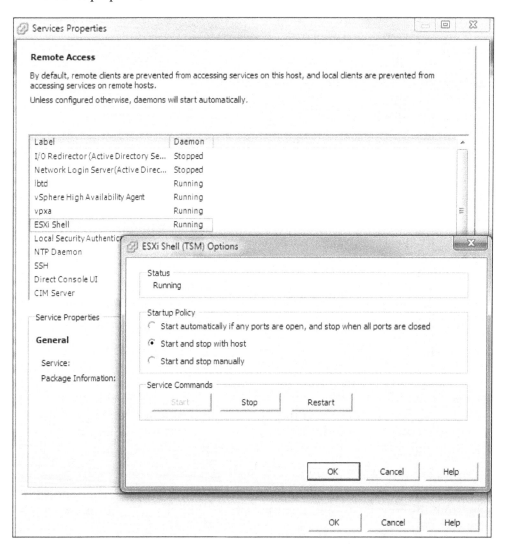

Once ESXi Shell access is enabled from the machine's physical console, you can press *Alt + F2* to access the login page. Once the correct username and password are entered, you'll get a CLI prompt. This mode can be used for configuration and troubleshooting. Many administrators, however, find it more convenient to configure hosts via vSphere Client. At the same time, troubleshooting sometimes requires CLI. VMware recommends using vSphere Client or vSphere CLI instead of shell access.

Summary

There are two categories of users in vSphere. The first category is the vCenter users, that is, users authorized to access the environment through vCenter. These are either users of the Windows domain that this vCenter belongs to, or the local Windows users on the host where vCenter Server is installed.

The second category is direct access users, that is, users who are able to log in to ESX hosts directly. These users are maintained locally on ESX hosts and are separate from vCenter users.

A role is a predefined set of privileges. When you assign a role to a user or a group, you assign a group of permissions for the object to this user or group.

The primary objective of a firewall is to control network traffic by analyzing it and making a decision if this traffic should be allowed or blocked.

ESXi and vCenter support the X.509v3 certificates. By default, SSL is enabled and all traffic is encrypted.

As an additional security measure, ESXi has a lockdown mode. When this mode is enabled, only vpxuser can authenticate against a host, which means that all operations on the ESXi host can be performed only through vCenter.

6

Resource Management

This chapter focuses on managing available host and storage resources with vCenter.

We will discuss different aspects of resource allocation, such as shares, reservations, limits, and resource pools.

We will also discuss **Dynamic Resource Scheduler (DRS)**, its requirements, and creating and disabling this feature.

Another topic we will touch on here is power management—a useful feature in vCenter that allows you to reduce power consumption in the datacenter.

In this chapter, we will cover the following topics:

- Resource allocation—shares, reservations, and limits
- Resource pools
- DRS requirements
- Creating DRS cluster and disabling DRS
- Power management
- Cluster validity and affinity rules

Resource management is the distribution of resources available from resource providers among resource consumers. These resources are CPU, memory, storage space, power, and network resources. Resource providers are hosts and groups of hosts (also called clusters), as well as datastores. Resource consumers are virtual machines.

In a vSphere environment, all resources are shared among the resource consumers. This brings up the following challenges that need to be dealt with:

- **Performance isolation**: We need to ensure that virtual machines don't monopolize resources and predictable service rates can be guaranteed
- **Efficient utilization of available resources**: We need to ensure that resources can be gracefully overcommitted, and undercommitted resources can be used
- **Ease of administration**: We need to ensure that resources can be prioritized and service-level agreements can be met

Resource management allows for the dynamic reallocation of resources, which gives it the ability to use the available resources more efficiently and address the previously stated challenges.

Resource allocation

Each virtual machine is allocated a certain amount of the host's hardware resources based on a number of factors as follows:

- The host's or cluster's available resources
- The number of virtual machines running at the same time, and the total resources consumed by them
- The resources required to manage virtualization
- User-defined resource limits

When you turn a virtual machine on, vCenter checks if there are enough resources available for it to run and allows you to turn it on only if there are enough resources. In case the available amount of resources don't meet the requirements, the amount of resources allocated to a VM or a resource pool may need to be adjusted.

Resource allocation settings, such as shares, reservations, and limits are used to determine the amount of CPU, memory, and storage resources available to for a virtual machine. There are several options available to administrators for allocating resources, listed as follows:

- Reserving the host's or cluster's physical resources
- Making sure that the needed amount of memory is backed up by the available host's physical memory
- Making sure a particular virtual machine is always allocated more physical resources than other VMs
- Setting an upper limit on the amount of resources that can be allocated to a virtual machine

Understanding shares

With shares, administrators can specify the relative importance of virtual machines or resource pools. Shares make sense only within the same level of hierarchy, that is, for VMs or resource pools with the same parent. A VM's priority is always relative to other VMs on the running machines.

Shares are usually specified as high, normal, and low and relate to each other at a 4:2:1 ratio. Values for resource allocation shares are listed in a table in the following VMware documentation article `http://pubs.vmware.com/vcd-51/index.jsp?topic=%2Fcom.vmware.vcloud.users.doc_51%2FGUID-CA70F12C-6650-4AF0-8650-BA051F551C5B.html`.

There is also a **Custom** option to set up **custom** values.

For example, a virtual machine with two vCPUs, 2 GB of RAM, and memory shares set to normal is assigned the following values:

2 x 1000 = 2000 CPU shares

10 x 2048 = 20480 memory shares

Shares can be used when frequent changes in total available resources are expected when VMs or resource pools are competing for available resources. For example, when more memory is added to a host, virtual machines stay at the same priority; however, they get a larger portion of memory.

Actual resource allocations for all VMs in a pool change each time a new VM is powered on. When two VMs have all the available hosts' CPUs allocated to them, they get fewer CPU resources once a third VM is powered on. Consider the following scenario :

- Two VMs run on a host that has 8 GHz of CPU capacity available for VMs. Their CPU shares are set to Normal and, therefore, each VM gets 4 GHz.

- On the same host, the third virtual machine is powered on with the CPU shares' value set to `High`. A High share value, as opposed to Normal, means that this VM should have twice as many shares. Therefore, the new virtual machine gets 4 GHz while the other two get only 2 GHz each. The same result can be achieved by specifying a custom share value of `2000` for the third virtual machine.

Understanding reservations

A reservation is the minimum guaranteed amount of resources allocated to a virtual machine. It's expressed in concrete units: MHz for the CPU and MB for RAM. vCenter server makes sure that there are resources available to provide the minimum allocation of resources required before powering on a VM. This operation will be denied if there are not enough resources.

When a virtual machine is turned on, vCenter also checks the resources available for the CPU and memory reservations, also considering the admission control settings, and not just the available host or cluster resources.

At the same time, once a VM reaches the limit for the reserved amount of memory, it is allowed to keep it. ESX allows memory overcommitment . This means that the total memory assigned to running virtual machines can be higher than the total memory available on the host or cluster. ESX hosts accomplish memory oversubscription due to their ability to transfer memory from idle virtual machines to VMs that need more memory. Because of a preset reservation, however, memory will be wasted if a virtual machine has reached its reserved amount but is idle at that moment.

Therefore, it's a good practice not to reserve all of the available resources right away. As you get closer to using all of the available resources, it will become more difficult to manage reservations.

VMs may consume more resources if they need to and these resources are available.

The default value for all resource allocations is zero.

Consider the following example:

- A host with 4 GHz of CPU has two VMs running, each with a 2 GHz reservation each.

- Both VMs will be able to run and will be guaranteed 2 GHz of CPU. One of them may be using only 1 GHz; in this case, the other may consume more than 2 GHz.

- If you try to power on a third machine with 1 GHz reservation, you will not be able to do that as the CPU power reserved for two running VMs is 2 GHz + 2 GHz = 4 GHz, which is all that's available on this host.

Understanding limits

Limits specify the maximum amount of resources that can be consumed. Limits as well as reservations are expressed in MHz and MB. Default values are unlimited. For memory, however, the configured RAM amount becomes its limit.

If you specify a memory limit lower than the amount assigned to a VM, it will result in excessive swapping as soon as the guest OS needs more RAM than the limit which, in turn, results in performance degradation. This happens because the guest OS can only see the allocated amount of memory and not the limit. If you need to control the maximum amount of memory that can be consumed by a VM, change the memory allocation in the VM's settings.

Limits can be used to simulate resource shortage, or to manage user expectations. In most cases, however, they cause wastage of idle resources, as VMs will not be able to use more than the limit. Therefore, limits should be used carefully.

All three resource allocation settings can be specified for **CPU** in each virtual machine under its settings in the **Resources** tab, as shown in the following screenshot:

Resource allocation settings that can be specified for **Memory** are shown in the following screenshot:

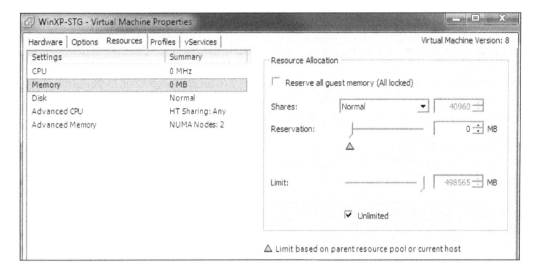

Resource pools

Resource pools are used for the flexible management of CPU and memory resources. Administrators can group them into hierarchies to partition the available resources hierarchically.

In this sense, resource pools can be considered as not only resource providers, distributing resources to virtual machines and child pools, but also resource consumers, consuming parents' resources either from parent pools or from clusters and hosts directly.

Advantages

One of the main advantages of resource pools is the ability to manage all available resources independently from existing hosts and clusters. By assigning VMs to a resource pool, administrators are able to control resource allocation to the set of virtual machines rather than per VM. This eliminates the need to set resource allocations and limits for each virtual machine.

Resource pools can be very useful when you need to manage a set of servers with different requirements for CPU and memory availability. For example, servers with high CPU requirements can be grouped under a resource pool, with high priority for CPU shares. Non-mission critical servers can be grouped under a resource pool with low memory and CPU priority.

Administrators are also able to delegate control and access to resources. For example, a top-level administrator can create a pool and make it available for administration to a department-level administrator who, in turn, will be able to create virtual machines and manage them within the boundaries of the resource pool that was delegated by the top-level administrator. This is illustrated in the following diagram:

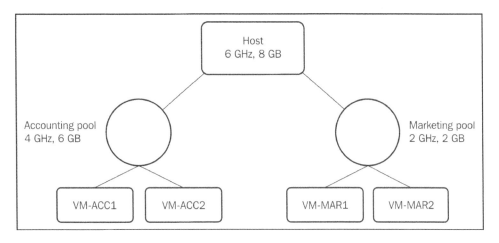

Creating and editing pools

Each standalone host and DRS cluster already contains a resource pool that has all the host's or cluster's resources. Because this resource pool and its available resources are always the same, it doesn't appear in the hierarchy.

A child resource pool can be created for this root resource pool or for any other existing child pool. Resource pools can be created only in vCenter and not directly for hosts, and they can't be created for a single VM. It's considered best practice to manage VMs' resources with resource pools, even if they have to be created for only one VM, than to use shares.

To create a resource pool, select an object in the inventory, right-click on or go to the **File** menu, and choose **New Resource Pool**. An additional window will open where you can assign the name of your resource pool and specify CPU and memory reservations, shares, and limits for the new resource pool, as shown in the following screenshot:

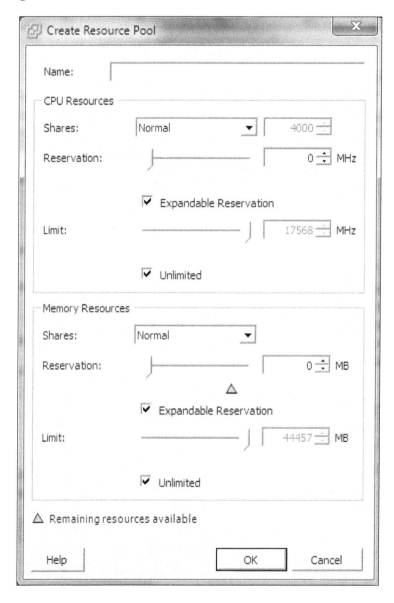

For more information about shares, reservations, and limits, see the previous section in this chapter.

To edit the settings for a resource pool, right-click on and choose **Edit Settings,** as shown in the following screenshot:

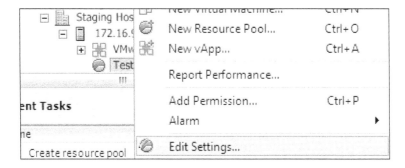

The easiest way to assign an existing virtual machine to a pool is to simply drag-and-drop it into a resource pool object. The following rules apply when you assign a VM to a resource pool:

- VMs' reservation and limit do not change. The move will fail in a situation where a VM is powered on while the resource pool doesn't have enough resources available to guarantee an existing reservation.

- The share value changes depending on the VM settings so that it reflects the total number of shares in the new resource pool. As share allocations are relative, you may need to change the VM's shares manually when you move it to a new pool.

- At the same time, custom share values are maintained.

When you move a VM between hosts or datastores, you will be asked which resource pool it should be assigned to, therefore, you may need to make a note of the VM's current resource pool before starting the migration wizard as you will not be able to see its current pool once the wizard opens up.

When you create a new VM, the wizard will ask you to specify a pool location.

To remove a VM from a resource pool, simply move it to another object or delete it.

When a VM is removed from a resource pool, each remaining share corresponds to more resources as the total number of shares of the resource pool is lower.

To remove a resource pool, right click on it and select **Remove**.

An additional admission control check happens when a VM is powered on in a resource pool. This is to make sure that all service-level guarantees will still be met once this VM is on. The decision whether to allow or deny the operation is made based on the VM's reservation setting and the resources available in the pool. The way in which the available pool's resources are calculated depends on the reservation type chosen for the pool:

- **Expandable** (default): The system checks the resources available in the pool as well as in its parent. The current pool can borrow resources from its parent which, in turn, is also set to expandable, and can borrow resources from its parent, and so on. This option gives more flexibility; however, it provides less protection because a child pool may be able to reserve more resources than it is expected to.

- **Fixed**: The system checks the resources available in the VM's pool only. If there are not enough available CPU and memory resources, the operation is not allowed.

DRS

DRS may be referred to as a joint load balancing and failover solution. It enables vCenter to manage host members of the cluster as an aggregate pool of resources.

Once a host is added to a DRS cluster, its resources become part of the cluster. In addition to resource aggregation, administrators are able to use the following features:

- **Load balancing**: DRS analyzes current resource usage for host and resource pools and compares that to the current demand. Based on this, it recommends or performs VM migrations. For example, the cluster on the left-hand side of the following diagram, assuming that all VMs are the same, is unbalanced. DRS may recommend migration or may perform the migration of VMs by itself to host 2 and 3, as shown in the following diagram, so that host resources are used more efficiently:

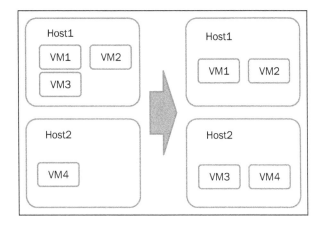

- **Power management**: If the DPM feature is turned on, DRS compares the current resource usage to the cluster's capacity. If there is excess capacity, DRS places hosts in standby power mode or recommends doing so. If there is a need for additional capacity, DRS powers on additional hosts or recommends increasing the number of powered-on hosts.

- **Affinity**: These rules help to control the placement of VMs on hosts.

Depending on the settings, DRS can place or recommend placement for VMs that are about to be powered on. Recommendations consist of mutually exclusive options for placement. In case prerequisite actions are required, for example, powering on a host from standby mode, the recommendations will have multiple lines with each action listed separately.

In the case of powering on multiple VMs that belong to different DRS clusters, recommendations are provided for each cluster separately.

Understanding the DRS cluster requirements

The following requirements must be met by hosts that are being added to a DRS cluster:

- Each host uses storage shared by all hosts

- All VMs are located on volumes shared by all hosts' volumes

- All storage volumes have names assigned and VMs use those to specify VM virtual disks

- The host's processors should meet the compatibility requirements in that, after a VM is vMotioned to a new host, it is supposed be able to run using equivalent instructions. vCenter provides features that allow administrators to use hosts with different CPUs and still be able to vMotion virtual machines. Administrators can use CPU masks or a feature called **Enhanced vMotion Compatibility (EVC)**. For more information about EVC, please see the section about managing hosts with different CPUs in *Chapter 2, Managing ESXi Hosts*. More information on CPU masks can be found in the VMware documentation.

- Hosts participating in a DRS cluster are members of a private, dedicated gigabit network connecting all member hosts. Having a vMotion network is an optional requirement, as DRS can still make recommendations even if actual vMotion is not possible.

Creating a DRS cluster

DRS can be enabled in cluster properties. The following screenshot shows the **PRD-CLUSTER Settings** tab with the option to check the **Turn On vSphere DRS** option:

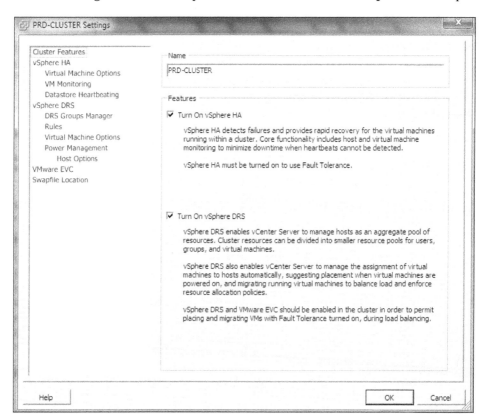

Once the **Turn On vSphere DRS** option is checked, as shown in the preceding screenshot, you get additional options to the left-hand pane where DRS settings can be specified.

There are three automation level options, as shown in the following bullet list and screenshot:

- **Manual**: This means that DRS will only suggest a VM placement
- **Partially automated**: This will place VMs automatically during power on and suggest options for VM placement when resource usage changes
- **Fully automated**: This option is for when the DRS performs the actual reallocation of VMs

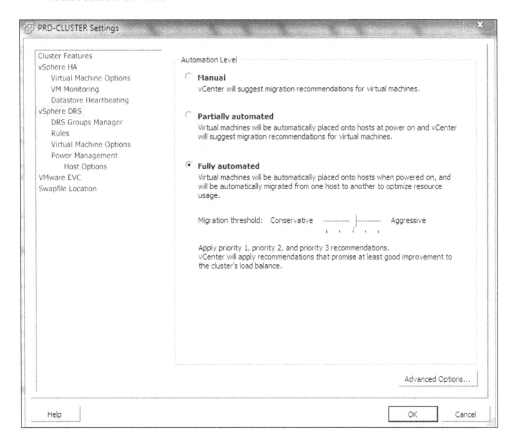

Additionally, the automation level can be set individually for each virtual machine in **Virtual Machine Options,** as shown in the following screenshot:

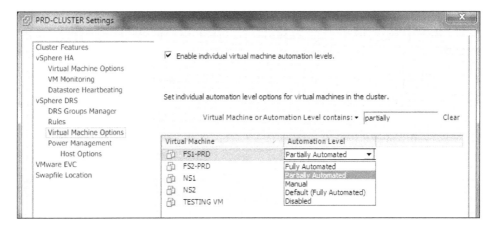

VMs can be assigned any of the three levels available under general settings as well as have automation disabled.

The **Migration threshold** setting defines recommendations that are generated and then applied, or that are shown when in the **Manual** mode. It also defines how much cluster imbalance is allowed across the host CPU and the memory load. It has five settings ranging from **Conservative** to **Aggressive**. As you move the slider to the right-hand side, the migration priority level is raised.

The priority level for each migration is calculated based on the load imbalance metric set for the cluster. A higher imbalance metric causes higher priority recommendations. Once the migration priority has been assigned, it is compared to the migration threshold setting and if the difference is equal to or higher than the current priority level setting for the cluster, this recommendation is either applied or displayed.

The cluster imbalance metric is calculated as the standard deviation of the host load and is displayed under the **Summary** tab in the vSphere client.

To add a host to a DRS cluster, simply drag-and-drop it into the cluster object. You will be provided with two options for the VMs running on this host:

- Put VMs into the cluster's root resource pool. If there were any resource pools on this host, they will be removed.

- Create a new resource pool for these VMs. In this case, vCenter creates a top-level resource pool. You can supply its name.

The host should already be managed by the vCenter server in order to be added to the DRS cluster.

When a host is removed from a cluster, the following resources are affected:

- Resource pool hierarchies will be changed
- Virtual machines need to be either migrated from the host, turned off, or suspended
- Clusters may become invalid as available resources decrease

To remove a host from a cluster, it needs to be placed into the **Maintenance** mode first. Once this is done, it can be dragged to a different inventory location. After that, the host can be removed from vCenter, added to another cluster, or you can make it exit the maintenance mode to run it as a standalone host.

Disabling DRS

DRS can be disabled in the cluster setting. Once disabled, both affinity rules and the hierarchy of resource pools will be lost, and will not be re-established even if DRS is turned back on. Therefore, it is suggested that you switch DRS to manual mode instead of turning it off, to avoid losing resource pools and other settings.

Using power management

This feature allows for reducing the DRS cluster's power consumption by enabling hosts to go into standby mode when resource utilization allows them to do so, and powering hosts back on when additional resources are needed. DPM considers current resource demand as well as any virtual machine resource reservations.

There are, additionally, the **Power Management** settings available under the cluster settings when DRS is enabled, as shown in the following screenshot:

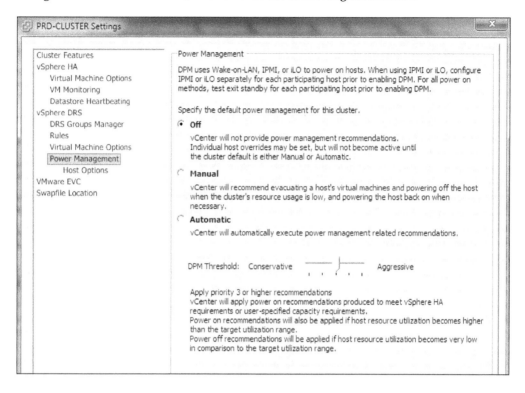

Obviously, the **Automatic** option means that changing the host's power state and VM vMotioning to the recently turned-on host will be done automatically.

The DPM threshold setting works pretty much the same way as the DRS Migration threshold. The more aggressive this setting is, the more priority levels are used to make a decision.

The **Power Management** settings can be changed on a per-host basis under **Host Options,** as shown in the following screenshot:

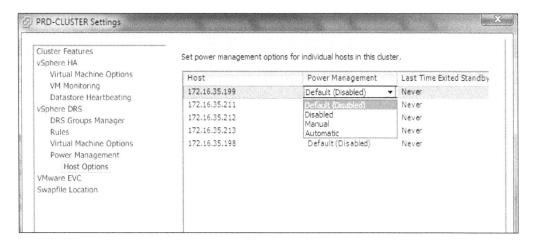

 Note that if a host that is currently in standby mode, it needs to be disconnected or moved to a different cluster. It has to be powered on first, as vCenter will not be able to power it back on.

To bring a host back from standby mode, the vSphere DPM uses one of three power management protocols: **Wake-On-LAN (WOL)**, **Intelligent Platform Management Interface (IPMI)**, or Hewlett-Packard **Integrated Lights-Out (iLO)**. Hosts should support at least one of these protocols so that they can be powered on by vSphere. In case a host supports more than one protocol, they will be used in the following order: IPMI, iLO, and then WOL.

The first two protocols—IPMI and iLO—require the **Baseboard Management Controller (BMC)** hardware and can be configured in the **Power Management** properties under the **Configuration** tab. If these features are supported by a host, there will be an option to type the BMC account credentials, and IP and MAC addresses of the NIC associated with BMC.

To test if a host supports WOL, click on **Enter Standby Mode** on the host's **Summary** tab to power the host down. Choose the **Power On** command and make sure the host comes back from standby mode, as shown in the following screenshot:

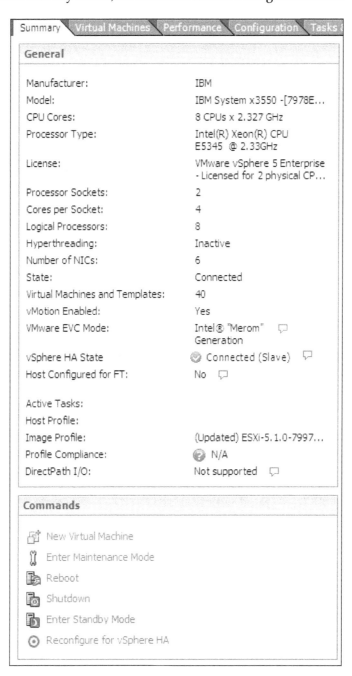

In case the VM didn't exit standby mode successfully, disable power management on this host from the DRS **Power Management** settings, as shown in the following screenshot:

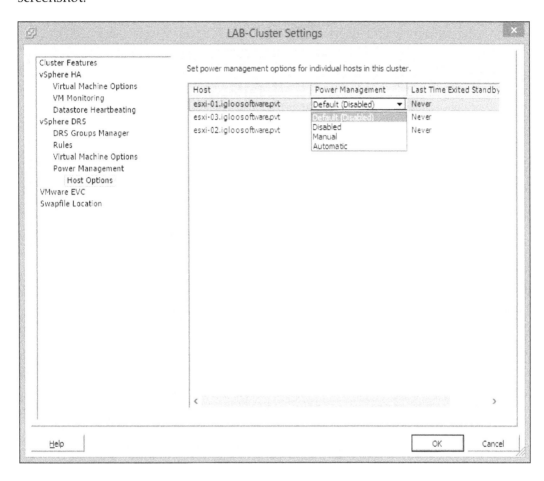

Once power management is disabled on this host, DPM doesn't consider it a candidate to be powered off and you can turn it back on manually.

To be able to monitor DPM activity, you can create a vCenter alarm for the following events listed in the VMware documentation available at `http://pubs.vmware.com/vsphere-4-esx-vcenter/index.jsp?topic=/com.vmware.vsphere.resourcemanagement.doc_41/using_drs_clusters_to_manage_resources/c_monitoring_vmware_dpm.html`.

For more information about creating alerts in vCenter, please see *Chapter 7, Events, Alarms, and Automated Actions*.

Cluster validity

A DRS cluster can be in one of three states which are indicated in vSphere:

- **Valid**: If all of the cluster requirements are met, the cluster is able to support all reservations and all running VMs.

- **Overcommitted** (yellow): This is when a cluster doesn't have enough resources to support all reservations, including child resource pools. This usually happens when cluster capacity is suddenly reduced, for example, because of host failure. A cluster will also turn yellow in case some changes are made to a VM while the vCenter server isn't available.

- **Invalid** (red): It typically happens when a tree is no longer internally consistent even though there are enough resources to support the necessary service levels. This happens, for example, if the vCenter server is not available. The cluster will also become red if reservations on a parent resource pool are reduced while a VM is in the process of failing over as the failing over of the VM doesn't count towards the parent resource pool's reservation.

Affinity rules

With affinity rules, administrators can control VM placement on hosts within a cluster.

There are two types of rules that can be used:

- **VM-to-Host affinity rules**: This specifies whether or not members of particular VM groups should be run on a particular group of hosts

- **VM-to-VM affinity rules**: This causes DRS to keep the specified VMs together on the same host, for example, because of performance considerations

If after the rules are followed, the creation of a cluster is in violation of a rule, it will operate further to show an alert.

Affinity rules can be created under the **Rules** section in the cluster properties, as shown in the following screenshot:

To create a VM-to-Host rule, you'll need to create VM and host groups under the **DRS Groups Manager** tab first, and then choose the **Virtual Machines to Hosts** rule type. Then assign a VM group to a host group, as shown in the following screenshot:

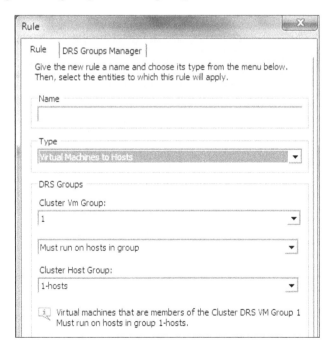

There are four specifications for the VM-to-Host rule which are listed as follows:

- Should run on hosts in group
- Must run on hosts in group
- Should not run on hosts in group
- Must not run on hosts in group

The "Should" and "Should not" options mean that affinity or anti-affinity will be maintained where possible. The "Must" and "Must not" options define the required rules. vCenter will never take an action that violates the required rule:

- DRS will not place virtual machines on a host in maintenance mode
- DRS will not place powered-on or load-balanced virtual machines
- vSphere HA will not perform failovers
- vSphere DPM will not enable hosts to go into standby mode to optimize power management

These types of rules should be used with caution. You should be especially careful when creating more than one required rule.

One of the possible scenarios in VM-to-Host affinity rules usage is when VMs run software with license restrictions. These VMs can be placed on a host that fulfills the necessary requirements. For example, a VM running an MS SQL server that is licensed for only 2 CPUs should be placed on the host that has no more than 2 CPUs.

When two VM-to-host rules conflict, the older one takes precedence. If a VM is part of two different VM groups that are assigned to two host groups, this VM will be able to run only on those hosts which belong to both host groups.

To create a VM-to-VM rule, select the appropriate rule type—either **Keep Virtual Machines Together** or **Separate Virtual Machines**. Then click on **Add** and select VMs, as shown in the following screenshot:

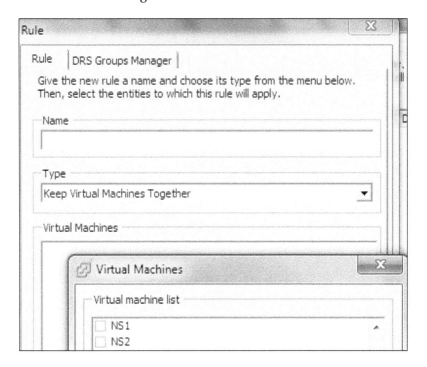

You can create more than one VM-to-VM rule. When two VM-to-VM affinity rules are in conflict, it's not possible to enable both of the rules. The older rule always takes precedence and new rules will be disabled.

CPU affinity rules

The CPU affinity VM setting allows you to limit the host's CPUs available to this VM. This setting can be changed from **VM Settings** under **Advanced CPU** settings in the **Resources** tab, as shown in the following screenshot:

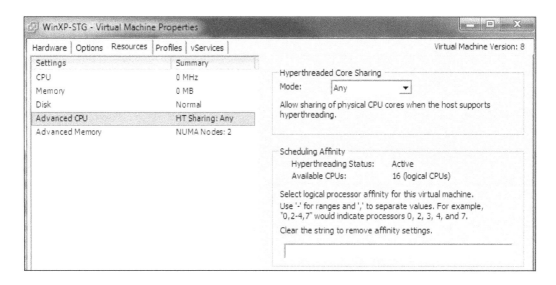

CPU affinity does not dedicate a physical CPU to a VM, but, limits which physical CPUs can be used by the VMkernel scheduler for this particular virtual machine. If a CPU has been chosen by an affinity rule for a particular VM, it doesn't restrict the scheduler to using this CPU for other virtual machines. CPU affinity can be used more for testing than anything else. In some controlled environments, however, certain specific workloads can benefit from CPU affinity. For example, CPU affinity was required when virtualizing Cisco Unity Messaging so that the one-to-one mapping of physical and virtual CPUs could take place. A VM can profit from aggregated caches when its workload is cache bound and has a larger cache footprint than the cache available in one CPU.

If the goal is to isolate a physical CPU, or, in other words, dedicate one of the physical CPUs to a single virtual machine as its logical core, also called LCPU, all of the VMs running on that particular host need to follow the CPU affinity rules as well. The physical CPU that needs to be dedicated has to be excluded from all other VMs with affinity rules.

It's important to keep in mind that if a VM with affinity rules is moved to another host, it loses its affinity settings and these settings will not be restored even when the VM is moved back. At the same time, if vMotion violates one of the VM-to-Host affinity rules, the cluster will reject this vMotion. In this case, affinity rules will have to be manually removed if there is a need to vMotion the VM. It's fair to say that CPU affinity doesn't work with vMotion and storage vMotion. A virtual machine with CPU affinity rules cannot be placed in a DRS cluster in fully automated mode because vMotion is not allowed for such VMs. Therefore, the DRS for the cluster or for this VM needs to be set to manual or partially automated, or the VM with affinity rules needs to be placed on a standalone host.

Many experts don't recommend using CPU affinity rules unless they are used in a controlled environment for applications that can benefit from them. Not only does it add management overhead, it can also be dangerous.

A virtual machine consists of multiple threads called worlds. Besides the vCPU world, worlds are created for other components that are associated with a VM and require processing power. Some of them include the CD-ROM, mouse, keyboard, screen, `.vmx` file, and so on. The CPU affinity setting affects not only the vCPU world, but all of the worlds associated with a VM. Therefore, if set incorrectly, it can reduce the VM's performance when different worlds have to compete for CPU time.

For best performance, if you have to use CPU affinity rules, it's recommended that you include one additional CPU to allow other VM threads to be scheduled concurrently with its virtual CPUs.

When CPU affinity is set on a VM running on **Non-Uniform Memory Access (NUMA)** architecture, this VM is treated as a non-NUMA client; but, at the same time, it gets executed by the NUMA scheduling. This may result in a VM running on a different NUMA node than that where its memory is located, which increases latency and causes higher waiting times while the memory is being fetched from a remote node.

It's important to remember that the admission control settings ignore affinity rules. Therefore, multiple VMs with affinity rules may have all cores reserved and still compete for resources with each other.

CPU power management

While DPM redistributes VMs among hosts to allow some hosts to be powered off, vSphere **Host Power Management** (**HPM**) allows for the saving of energy on running hosts by placing certain parts of the hosts' hardware into a reduced power state. When in this state, the system or device is inactive or runs at a lower speed.

There are several power management options available under the host setting that allow administrators to balance between performance and power use. These power settings can be controlled from **Hardware | Power Management** under the **Configuration** tab, as shown in the following screenshot:

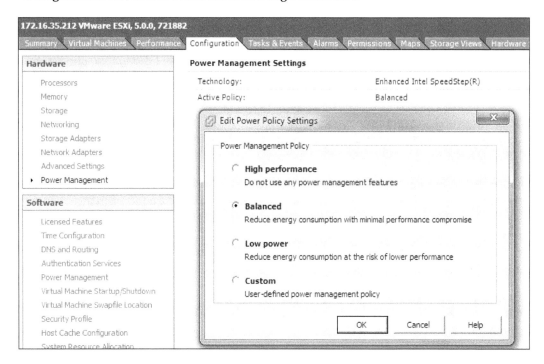

VSphere utilizes the **Advanced Configuration and Power Interface** (**ACPI**) standard to provide power management options. ACPI is an open standard. It allows the operating system to perform device configuration and power management. The standard defines platform-independent interfaces for hardware discovery and configuration, power management, as well as monitoring. Among other standards, ACPI defines processor and performance states.

Processor or CPU states are listed as follows:

- **C0**: It encapsulates the operating state, maximum performance, and power consumption of the processor.

- **C1 or Halt**: The processor is not executing instructions, but can be returned to an operating state almost instantaneously. Certain processors also support an enhanced C1 state (also known as C1E, or Enhanced Halt State). This is a hardware-managed state for lower power consumption. ESXi puts CPU into C1 and the CPU hardware determines whether or not this state can be switched to C1E to save more power. Usually, C1E allows you to reduce power consumption with little or no impact on the performance. When `Turbo Boost` is enabled, C1E can even increase the performance of certain single-threaded workloads. Under certain circumstances, however, for a very few multithreaded workloads that are highly sensitive to I/O latency, C1E can reduce performance. If that's the case, C1E should be disabled in BIOS, if the option is available.

- **C2 or Stop-Clock**: In this state, the processor maintains all software in the visible state; however, it takes longer to wake up.

- **C3 or Sleep**: In this state, the processor does not need to keep its cache coherent; however, it maintains other states. Some processors have variations on this state, such as Deep Sleep, Deeper Sleep, and so on. These variations differ in how long it takes to wake the processor up.

C-states are deeper than C1/C1E states managed by the software. Obviously, they allow greater power saving, but with the increased possibility of performance impact. Therefore, it's recommended to enable all C-states in BIOS and let vSphere control their use.

While a processor operates in C0 states, it can still be in one of several power-performance states. While these states are dependent on implementation, P0 is always the highest-performance state and states from P1 to Pn are lower-performance states; where n is an implementation-specific limit which can't be higher than 16.

 P-states in Intel processors are known as SpeedStep. In AMD processors, they are called PowerNow! or Cool'n'Quiet.

The P-states, in ascending order, are as follows:

- P0 maximum power and frequency
- P1 less than P0, frequency/voltage scaled
- P2 less than P1, frequency/voltage scaled
- Pn less than P(n-1), frequency/voltage scaled

Therefore, depending on the settings chosen, either the CPU frequency or CPU mode changes. Both of these setting's changes make the CPU and the host itself consume less voltage. ESXi, however, attempts to change the mode or frequency so that the VM performance is not affected.

The following table gives more details about available power options:

Power management	Policy description
Not supported	No power management features are supported by the host or power management is not enabled in BIOS.
High Performance	This setting maximizes performance by using only two C-states—C0 and C1/C1E—and the highest P-states all of the time. No deep C-states are used in this mode. This is the default mode for ESX/ESXi 4.0 and 4.1.
Balanced	This option is designed to reduce power consumption with little or no performance impact. It uses an algorithm that exploits the processor's P-states. This is the default mode for ESXi 5. In ESXi 5.5, deep processor power C-states (greater than C1) are also used, providing additional power savings.
Low Power	The VMkernel reduces host energy consumption at the risk of lower performance by aggressively using available deep C-states.
Custom	The power management policy is based on the values in the advanced configuration parameters. These parameters can be set in the vSphere **Client Advanced Settings** dialog box.

There are also additional custom power parameters that can be set under the host's advanced settings. When **Custom** power management is chosen for a host, these power management parameters are used to control HPM behavior. The VMware documentation article lists them with descriptions, available at `http://pubs. vmware.com/vsphere-51/index.jsp?topic=%2Fcom.vmware.vsphere.resmgmt. doc%2FGUID-474AB73D-9105-43E3-A8E2-4C156EF78B69.html`.

Host power usage as well as other power information can be obtained from the command-line window using the esxtop utility by pressing the *P* key. The following screenshot shows an example of the esxtop power screen:

```
12:07:54am up 220 days  7:36, 509 worlds, 27 VMs, 74 vCPUs; CPU load average: 0.12, 0.15, 0.13
Power Usage:   248W, Power Cap:  N/A
PSTATE MHZ: 2794 2793 2660 2527 2394 2261 2128 1995 1862 1729 1596

CPU %USED %UTIL %C0 %C1 %C2 %P0 %P1 %P2 %P3 %P4 %P5 %P6 %P7 %P8 %P9 %P10
   0   9.3  12.1  14  86   0  89   0   0   0   0   0   0   0   0   0  10
   1   3.9   5.9   7  93   0  71   0   0   0   0   0   0   1   0   1  27
   2   4.1   5.5   7  93   0  60   0   0   0   0   0   0   0   0   0  39
   3   5.1   6.7   8  92   0  85   0   0   0   0   0   0   0   0   0  14
   4   7.8   9.8  12  88   0  95   0   0   0   0   0   0   0   0   0   5
   5   5.0   6.9   9  91   0  80   0   0   0   0   0   0   0   0   0  19
   6   2.9   4.0   6  94   0  62   0   0   0   0   0   0   0   0   0  38
   7   4.5   6.0   8  92   0  89   0   0   0   0   0   0   0   0   0  11
   8   4.9   6.7   8  92   0  86   0   0   0   0   0   0   0   0   0  13
   9   6.6   8.4  10  90   0  89   0   0   0   0   0   0   0   0   0  11
  10   4.0   5.8   7  93   0  78   0   0   0   0   0   0   0   0   0  21
  11   4.7   6.4   8  92   0  86   0   0   0   0   0   0   0   0   0  14
  12  13.9  15.3  18  82   0  53   0   1   0   0   1   1   0   1   1  42
  13   5.9   7.6   9  91   0  58   0   0   0   0   1   1   0   1   1  39
  14  10.5  12.0  15  85   0  67   0   0   0   0   0   0   0   0   0  31
  15   8.2   9.8  12  88   0  65   0   0   0   0   0   0   1   0   1  33
  16  11.1  12.4  15  85   0  65   0   0   0   0   0   1   0   0   0  36
  17   8.6   9.9  12  88   0  59   0   0   0   0   1   1   0   1   1  37
  18   5.5   6.7   8  92   0  61   0   1   1   1   0   1   0   1   1  33
  19  12.1  13.4  16  84   0  55   0   1   0   0   0   0   0   0   1  42
  20   7.1   8.4  10  90   0  63   0   0   0   0   0   0   0   0   0  35
  21   7.8   9.1  11  89   0  45   0   0   0   0   0   0   0   1   1  52
  22  12.5  13.8  17  83   0  51   0   0   1   2   0   1   1   2   1  41
  23   7.2   8.4  10  90   0  56   0   0   0   0   1   0   1   1   1  38
```

The power usage value (in the second row, as shown in the preceding screenshot), is obtained from the power sensor in the server's power supply. A zero value will be shown if the sensor doesn't exist or ESXi is not able to read the sensor.

The third row in the preceding screenshot shows the frequencies of each available P-state.

The table after the third row shows information for each virtual CPU. %**UTIL** is the percentage of real time during which the logical CPU has been non-idle. %**USED** is the percentage of nominal speed at which the logical CPU has been operated. Idle time is counted as operation at zero speed. %**USED** can be lower than %**UTIL** in P-states lower than P0. %**USED** can also be higher than 100% if the CPU has been in Turbo mode.

Esxtop is able to compute and estimate power usage per virtual machine, distinguished by processes running on the host. This feature needs to be enabled first by setting the `/config/Power/intOpts/ChargeVMs` advanced configuration option to 1. After it's enabled, run esxtop, and press the *F* key and then the *J* key.

Per-VM power usage is still considered experimental in ESXi 5.

Summary

Resource management is the distribution of resources available from resource providers among resource consumers. In the vSphere environment, all resources are shared between resource consumers. Each virtual machine is allocated a certain amount of the host's hardware resources based on a number of factors. With shares, administrators can specify the relative importance of virtual machines or resource pools. A reservation is the minimum guaranteed amount of resources allocated to a virtual machine. Limits are the maximum amount of resources that can be consumed. Resource pools are used for the flexible management of CPU and memory resources. Administrators can group resource pools into hierarchies to partition available resources hierarchically. DRS may be referred to as a joint load-balancing and failover solution. It enables vCenter to manage hosts as an aggregated pool of resources.

7
Events, Alarms, and Automated Actions

This chapter focuses on the monitoring options available in vCenter, including performance and storage monitoring, as well as possible response actions including e-mail alerts.

We will also discuss automation options, such as scheduled tasks and the Update Manager plugin, which can simplify patch management tasks.

In this chapter, we will cover:

- Alarms and events
- Monitoring host health, guest performance, storage usage, and snapshot size
- Viewing and scheduling tasks
- The Update Manager plugin—installation, baselines, scanning, and remediation

Events, alarms, and system monitoring

vSphere includes a configurable subsystem of events and alarms. This subsystem is able to track what's happening in the environment, let administrators know about unusual activity, and respond automatically to certain situations. Important system events that are matched to appropriate alarms and the responses that are configured properly all together play an important role in system monitoring.

Alarms and events

Each time a user or system action occurs, vSphere records this as an event and stores this data in the event log and vSphere database.

Examples of such events are as follows:

- High host or VM memory or CPU usage
- Lost connection to a host or datastore
- User log ins
- A virtual machine is powered on

Each event record consists of different details about the event, such as the following:

- Who generated the event
- Timestamp
- What type of event it is: information, warning, or error

Alarms are notifications about events. Each alarm has a definition that consists of the following details:

- Name and description.
- Alarm type—the object that is monitored.
- Trigger—what triggers the alarm: an event, its condition or state, or notification severity.
- Tolerance thresholds—trigger thresholds which must be exceeded to trigger an alarm.
- Actions—what occurs in response to triggered alarms. There is a set of predefined actions, including notification e-mail or trap and operations on hosts, such as reboot, shut down, put into maintenance mode. Usually, available actions are specific to objects from the inventory.

Alarms can have one of the following severity levels:

- Normal—green color
- Warning—yellow color
- Alert—red color

Events and alarms are part of a user-configurable subsystem in vSphere. The administrator can specify the conditions that trigger the alarm, as well as the severity levels and automated actions that should happen when certain events occur.

Alarms can be defined for different objects from the inventory. Once an alarm is defined for a certain object, all child objects inherit it; however, this alarm can only be changed in the object where it's defined.

Events can be viewed for either the whole vSphere environment or a single object from the inventory with which they are associated. All events can be viewed under **Events** in the **Management** section on the home page.

To see all the events associated with a particular object, select that object in the inventory, go to the **Tasks & Events** tab, and click on **Events**:

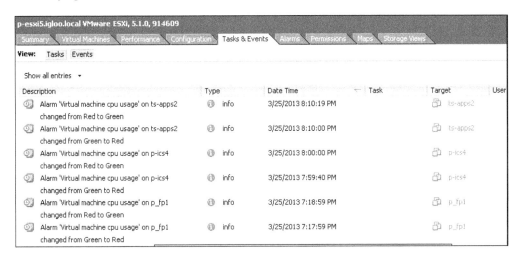

As we've mentioned before, vSphere stores events in the vCenter database. These records include information about who generated the event, when it was generated, and the type of event. To access them, go to **System Logs** in the **Administration** section on the home page. These log entries can be filtered by logfile and exported using the **Export System Logs** button.

vCenter exports them as text logfiles archived in a separate volume for each host and vCenter Server. This information can also be requested by VMware support for troubleshooting purposes.

Acknowledging and resetting triggered alarms

In vSphere Client, all triggered alarms can be viewed in the status bar when you click on **Alarms**. To view the triggered alarms for a specific object, select this object in the inventory and click on **Triggered Alarms** in the **Alarms** tab.

Alarms associated with a specific object, that is, alarm definitions, can be viewed from the **Alarms** tab if you click on **Definitions**.

Triggered alarms can be acknowledged by an administrator. Once an alarm is acknowledged, it stops all actions associated with this alarm; for example, no more e-mail notifications will be sent. To other users and administrators, it means that this issue is being taken care of. Acknowledgement doesn't clear or hide the alarm; it will be visible in the system until the condition is cleared.

To acknowledge an alarm, right-click on it in the list and choose **Acknowledge Alarm**.

Sometimes, the triggered alarm might not reset automatically to its normal state once the condition has been cleared. In this case, it needs to be reset manually. To do that, right-click on the alarm and select **Reset Alarm to Green**.

Monitoring host health

vCenter Server comes with a large set of predefined alarms' definitions that can be used to monitor different components of the system.

When it comes to host monitoring, there is a separate tool that allows the monitoring of host hardware health, including those listed as follows:

- CPU processors
- Memory
- Fans
- Temperature
- Voltage
- Power
- Network
- Battery
- Storage
- Cable/interconnect
- Software components

VMware uses the **Systems Management Architecture for Server Hardware (SMASH)** protocol to gather data about the host's hardware state. SMASH is an industry standard suite of specifications and protocols for monitoring and managing a variety of systems in the datacenter.

The states of hardware components for a particular host can be viewed under the **Hardware Status** tab. Expand components to see more details about them.

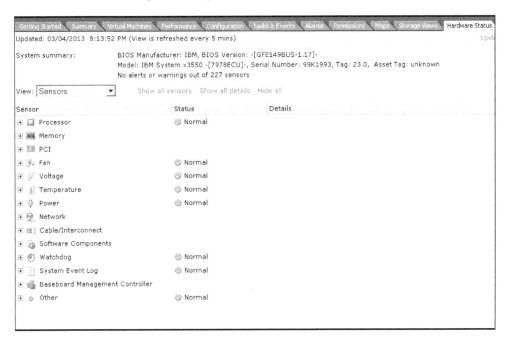

Certain hardware sensors display data that is accumulated over time. These counters can be reset by clicking on **Reset Sensor** at the top of the **Hardware Status** tab.

Hardware Status is actually a plugin in vCenter. Therefore, if the **Hardware Status** tab is not visible, go to the **Plugins** menu and then **Plugin Manager** to verify that it's installed and enabled.

Sometimes, the **Hardware Status** tab displays the following error message: **the remote name could not be resolved SERVER_NAME**, where SERVER_NAME is the domain name of the vCenter Server system.

This error appears when the client system is unable to resolve the domain name of the vCenter Server. You can either fix the domain name resolution problem or edit the file `Program Files\VMware\Infrastructure\VirtualCenter Server\extensions\cim-ui\extensions.xml` on the vCenter Server system and replace the vCenter Server domain name with its IP address.

Guest performance and storage usage

VMware collects data for many performance counters related to different aspects of the guest operating system. Because resources such as CPU and memory are allocated dynamically, it makes it more difficult to obtain correct information about resource utilization by running VMs. VMware provides virtual machine-specific performance counter libraries for the Windows Perfmon utility. Therefore, if the guest OS is Microsoft Windows, administrators are able to access the resource utilization data from Windows using the Windows Perfmon utility. You will need to install VMware Tools before this data is available from Windows.

To view performance statistics, you can navigate to **Start | Run**. Type `perfmon` and press *Enter*. From the **Performance** dialog box, you can add counters by selecting performance objects that begin with VM.

If the performance object has multiple instances, you will need to select the instances that are to be displayed. Have a look at the following screenshot:

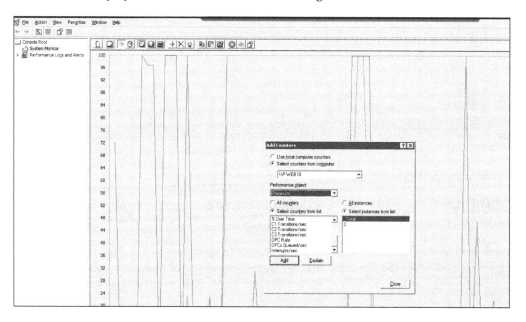

When it comes to storage monitoring, there are two options available in vCenter—**Reports** and **Maps**—both found under the **Storage Views** tab for each inventory object except networking:

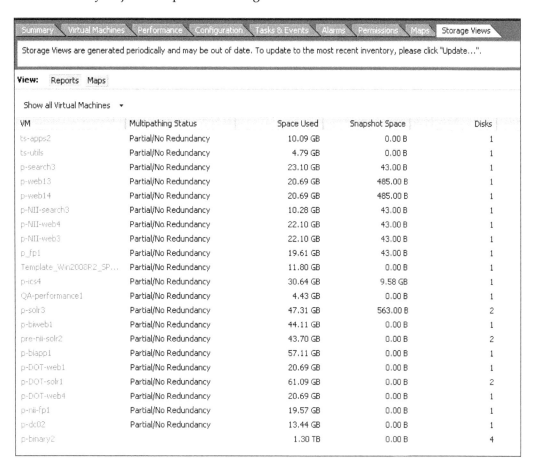

The **Reports** view shows a table with inventory objects and their relation to different storage entities. Storage usage data is available there as well for objects' virtual and physical storage resources. The **Reports** view can be used to analyze storage space utilization and availability as well as the multipathing status.

By default, the **Reports** table will be different depending on the inventory object selected. For example, for datastore, you'll see hosts that have access to this datastore as well as VMs and a number of virtual disks per VM. If a particular VM is selected in the inventory, the **Reports** table will show the datastore associated with this VM as well as the filesystem type, capacity, and connectivity status.

The **Reports** table can also be filtered by object types, such as datastores, VM files, LUNs, and so on, using the menu in the top-left corner. Have a look at the following screenshot:

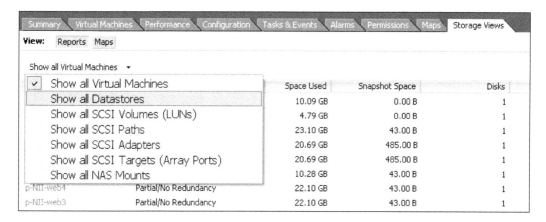

Storage reports can also be exported using the **Export List** option from the **File** menu.

The **Maps** view is a visual representation of the relationships between selected objects and associated storage entities. Have a look at the following screenshot:

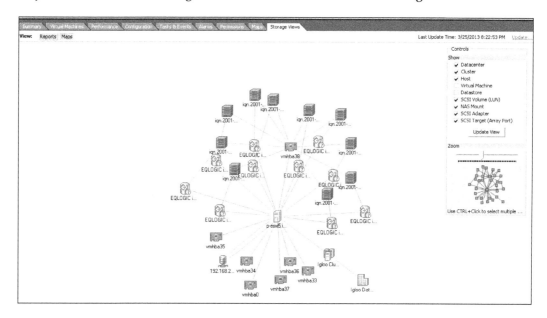

Maps are updated automatically by default every 30 minutes, and they can also be updated manually using the **Update** link.

Maps can be customized using the options in the show area. This can also be repositioned and zoomed in or out of.

Snapshot size monitoring

As described in *Chapter 3*, *Virtual Machine Management*, VM snapshots may become a problem, especially when they are kept for a long time. They grow, they take up space, and their deletion may affect performance and availability.

vCenter doesn't have a predefined alarm definition for monitoring snapshot size; however, there is a trigger that can be used to create an alert.

Choose the appropriate object in the inventory, go to **Definitions** under the **Alarm** tab, and add a new alarm as shown in the following screenshot:

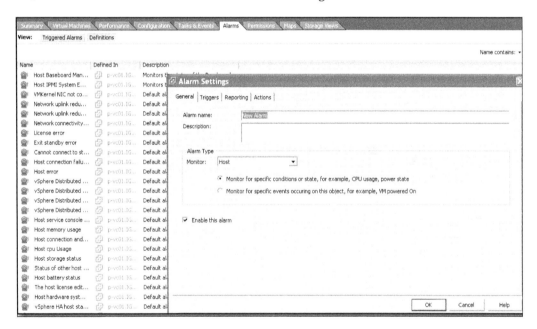

Name the new alarm and, under the **Triggers** tab, add a new trigger called **VM Snapshot Size (GB)** as shown in the following screenshot:

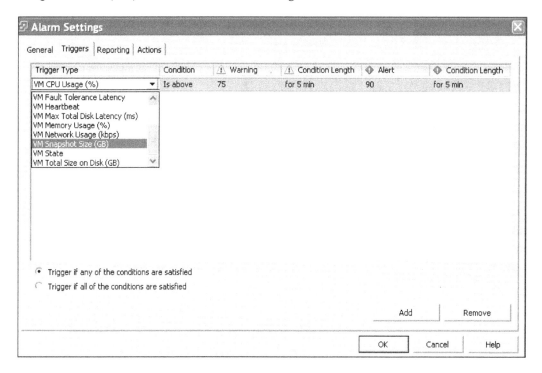

The minimum value for the snapshot size is 1 GB. Set appropriate values for the **Warning** and **Alert** levels. Configure the necessary **Actions** and **Reporting** parameters under other tabs.

Setting up e-mail alerts and SNMP traps

vCenter comes with an SMTP agent that can be used to send e-mail notifications when an alarm is triggered.

An e-mail notification can be configured as an alarm action under the **Actions** tab in **Alarm Settings**. Click on **Add** to add an action; in the **Actions** column, select **Send a notification email** from the drop-down menu. In the **Configuration** column, add the recipient's address. Multiple addresses can be separated with commas. Have a look at the following screenshot:

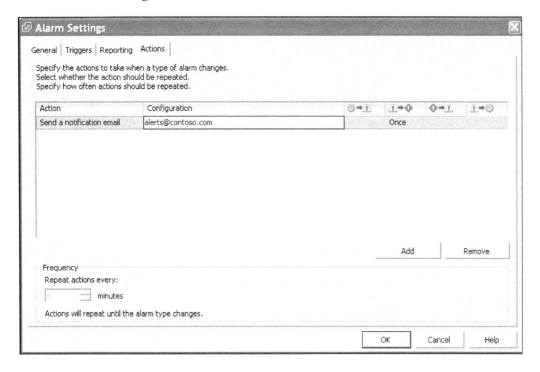

To be able to send e-mail notifications, vCenter has to be configured to use the correct SMTP server and sender account. This can be accomplished from **Administration | vCenter Server Settings**. From the navigation pane on the left, select **Mail** and enter the SMTP server information, such as IP address or FQDN and sender information, that is, from the e-mail address. Have a look at the following screenshot:

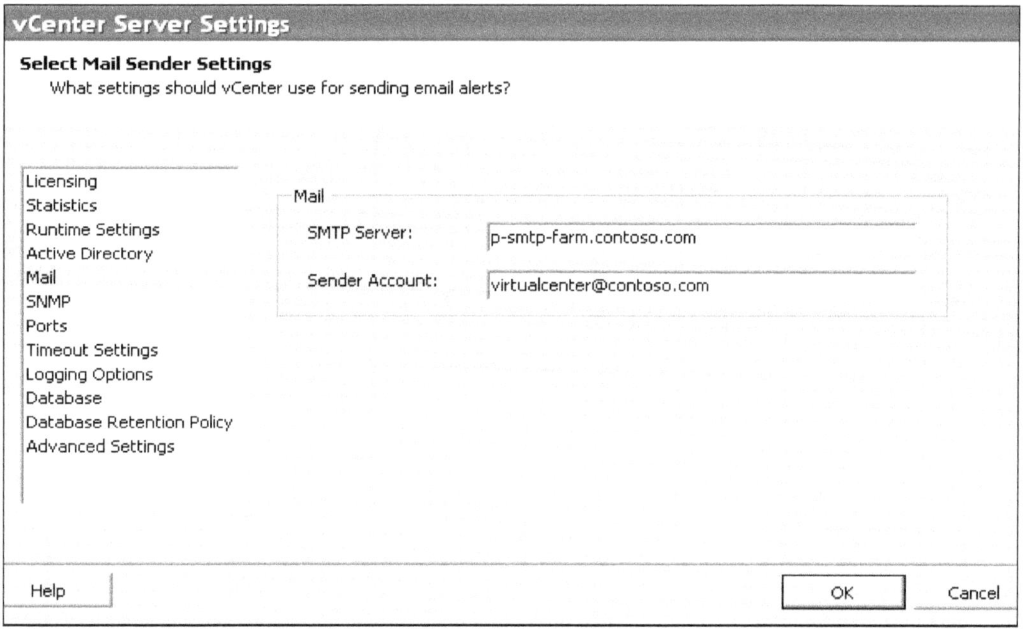

You can configure alerts to send SMTP traps when the alarm is triggered. To send traps, vCenter uses an SNMP agent that works only as a trap emitter and doesn't support any other SNMP functions.

To be able to send SNMP traps, besides configuring appropriate alarm actions, you need to configure SNMP in vCenter Server and also configure the management software to accept and understand the data from vCenter Server.

Alarm actions can be configured in a similar way as described earlier for e-mail alerts. The **SNMP** settings in vCenter are under **Administration | vCenter Server Settings**. Click on **SNMP** in the left navigation pane. Enter the primary receiver URL, port, and community names. Optionally, additional receivers can be configured as shown in the following screenshot:

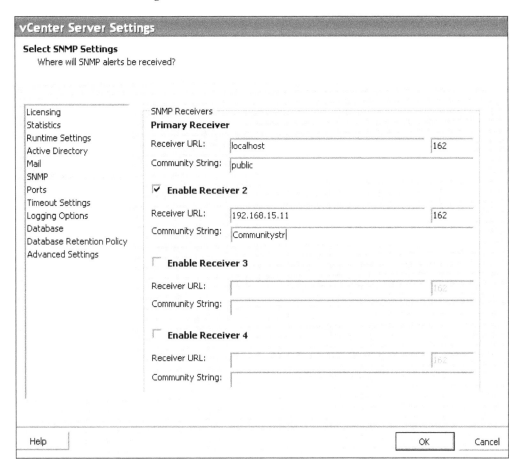

VMware comes with a set of MIB files that define information that ESXi hosts and vCenter Server provide to management software. MIB files can be downloaded from the VMware website and can be used to configure the SNMP management software to be able to read information from SNMP traps. Traps sent by vCenter Server are defined in the VMWARE-VC-EVENTS-MIB.mib file.

Viewing and scheduling tasks

A task is any system activity that takes time to complete; for example, VM migration or powering a VM on/off. Tasks can be started manually or scheduled using a built-in scheduler.

Tasks for a particular inventory object can be viewed under the **Tasks & Events** tab. Detailed information about the tasks can be viewed in the **Details** pane. A list of recent tasks can be viewed under **Recent Tasks** on the status bar as shown in the following screenshot:

Certain tasks can be canceled by right-clicking on them in the **Recent Tasks** list and choosing **Cancel**. This option cancels only the running task. In the case of a scheduled or recurring task, it needs to be edited or deleted from the **Scheduled Task** pane.

You can cancel the following tasks:

- Connecting to a host
- Cloning a virtual machine
- Deploying a virtual machine
- Migrating a powered-off virtual machine (only when the source disks have not been deleted)

If vSphere uses virtual services, the following tasks can also be canceled:

- VM power state change
- VM snapshot creation

Tasks can be scheduled to run in the future—either once or multiple times at certain intervals. The types of tasks that can be scheduled can be found in the VMware documentation at `http://pubs.vmware.com/vsphere-51/index.jsp?topic=%2Fcom.vmware.vsphere.vcenterhost.doc%2FGUID-F9DC9B18-625E-4ACB-AA3A-17BEB109A206.html`.

vCenter Client needs to be connected to vCenter Server before a task can be scheduled. A scheduled task is created by navigating to **Home | Management | Schedule Task** and running the **Schedule Task** wizard. The wizard may look different depending on the type of task you are trying to create.

The Schedule Task.Create Tasks privilege is required to create new scheduled tasks. The available **Frequency:** options are **Once**, **After Startup**, **Hourly**, **Daily**, **Weekly**, and **Monthly**. The **After Startup** option allows for a task to be delayed for an interval (in seconds) that you enter below the option. Have a look at the following screenshot:

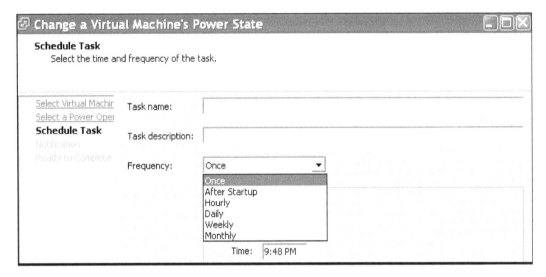

There is also an option to send an e-mail notification once the task is complete. Your e-mail address can be added in the last step of the **Schedule Task** wizard. In order for vCentre to be able to send this notification e-mail, it needs to be configured to use the correct SMTP server and address as described in the *Setting up e-mail alerts and SNMP traps* section.

Unfortunately, it's not possible to create a task for multiple objects. For example, it's not possible to create a task that shuts down all VMs on a host; you will need to create tasks separately for each VM.

Once a scheduled task runs, it can be scheduled again for another time. To do that, go to **Properties** and change the task attributes as required.

The following are a few things to keep in mind when working with scheduled tasks:

- It's not recommended to schedule more than one task at the same time for the same object; the results are unpredictable.

- The user who is going to perform the task has to have the required permissions on the relevant objects. A scheduled task, once created, will be performed even if the user no longer has permission to perform the task.

- In case of conflicting tasks, the task that is scheduled to run first will be started first.

- If a virtual machine or a host is in a state that prevents it from performing the task, the task will not be run and a message will be recorded in the event log.

- All associated tasks are removed when the object is removed from vCenter Server or the ESXi host.

- vSphere Client and vCenter Server use UTC time to determine the start time of a scheduled task. Therefore, vSphere Client users see scheduled tasks at their local time.

The Update Manager plugin

VMware vSphere Update Manager 5 allows administrators to manage patches for ESX and ESXi servers, VMs, and virtual appliances. It allows centralized and automated patch management.

The following tasks can be performed with Update Manager:

- Patching and upgrading ESXi hosts
- Upgrading VM hardware and VMware Tools

To be able to install patches on an ESX/ESXi server, you will need at least ESX/ESXi Version 3.5. If you want to upgrade or migrate hosts to a newer version of the operating system, Update Manager requires at least ESX/ESXi Version 4. VMware Tools and VM hardware updates are also supported on Version 4 and higher.

Installation

Update Manager 5 is a vCenter Client plugin that needs to be installed on each client that needs the ability to manage updates. It also consists of a server component; therefore, clients need to be able to connect to the vCenter server.

The Update Manager installer can be downloaded from the support section on the VMware website.

Requirements for the server part include:

- An Intel or AMD x86 processor with at least two 2 GHz cores
- A 10/100 Mbps or Gigabit network connection between the server running Update Manager and the ESXi hosts
- At least 2 GB of RAM if Update Manager is installed on a different machine from vCenter Server and at least 4 GB of RAM if they are running on the same server
- A 64-bit Windows operating system
- An Oracle or MS SQL database; for small deployments with less than five hosts and 50 virtual machines, the express version of MS SQL can be used
- vCenter Server 5

Also, the server part can't be installed on a server that is the Active Directory domain controller.

Plugin installation requires .NET Framework 3.5 or higher and Windows administrative privileges on the machine that is running vCenter Client.

To install it, go to **Manage Plug-ins** in the **Plug-ins** menu. In the **Plug-in Manager** window, click on the **Download and Install** link next to the VMware vSphere Update Manager extension. Follow the installation prompts. Once the installation is complete, click on **Finish**. Make sure that the status for the Update Manager extension is shown as enabled. If it's disabled, right-click on the extension in the list and click on enable as shown in the following screenshot:

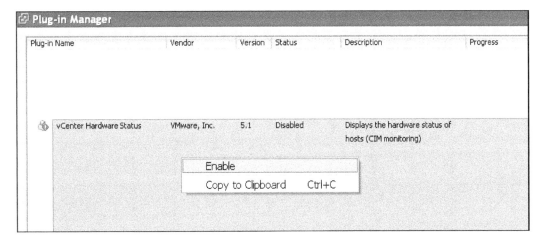

Once the plugin is installed, you will see a new tab in vSphere Client called **Update Manager**. There are two main views there: the compliance (default) view and the administration view. Have a look at the following screenshot:

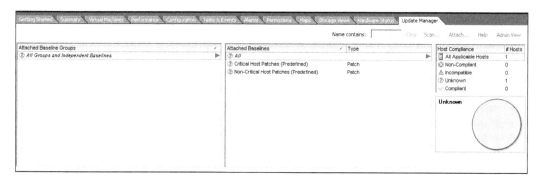

In the **Compliance** view, you can perform the following actions:

- View the inventory object scan results and compliance view
- Attach and detach baselines and baseline groups
- Scan inventory objects
- Remediate inventory objects
- Stage patches or extensions

In the administration view, it's possible to perform the following actions:

- View Update Manager events
- Create and manage baselines and baseline groups
- Review the patch repository and available upgrades
- Check notifications
- Configure Update Manager settings
- Import ESXi images

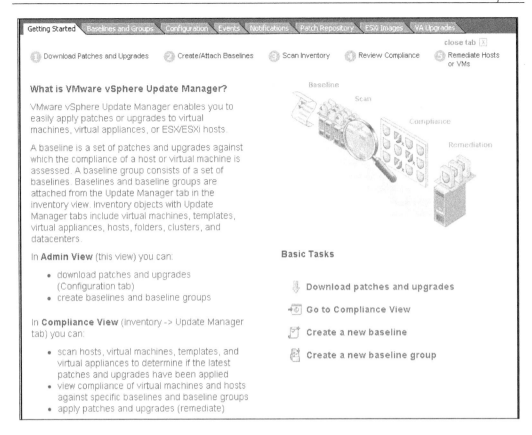

Once all prerequisites are met and the Update Manager server part and plugin are installed and configured, the next tasks that need to be accomplished include the following:

- Creating baselines and baseline groups
- Attaching baselines or baseline groups to objects
- Scanning objects and reviewing scan results
- Remediating selected objects
- Staging patches and extensions for hosts

We will briefly review some of the previously listed steps in the following sections.

Working with baselines

A baseline is a collection of patches, extensions, and upgrades.

Update Manager includes three upgrade baselines and two dynamic patch baselines.

The default baselines can be found under the **Baselines and Groups** tab in the Update Manager Client administration view. Administrators who have the Manage Baseline privilege can edit existing baselines and create new ones using the **New Baseline** wizard.

Two or more non-conflicting baselines can be added to a baseline group. Groups allow for scanning and remediating objects against more than one baseline at the same time.

A baseline group containing the following baselines can be used to update more than one VM:

- VM Hardware upgrade
- VMware Tools upgrade

A baseline group containing the following baselines can be used to update more than one host:

- Baseline groups for virtual machines
- Baseline groups for hosts

Administrators can create their own baselines and groups. This is accomplished from the administration view by right-clicking on the empty space and selecting **New Baseline**. This opens the **New Baseline** wizard that allows us to choose the baseline type and the criteria used to include or exclude patches as well as add additional patches.

There are two baseline options available: **Fixed** and **Dynamic**, as shown in the following screenshot:

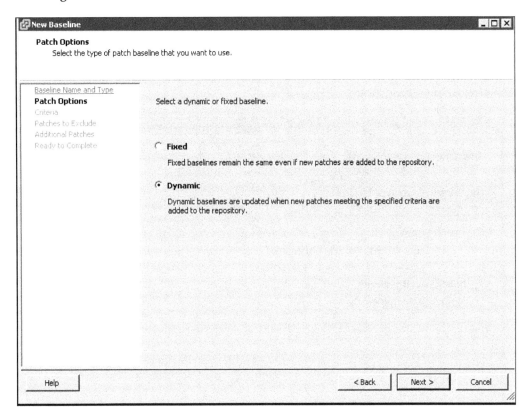

Fixed baselines consist of patches that do not change as patch availability changes. Fixed baselines contain only patches that were initially selected, regardless of new patch downloads that become available.

Dynamic baselines consist of patches that meet the chosen criteria; therefore, they vary as patch availability changes.

Once baselines and baseline groups are created, they need to be attached to objects in the inventory so that you can check objects' compliance and remediate the baselines. Baselines and baseline groups can be attached to individual inventory objects, such as VMs or hosts, as well as containers (which may be more efficient). In this case, all child objects inherit this setting. Baselines and baseline groups can be attached to objects. This can be done in the Update Manager Client compliance view by choosing **Attach** and selecting the appropriate baselines or groups. Have a look at the following screenshot:

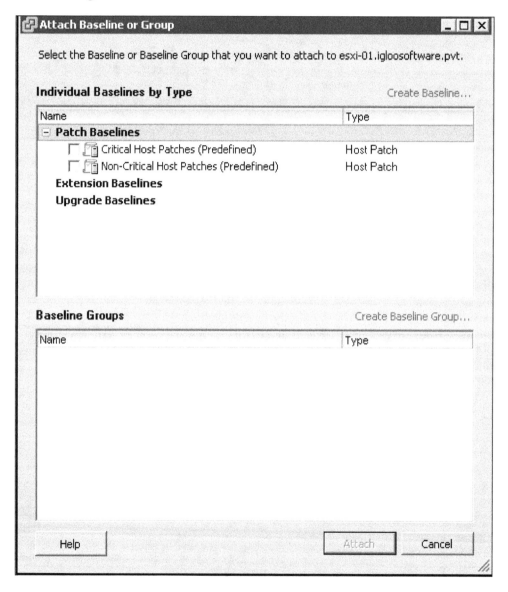

Attached baselines and groups can be viewed or detached from the same view. To detach a baseline or group, simply right-click on it and choose **Detach Baseline** or, if it's a baseline group, **Detach Baseline Group**.

Scanning and remediating objects

After an object has some baselines attached, it can be scanned for compliance. Scanning evaluates an object by comparing the installed patches, extensions, and upgrades to those present in the baseline that is attached to the object.

Compliance scanning can be initiated manually by clicking on **Scan** from the compliance view. Scanning can also be scheduled using the vCenter built-in scheduler. This can be accomplished by creating a new scheduled task in the **Schedule Task** view that can be opened from the home page under the **Management** section. More information on working with scheduled tasks has been given earlier in this chapter.

Compliance scan results are displayed in the same view under the **Update Manager** tab as shown in the following screenshot:

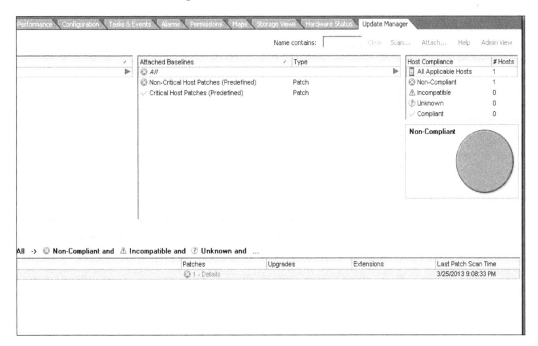

The compliance information shown under the **Update Manager** tab is based on the user's privileges. To view compliance information, a user needs **View Compliance Status** permissions. For example, if a user has permission to view the compliance information for a container but not for its child objects, he/she will be able to see only the aggregate compliance for all objects in this container. This means that if the parent object has a baseline attached and has two child objects, one that is compliant and one that is not, the aggregated status of this parent object will be noncompliant.

Users who have rights to remediate against patches, extensions, and upgrades or to stage patches automatically have rights to view the compliance status, even if they don't have this permission explicitly assigned to them.

Updates for each object can be in one of the compliance states listed in the article from the VMware documentation at `http://pubs.vmware.com/vsphere-51/ index.jsp?topic=%2Fcom.vmware.vsphere.update_manager.doc%2FGUID- EBAA4F4A-57E0-45ED-8730-4B851FC846A9.html`.

An object itself can be compliant to either a baseline or baseline group, noncompliant, unknown, or incompatible.

An unknown status generally means that a compliance scan is required. An object will have an unknown status when either a baseline or baseline group has been attached to it but no compliance scan has been performed, or when there are new updates that have an unknown status.

An incompatible status, in most cases, requires further investigation. Usually, an object has an incompatible status when a baseline or group attached to this object has updates in one of the following states: Conflict or Conflicting New Module, Not Installable or Missing Package, Incompatible Hardware, or Unsupported Upgrade.

Usually, Update Manager provides enough details about an incompatible compliance state.

Noncompliant objects can be remediated. Remediation can be initiated manually or scheduled. Remediate to apply patches, extensions, and upgrades; privilege is required to do that.

To start the process manually, click on the **Remediate** button. This brings up the wizard where you can choose options for the remediation process. To schedule remediation, select a specific date and time for the update. Once the task is scheduled, it can be edited. You will need to remove it and create a new one if changes are required.

In most cases, host remediation requires the host to be able to go into maintenance mode and, often, a reboot is required as well. However, it depends on the updates that are being installed. In some cases, you may need to take care of the VMs running on this host. For example, if this host is part of a cluster, you may need to migrate the VMs to another host before installing any updates.

Under normal circumstances, Update Manager is able to take care of dependencies and conflicts that occur during patch installation. When extensions are remediated, prerequisites are not installed automatically; therefore, if they are required, remediation will fail.

Updates for ESXi hosts contain patches from all previous releases. There are two copies of the ESX image on each host: active boot and standby boot. When a patch is installed, Update Manager creates a new image based on the active boot and places it into the standby boot. Once the active boot is designated as standby, the standby boot becomes active and the host is rebooted. After the reboot, the standby boot contains the previous image which can be used for rollback if necessary. If an update fails and ESXi is not able to boot from the new image, the host will revert to booting from the original build.

With ESXi hosts, remediation from Version 4 to 5 will be considered an upgrade.

Host remediation for a cluster is sequential by default. If one host fails to update, the whole process stops and fails. If Update Manager runs on a VM in a DRS-enabled cluster, this VM will be migrated to another host. If migration fails, remediation for the host where this VM is currently fails as well; however, the whole process does not stop. Update Manager will remediate the next host in the cluster.

Remediation of hosts in a cluster can happen only if all hosts can be updated. Features such as HA admission control, DPM, and FT, if enabled on at least one VM, need to be turned off before host remediation can proceed. Also, all removable devices connected to the VMs need to be disconnected.

With Update Manager 5, it's possible to run host remediation in parallel, meaning that Update Manager will remediate hosts concurrently. In this case, if one host fails or gives an error, it will be ignored and Update Manager will remediate the next host. In this mode, using DRS settings, Update Manager continuously evaluates how many hosts can be remediated at the same time. The number of concurrently remediated hosts can also be limited to a specific number.

To remediate multiple VMs, they need to be located under the container that has the appropriate baseline attached. There is also an option to update VMware Tools the next time a VM restarts. To accomplish that, go to the VMs and templates view in vCenter and select a VM, or its parent container if you want to change this setting for multiple VMs. Then, go to the **Update Manager** tab and click on **VMware Tools upgrade settings**. This will bring up a list of VMs that are available, where you can select which VMs will get their VMware Tools updated during the next power cycle.

Another way to accomplish this is from VM settings. Go to the **Options** tab, select **VMware Tools**, and then, in the **Advanced** section, mark the **Check and upgrade Tools during power cycling** checkbox and click on **OK**.

As an optional step, you can stage patches and extensions to ESX hosts before remediation. Staging allows the downloading of patches and extensions without applying them immediately after that, which speeds up the remediation process and reduces downtime. Update Manager performs a compliance scan and updates compliance information during the stage operation. After successful remediation, all staged patches are deleted.

Deploying Windows updates

If you are running earlier versions of Update Manager, it can also be used to install OS updates on Windows guests. Windows updates are listed the same way as ESX updates; there are baselines that can be attached to Windows VMs or their parent containers. Windows updates are applied in a similar way to VMware Tools updates. Based on selected updates, vCenter creates an ISO image, connects it to a VM as a virtual CD-ROM, installs patches, and reboots the VM if necessary. Unfortunately, this feature is not available in Update Manager 5 anymore.

Summary

Events and alarms are part of the user-configurable subsystem in vSphere. The administrator can specify conditions that trigger the alarm as well as the severity levels and automated actions that can happen when certain events occur.

vCenter Server comes with a large set of predefined alarms' definitions, which can be used to monitor different components of the system.

A task is any system activity that takes time to complete, for example, VM migration or powering a VM on/off. Tasks can be started manually or scheduled using the built-in scheduler.

VMware vSphere Update Manager 5 allows administrators to manage patches for ESX and ESXi servers, VMs, and virtual appliances. It allows centralized and automated patch management.

A baseline is a collection of patches, extensions, and upgrades.

After an object has some baselines attached, it can be scanned for compliance. Scanning evaluates an object by comparing the installed patches, extensions, and upgrades to those present in the baseline that is attached to the object. Non-compliant objects can be remediated.

8
VMware vCenter Operations

This chapter focuses on vCenter Operations — the software that does real-time performance monitoring and management of the vSphere environment.

We will discuss its requirements, installation, and configuration. We will also focus on the way this software is organized and the logic behind it.

Finally, at the end of the chapter, we will talk about memory pressure and ballooning.

In this chapter, we will cover the following topics:

- Installing and configuring vCenter Operations
- Evaluation tasks: badges and scores
- Evaluation tasks: hierarchy views
- Evaluation tasks: health details
- Evaluation tasks: scorecards
- Evaluation tasks: analyze using heat maps
- Memory pressure and ballooning

Installing and configuring vCenter Operations

It is important to know the features and requirements of the software before making a decision if this software may be useful in your environment. The next sections are focused on the features and requirements of vCenter Operations as well as on its basic and additional configuration tasks.

What is vCenter Operations?

VMware vCenter Operations is a software suite for real-time performance management of the virtual environment. Its role is to diagnose and fix performance issues of individual components as well as the entire virtual infrastructure.

There are four editions available. Components available with the editions of the suite include vCenter Operations Manager, vCenter Configuration Manager, vCenter Infrastructure Navigator, and vCenter Chargeback Manager.

Standard and Advanced editions targeted at small and medium-sized businesses include only vCenter Operations Manager. Enterprise and Enterprise Plus editions targeted at large enterprises include all four components.

The Standard edition is suitable for small vSphere environments with less than 1,500 virtual machines. This version is capable of doing performance analysis, capacity metering, and sending alerts. It collects performance data related to the CPU, memory, disk, and network. It combines this data into single performance scores, and represents the current and historical information as graphical views, scorecards, and heat maps. The software calculates the normal range for each metric and highlights abnormalities as well as changes to the virtual infrastructure.

The Advanced edition can be used for larger vSphere deployments, and besides, the Standard version's functionality is capable of building trends, working with scenarios and models, and creating reports.

Enterprise and Enterprise Plus editions are suitable for large virtual, cloud, and heterogeneous environments. These versions not only allow collection and diagnostics, but also management and configuration, and include the following features:

- OS and application-level monitoring
- vSphere host configuration
- Dashboard customization
- Compliance management for hosts, VMs, and guests
- Automated discovery
- Relationship virtualization
- Cost modeling, analysis, and reporting

The following table shows the available editions of vCenter Operations, their targeted environments, and included modules:

	Standard and Advanced editions	**Enterprise and Enterprise Plus editions**
Target users	Small and medium-sized businesses	Large enterprises
Suitable for	Small vSphere environments	Large cloud and heterogeneous environments
Modules included	vCenter Operations Manager	vCenter Operations Manager
		vCenter Configuration Manager
		vCenter Infrastructure Navigator
		vCenter Chargeback Manager

Let's briefly review the capabilities of each module:

- **vCenter Operations Manager** provides the following operations management capabilities of the suite:
    - A comprehensive look into the health, risk, and efficiency of your infrastructure and applications
    - Proactive management of vSphere health
    - Early determination and remediation of potential performance issues and bottlenecks before they become noticeable to the end users
    - Management of virtual machines, physical servers, and applications across multiple datacenters from a single console
    - Automatic correlation and analysis of monitoring data across the infrastructure

Please refer to the later sections in this chapter for more details about the vCenter Operations Manager module.

- **vCenter Infrastructure Navigator** provides application discovery and dependency mapping. It seamlessly integrates into vCenter and allows you to perform the following tasks:
    - Automatically discover applications and visualize their dependencies
    - Identify and correlate application services with existing infrastructure components (VMs, hosts, storage resources, and networks)
    - Identify workloads, relationships, and changes within the application environment

        °   Filter and search VMs associated with specific application criteria

- **vCenter Chargeback Manager** provides the ability to track the costs related to virtual infrastructure services. With this module, you will be able to perform the following tasks:

        °   Define how virtual machines and hosts are shared between departments and business units within your organization

        °   Define pricing models, cost templates, and billing policies including fixed costs, allocation-based costing, utilization-based costing, or a combination

        °   Generate cost reports including summaries and comparison of costs and resource usage for specified periods

        °   In addition to standard resources (CPU, memory, storage, and network) metering, thin/thick provisioning, raw disk mapping, and tiered storage

- **vCenter Configuration Manager** is for change, configuration, and compliance management. It is capable of continuous configuration, data collection, assessment, and auditing. This module includes compliance toolkits for a broad range of standards including NIST, PCI, SOX, HIPAA, and so on. It can also be used to build your own IT standards and automatically remediate non-compliant configurations.

Each component can also be downloaded separately as a 60-day trial from the VMware website.

vCenter Operations Manager Standard deployment

Further on in this chapter, we will give a brief overview of vCenter Operations Manager Standard 5.0.3, its requirements, installation, and functionalities.

vCenter Operations Manager uses vSphere APIs to collect data. It begins collecting data shortly after installation, collects continuously until stopped, and stores this raw data in its scalable File System Database (FSDB).

The software comes as a virtual appliance. It needs to be imported into the existing environment and connected to the vCenter Server. There are no changes necessary for vCenter configuration. The software can be bought online. Also, a 60-day trial version can be downloaded from VMware website.

The minimum system requirements for successful deployment include the following:

- ESXi 4.0.2 or higher
- VMware vCenter Server 4.0.2 or higher
- Some storage-related performance metrics such as Host I/O Commands, Host Throughput (Kbps), and Host Latency (ms) are available only if both the vCenter Server and the ESXi host version are 4.1 or later
- One Windows workstation or laptop with at least Internet Explorer 7 or Mozilla Firefox 3 that should be used to connect to the VMware vCenter Server using the locally installed VMware vSphere Client, and to access VMware vCenter Operations Standard using a web browser

The virtual appliance requirements are as follows:

- 4 vCPU on 2.4 GHz or faster.
- 16 GB of RAM.
- 1,000 disk I/O.
- 128 GB HDD for a UI virtual machine and 208 GB for analytics VM. Thick provisioning is recommended for best performance. Thin provisioning can be used but is not recommended.
- The following TCP ports need to be opened on your firewall:
    - ○ 22: It is used to obtain SSH access to the VMware vCenter Operations Standard virtual appliance
    - ○ 443: It is the administrator portal's HTTPS server port
- DRS needs to be enabled in order to import the appliance into the cluster. The appliance can be deployed outside the cluster directly on ESXi; however, ESXi needs to be managed by vCenter Server.
- The IP pool needs to be associated with the virtual network that it's going to use. The pool doesn't need to be enabled; however, for vCenter Operations to work, the IP pool can be created in a Datacenter object under the **IP Pools** tab.
- The two IP addresses that will be assigned to the appliance and IP pool should be within the same subnet as vCenter Server.

The following screenshot shows an example of the IPv4 configuration:

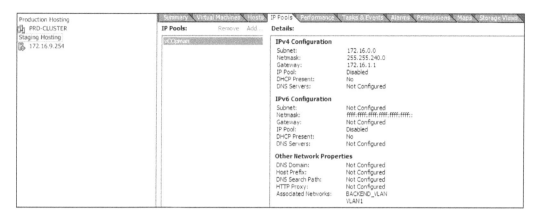

Basic configuration

Once the virtual appliance has been imported and powered on, assuming you assigned the IP addresses during deployment, go to `http://<ipaddress>` (UI IP) and log in using the following default credentials:

- Username: `admin`
- Password: `admin`

Before vCenter Operations can be used, you will be required to do a quick configuration. The steps are as follows:

1. Set up vCenter server address and credentials.
2. Change the default administrator's password.

Follow the configuration wizard prompts after accessing the web interface for the first time.

Also, to be able to start properly, the software requires license key to be applied in vCenter through the vSphere client. To apply the **License key**, the steps are as follows:

1. From the home page, select the **Licensing** tab under **Administration**.
2. Select the **View by Asset** option and you will see **vCenter Operations Standard** listed. If it doesn't show up, refresh the page.
3. Right-click on the **Asset** and select **Change License key** and enter the license key.

4. If there are no errors, then your VMware vCenter Operations Standard installation has been licensed and is ready to be used, as shown in the following screenshot:

Additional configuration and usage

vApp should be used to power-on and power-off the appliances; however, it's not recommended to use power actions directly on the appliances. Instead, it's better to use power actions available for the VMware vCenter Operation vApp as shown in the following screenshot:

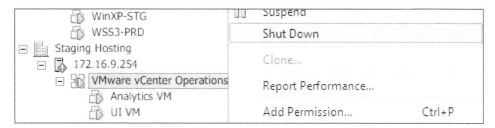

It is not recommended to manually change the IP addresses inside the virtual appliances. The proper way to do this is to use the Admin UI instead. If the dynamic address assignment was selected during installation and needs to be changed to the static IP, redeployment is preferred over changing the settings manually. IP addresses can be changed in the **vApp Properties** option as well, as shown in the following screenshot:

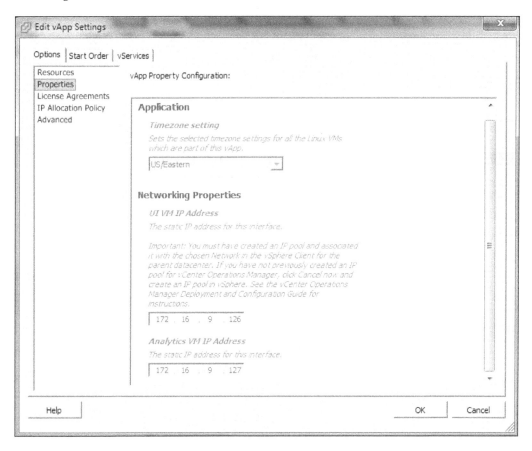

Additionally, appliance configuration can be done from the administrative interface, http://<ipaddress>/admin, where <ipaddress> is the UI IP of the virtual appliance.

The default login credentials, unless they've been changed during basic configuration, are as follows:

- Username: root
- Password: vmware

From the administrative interface, you can change the connection in the mail server settings of the vCenter Server, install an SSL certificate, check the service status, and update the software, as shown in the following screenshot:

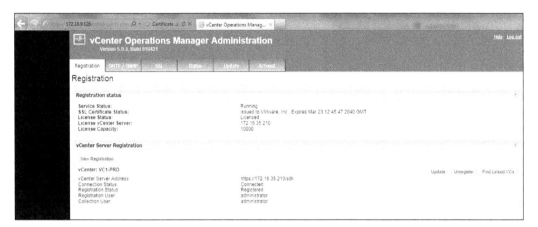

The mail server has to be configured in order to set up e-mail alerts for your environment. This can be accomplished from the **SMTP/SNMP** tab, as shown in the following screenshot:

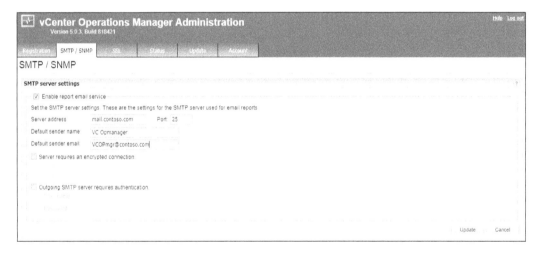

E-mail alerts can themselves be configured from the **Notifications** section in the main UI Dashboard. For each notification rule, you will need to specify the e-mail address for alerts, as well as **Alert types**, **Criticality Levels**, and objects that will be reported, as shown in the following screenshot:

The time zone can be changed from the **UI VM** console using the command-line interface, as shown in the following screenshot:

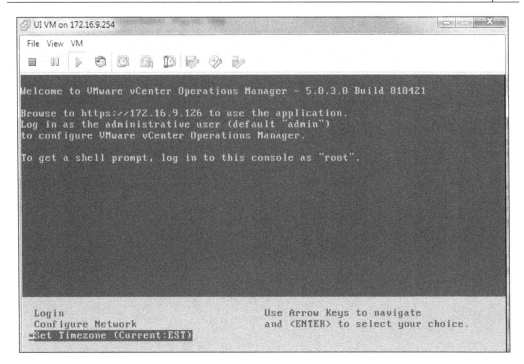

Evaluation tasks

In the following section, we will review the basic evaluation tasks and the steps involved in each of them.

After logging in to UI, you will see the main dashboard that contains three sections. The section to the left has a hierarchy of available resources in your environment. It looks similar to vCenter's view of Hosts and Clusters, and additionally, lists the storage resources under each host that they are connected to, as shown in the following screenshot:

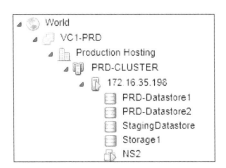

The main section in the center contains information of available diagnostics. It has six main tabs, many of which have additional tabs and menus inside. Data shown in the main section is related to the object selected on the left section of program window.

The section to the right contains warnings and alerts as well as baselines for three main metrics: health, risk, and efficiency.

Both the left and right-hand sections can be hidden.

Badges and scores

In vCenter Operations Manager, the virtual environment can be viewed from three different perspectives: **Health**, **Risk**, and **Efficiency**. Each object in your environment is assigned these three scores, and appears in one of the predefined colors based on the score, as shown in the following screenshot:

Each of the three major **badges** are calculated by vCenter Operations Manager as a weighted combination of additional metrics. Their icons and description are listed as follows:

* **Health**: It is a general assessment of the behavior of performance metrics, combined with a best practice understanding of key metrics; values range from 0 (very abnormal behavior) to 100 (very normal behavior). In most cases, if there are any problems shown in this section, they require immediate attention.

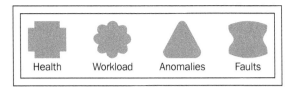

- ° **Workload**: It is an assessment of the level of work being done by a virtual element based on the four key potential constraints of CPU, memory, disk I/O, and network I/O. Values range from 0 (no usage of these resource characteristics) to more than 100 (one or more of these resource characteristics are seriously constrained).

- ° **Anomalies**: It is an expression of the number of metrics trending above or below normal, which is the main indicator of upcoming performance issues.

- ° **Faults**: It is the number of hard thresholds that have been reached when there is an availability issue or when hardware failure has occurred.

- **Risk**: It describes the potential future problems. It is based on the following factors:

  - ° **Time**: It is the time remaining before resources are exhausted

  - ° **Capacity**: It is the capacity remaining before the resources are exhausted

  - ° **Stress**: It is the metric that shows patterns of chronic strain

- **Efficiency**: It is an assessment of resource utilization in your environment

  - ° **Reclaimable waste**: It is the idle time, over and under provisioned virtual machines

  - ° **Density**: It shows the current consolidation ratio versus the maximum possible ratio without performance degradation

Score thresholds for different colors can be changed in the configuration manager as shown in the following screenshot:

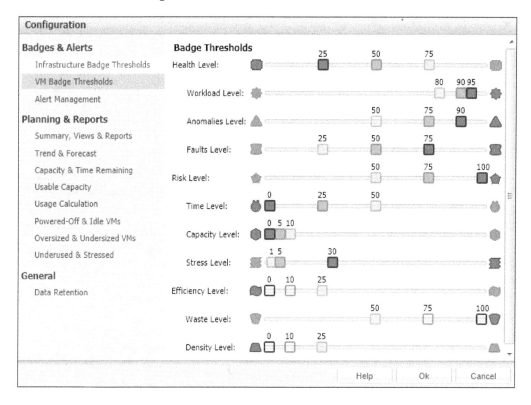

Additional details on each of the metrics in the preceding screenshot can be viewed under the **Operations** and **Planning** tabs.

Hierarchy views

Environment views under the **Operations** and **Planning** tabs show the hierarchy of vSphere objects. Depending on the selection on the left-hand side panel, objects will be highlighted or dimmed. Context-focus can also be changed by selecting an object in the hierarchy. The following screenshot shows an example of the **Environment** view:

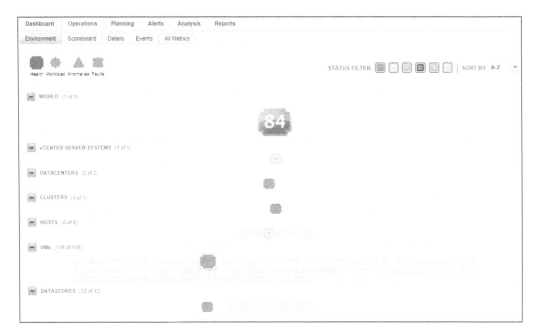

To filter objects by state, use the **STATUS FILTER** buttons in the upper-right corner of the **Environment** view, as shown in the following screenshot:

Each status can be either turned on or off. For example, in the earlier screenshot, the powered-off object and the objects in a good state are excluded.

You can always move your mouse over any object to see its name and scores, as shown in the following screenshot:

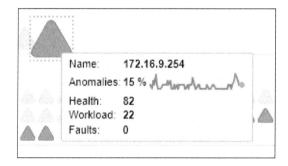

Health details

The following screenshot shows a quite healthy environment:

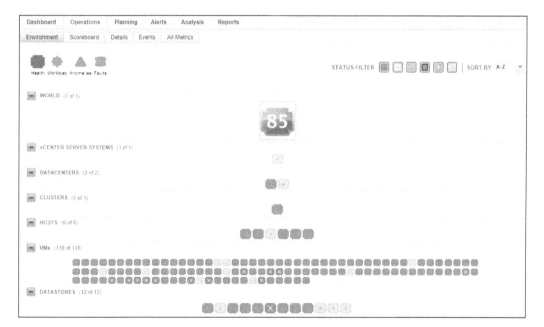

There are few yellow objects; among them there are datastores shown at the bottom. To be able to understand what's causing these warnings, highlight one of the objects and go to the **Details** tab:

As you can see, there are two exclamation marks under the **Key Metrics** section. In this case, the number of virtual machines running on the storage exceeds the threshold. This can also be confirmed if you go to the **All Metrics** tab and expand the highlighted containers, as shown in the following screenshot:

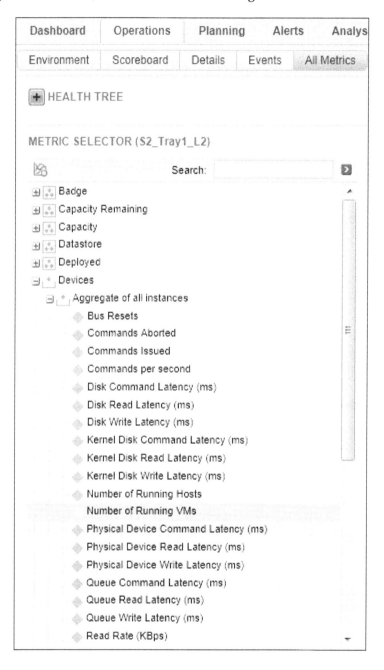

Scorecards

Scorecards can be used to determine the main contributors to metrics. For example, the following screenshot shows a scorecard for one of the ESXi hosts:

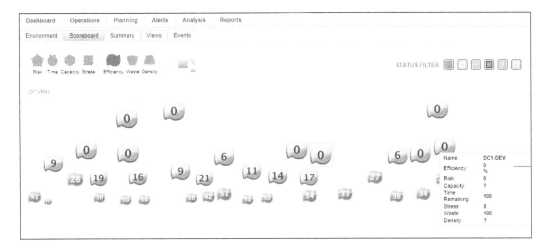

In this case, a larger icon means worse efficiency. As you can see, there are many virtual machines that have very low scores. Be careful with those that are shown as 0. They may be VMs that have recently been turned off.

DC1-DEV, however, is currently running, and it looks like we should be able to assign part of its resources to VMs that need them more.

Analyse using heat maps

A heat map is a collection of rectangles of different colors and sizes. Each rectangle represents a resource in the virtual environment. The color of each rectangle is defined by one metric, the size represents the value of another.

In vCenter Operations Manager, heat maps are available under the **Analysis** tab. They allow you to compare the performance of objects across the entire infrastructure in real time. There are more than 20 predefined heat maps that compare commonly used metrics. vCenter Operations Manager allows an unlimited number of custom heat maps to be defined that display specific metrics that are needed.

With heat maps, you can perform the following tasks:

- Compare the performance of selected metrics across the whole infrastructure, and use this information to balance load across hosts and storage

- Find objects with the highest or lowest values for particular metrics

- Analyze if the operation of different objects is within or outside the desired range of each metric

In the following screenshot, we compare the virtual machine's capacity versus the workload for ESXi hosts in our virtual environment:

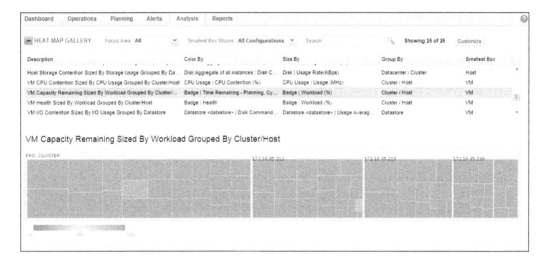

Such analysis allows us to understand how risk is allocated across the cluster. For example, high workloads combined on one host present a risk and may need to be distributed.

In the preceding screenshot, the first host has the most virtual machines with the highest workload. In spite of the fact that these VMs have the most capacity remaining, they may need to be redistributed better between the other hosts.

If none of the predefined heat maps show the information that you are looking for, you can create a custom one. It's possible to customize every aspect of future heat maps, including objects and metrics, their tracks the, colors they use, and the endpoints for their value range, as shown in the following screenshot:

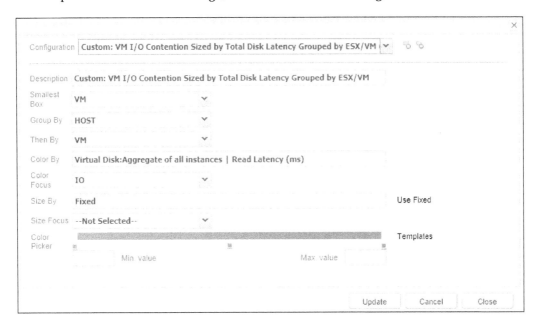

The preceding screenshot shows the creation of a custom heat map to determine VM disk latency combined by ESXi hosts. The result is displayed in the following screenshot:

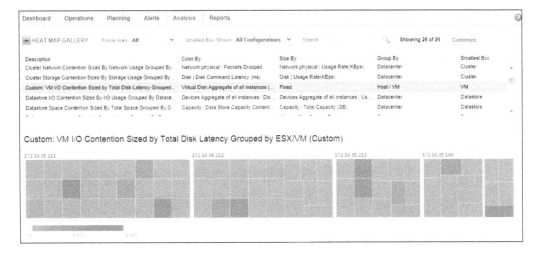

The color bar at the bottom is a legend that gives an idea about the values behind the colors. In this case, virtual machines marked in red still have less than 9 ms latency, which is an acceptable value.

Min.value and **Max. value** fields can be set to the top and bottom values of the desired metric range, as shown in the following screenshot:

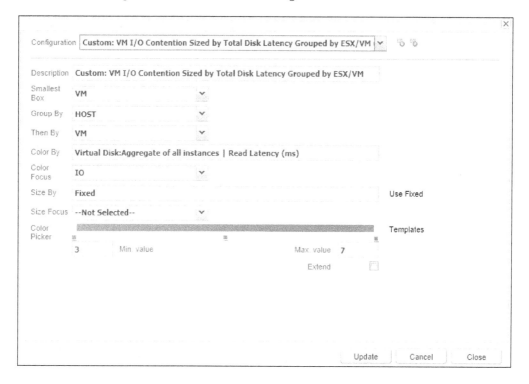

When these fields are defined, any object that is showing endpoint colors — either red and green, or orange and blue — is outside the desired range.

In the following screenshot, you can see the same heat map with defined endpoints. As you can see, the legend has changed as well as with the heat map itself:

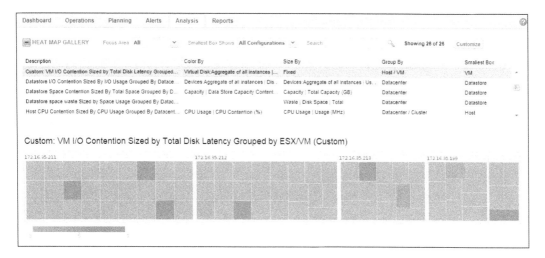

Memory pressure and ballooning

VMware Operations Manager is not the only solution for performance monitoring and management. There are other tools available from different vendors. Depending on the existing environment and requirements, other tools may be more suitable.

Third-party tools may also have different metrics. An example of such metrics is host memory pressure and high balloon memory utilization, which are monitored and reported by Veeam ONE for VMware.

The following screenshot shows Veeam ONE reporting **Host memory pressure**:

When the OS components and processes have used all the available memory, and there is another process that needs to do I/O, it tells the OS to free some memory or cache. This is called memory pressure, and when it happens, the OS determines which memory pages are safe to get rid of, in order to free some resources.

The Memory pressure metric is useful while troubleshooting performance issues as well as planning the capacity of your environment. Essentially, it tells you how overcommitted your host memory is. If memory pressure is high, it means that a lot of memory has been allocated to VMs, and if they all were to use this memory at the same time, ESXi may start memory ballooning, or you may get performance issues such as swapping.

Ballooning is the process of reclaiming unused memory from a VM by the ESXi hypervisor. In most cases, it's used by the host when its memory resources are overcommitted, and allows memory to be redistributed between consumers. The process is shown in the following diagram:

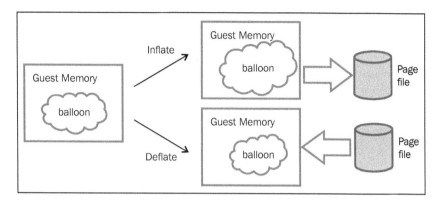

ESXi server controls assign memory by communicating with the guest OS module—the pseudo-device driver or kernel module. It instructs the driver to inflate or deflate the memory balloon that makes the guest OS invoke its own memory management algorithms, or deallocate previously allocated pages.

Memory ballooning itself in most cases is not a problem. It indicates that ESXi is maximizing the memory usage.

If a host has high memory pressure, you may need to migrate VMs to a different host. If this is the case for all hosts, adding a new ESXi host or upgrading memory on existing ones may be necessary.

Summary

VMware vCenter Operations is a software suite for real-time performance management of a virtual environment. Its role is to diagnose and fix the performance issues of individual components as well as the entire virtual infrastructure.

vCenter Operations Manager uses vSphere APIs to collect data. It begins collecting data shortly after installation, and collects continuously until stopped.

In vCenter Operations Manager, the virtual environment can be viewed from three different perspectives: health, risk, and efficiency. Each object in your environment is assigned these three scores and appears in one of the predefined colors based on the score.

Scorecards can be used to determine main contributors to metrics.

The heat map is a collection of rectangles of different colors and sizes. Each rectangle represents a resource in the virtual environment. The color of each rectangle is defined by one metric, the size represents the value of another.

VMware Operations Manager is not the only solution for performance monitoring and management. There are other tools from different vendors available.

Third-party tools may also have different metrics. An example of such metrics is host memory pressure and high balloon memory utilization, which are monitored and reported by Veeam ONE for VMware.

VMware vCenter Orchestrator

9

The intention of this chapter is to give a brief overview of VMware vCenter Orchestrator. We will discuss its requirements and installation process as well as the initial configuration or networking, LDAP configuration, database connectivity, and SSL security.

The second part of this chapter describes several administration aspects of vCenter Orchestrator. In particular, we will talk about workflows, elements, and actions.

In this chapter, we will cover the following topics:

- System requirements and components setup
- Installing and upgrading Orchestrator
- Initial configuration: network access, SSL Certificate, LDAP configuration, database connection, and plugin configuration
- Administering vCenter Orchestrator
- Overview of workflows
- Resource elements and actions

Installing and configuring vCenter Orchestrator

VMware vCenter Orchestrator is an automation tool that provides a set of workflows that can be used to automate the configuration and management of vSphere infrastructure. It uses vCenter Server APIs that cover almost every operation.

The table at the following link leads to an article from the VMware documentation that lists key Orchestrator features:

```
http://pubs.vmware.com/vsphere-50/index.jsp?topic=%2Fcom.vmware.
vsphere.vco_appliance.doc_42%2FGUID015CC419-7F9B-4269-B0B1-
F1E9B3B842C9.html
```

Two main components of vCenter Orchestrator are the **workflow library** and **workflow engine**. They allow the creation and running of workflows to automate processes. Workflows can be run on different objects accessible to Orchestrator via plugins.

There is a standard set of plugins. Because of the open architecture of Orchestrator, third-party plugins can be used as well.

The following diagram shows the Orchestrator architecture:

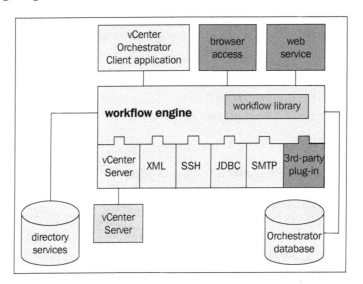

System requirements and components setup

Before installing Orchestrator, make sure you've fulfilled the following requirements:

- You have at least two CPUs 2.0 GHz or faster — Intel or AMD x86
- You have at least 4 GB of RAM
- You have at least 2 GB of disk space available
- You have a free, static IP address
- You run a 64-bit operating system

As well as the preceding requirements, you also need a working LDAP server in your network with one of the following directory service types:

- Windows Server 2003 Active Directory
- Windows Server 2008 Active Directory
- Novell eDirectory Server 8.8.3
- Sun Java System Directory Server 6.3

To be able to access Orchestrator's configuration interface or Web Views, you will need one of the following browsers:

- Microsoft Internet Explorer 7.0
- Mozilla Firefox 3.0 (build 3.0.6 or later)
- Mozilla Firefox 3.5

For configuration and performance purposes, it is recommended to install Orchestrator on a computer different from where vCenter Server runs.

When configuring Orchestrator, make sure you don't go over the following supported maximums:

Item	Maximum
Connected vCenter Server systems	10
Connected ESX/ESXi servers	300
Connected virtual machines spread over vCenter Server systems	15,000
Concurrent running workflows	300

The more vCenter Server instances you manage, the more sessions Orchestrator needs to handle. Each session means an additional activity on the corresponding vCenter Server; therefore, too many sessions will cause Orchestrator to timeout. This becomes an issue if you are running more than 10 sessions.

If you need to manage more than 10 vCenter Server instances, you will need to use different machines. For communication with vCenter Server via network, a network connection of 100 MBps is required.

Orchestrator authentication requires an LDAP server. It is recommended to connect the Orchestrator server to the closest LDAP server and avoid remote connections since long response times for LDAP queries can cause slower overall performance.

To improve the performance of Orchestrator, it's recommended to keep the user and group lookup base as narrow as possible by limiting users to only targeted groups that need access.

Orchestrator requires a database. VMware recommends using a database separate from vCenter Server's database. Orchestrator supports Oracle and Microsoft SQL Server databases. For small deployments with less than five hosts and 50 virtual machines, SQL Server Express can be used.

To setup the Orchestrator database, you will need to create a database, enable a remote connection to it, and configure remote connection parameters. Almost every activity in Orchestrator triggers an operation in the database. Therefore, the database setup directly affects Orchestrator's performance so it's recommended to run the database on a server separate from the one where Orchestrator is installed. At the same time, the database should be closed to make sure that the network connection is not causing any performance issues.

Of course, it's recommended to use the fault-tolerant failover database server cluster to make sure that the database is not a single point of failure.

In case there is a need to manage geographically distant sites with VMware Orchestrator, it is recommended to run separate instances of Orchestrator and the database server for each site to avoid any performance issues.

It is also recommended to store database plugins in a separate database, which makes it easier to update the system. A dedicated database instance will allow you to perform updates without affecting any other products.

Installing and upgrading Orchestrator

Orchestrator consists of client and server components. The general requirements for Orchestrator are listed as follows:

- The server component needs a 64-bit Windows machine
- The client component works on both 32- and 64-bit systems
- You need local or domain administrator rights to install Orchestrator
- Orchestrator can be installed as part of the vCenter Server installation or separately
- When you install vCenter Server 5.0.1, Orchestrator 4.2.1 is installed by default as an additional component, unless you explicitly choose not to install it

Download the vCenter Server installer from the VMware website, run it, select **vCenter Server**, and click on **install**.

The next steps are straightforward. You'll need to enter the username, organization name, and license key, choose the database option, set the login information for vCenter Server, change the destination folder or accept the default option, and so on.

For more details about installing vCenter Server, see *Chapter 1, vCenter Deployment*.

Standalone Orchestrator is usually installed on a separate machine to improve its performance and make administration and updates easier.

To install the standalone version, you still need to download the vCenter Server installer. When you run it, choose the Orchestrator option, and not the vCenter Server option.

In the next steps, you will be prompted to accept the license agreement, choose or change the destination folder, select the type of installation, and specify the location of Orchestrator shortcuts.

Options for the installation type are listed in the VMware documentation article that you can find at the following website:

```
http://pubs.vmware.com/vsphere-50/index.jsp?topic=%2Fcom.vmware.
vsphere.vco_install_config.doc_42%2FGUID2DE5C17A-32AD-4565-9972-
DB4BCEB7166D_copy.html
```

If you need to install the Orchestrator client on a 32-bit machine, you'll need to download the vCenter Orchestrator Client distribution and run it to launch the installation wizard.

If you are running Orchestrator 4.1 either as a standalone installation or bundled with vCenter, you can upgrade it by either upgrading vCenter Server if it's installed on the same machine, or installing the newer version of Orchestrator in the case of a standalone installation.

Before running the installation of the newer version of Orchestrator or vCenter Server, you will need to stop the following Windows services:

- VMware vCenter Orchestrator Configuration.
- VMware vCenter Orchestrator Server.
- VMware Virtual Center Server. This service is installed only when Orchestrator is running on the same machine as vCenter Server.

Once it's done, run Orchestrator or the vCenter Server installer and follow the wizard. You will be prompted about whether or not you want to continue with the upgrade.

If the machine on which you are planning to deploy Orchestrator 4.2.1 already has Orchestrator 4.0 installed, keep in mind that the older version will not be detected automatically by the installer and two versions of Orchestrator will be installed and co-exist. Obviously, they will be using different SQL instances and/or different databases; however, you will end up running two different versions of the software on one server.

Therefore, you cannot upgrade Orchestrator 4.0 by running the Orchestrator 4.2.1 installation or upgrading vCenter Server, in case it's installed on the same server. You will need to export the Orchestrator configuration, uninstall the old version of the software, and install the new one.

To export the configuration, log in to **Orchestrator configuration** as a vmware user, go to the **General** tab, and click on **Export Configuration**. You will be prompted for a password to protect the configuration file.

To uninstall an older version of Orchestrator, go to **Add or Remove Programs**, select **vCenter Orchestrator**, and click on **Remove**. Once it's done, install Orchestrator as described earlier in the chapter.

Once the current version is installed, go to the **General** tab when logged in to the configuration interface as the vmware user, and click on **Import Configuration**. You will be prompted for the configuration file password that you will have chosen during export.

Initial configuration

If Orchestrator was installed together with vCenter Server, you will need to start the VMware vCenter Orchestrator Configuration service from the Windows Services snap-in in order to be able to access the **Orchestrator configuration** interface.

To access the interface itself, go to **Start | Programs | VMware** and run **vCenter Orchestrator Configuration**. Alternatively, you can open the web browser and go to https://localhost:8283 or http://localhost:8282.

Log in with the following default credentials:

- **Username**: vmware
- **Password**: vmware

When you log in with the default credentials for the first time, you will see the welcome page prompting you to change the password. The default username cannot be changed.

Network access

By default, you are only able to connect to the configuration interface locally. If you need to connect from different hosts through the network, you'll need to enable remote connections. This can be accomplished by editing the following line in the jetty.xml file:

```
<SystemProperty name="jetty.host" default="localhost"/>
```

Replace localhost with 0.0.0.0.

Once it's changed, you need to log in to the configuration interface and restart the configuration service by going to **Startup Options** and clicking on **Restart on the vCO configuration server**.

The default location of jetty.xml will be different depending on the way Orchestrator was installed. You can find more details in the article at the following link: http://pubs.vmware.com/vsphere-50/index.jsp?topic=%2Fcom.vmware. vsphere.vco_install_config.doc_42%2FGUID-C9CF14B8-722D-4D42-AA36- FEB3B2A52890.html

When you install Orchestrator, the IP address used by the server to communicate with clients may not be set automatically.

You can choose the IP address which Orchestrator binds to in the configuration interface under **Network** by selecting the correct address from the IP address drop-down menu.

You may also need to change the IP address which Orchestrator binds to when the machine it's installed on has more than one IP address assigned to it.

It is recommended to use a static IP address or the IP address provided by DHCP using reservations. This helps to avoid issues when dynamic IP addresses change.

SSL certificate

You may need to install an SSL certificate to avoid throwing a certificate error message when Orchestrator uses a secure connection. An SSL certificate can be installed in the configuration interface under the **Network | SSL Certificate** tab.

You can use a vCenter Server certificate which can be imported either from a file or a URL. The table in the VMware documentation article at the following link gives more details about these two options:

http://pubs.vmware.com/vsphere-50/index.jsp#com.vmware.vsphere.vco_ install_config.doc_42/GUID39C552FA-0225-4D29-A4AC-7680252A5EC8.html

Once you choose one of these options, click on **Import**.

LDAP configuration

Orchestrator requires an available LDAP server in the environment so that it can manage user permissions. Unfortunately, multiple domains from different trees are not supported by Orchestrator, even if they have a two-way trust between them.

To be able to use LDAP over SSL in Windows 2003 or 2008 Active Directory, disable the **LDAP Server Signing Requirements** group policy on the LDAP server.

To configure LDAP authentication, go to the configuration interface and click on **LDAP**. Choose the type of directory server from the **LDAP client** drop-down list. Specify **Primary LDAP host**, **Secondary LDAP host**, and which **Port** to use. You can use either the IP address or the DNS name.

In the **Root** textbox, you will need to specify the root element of the LDAP service. In other words, it's going to be the place where the LDAP service starts searching for users. In most cases, it will look something like `dc=company,dc=org` (if, your domain was called `company.org, for example)` as shown in the following screenshot.

You may need to narrow it down to a specific OU, for example, `ou=users,dc=company,dc=org`.

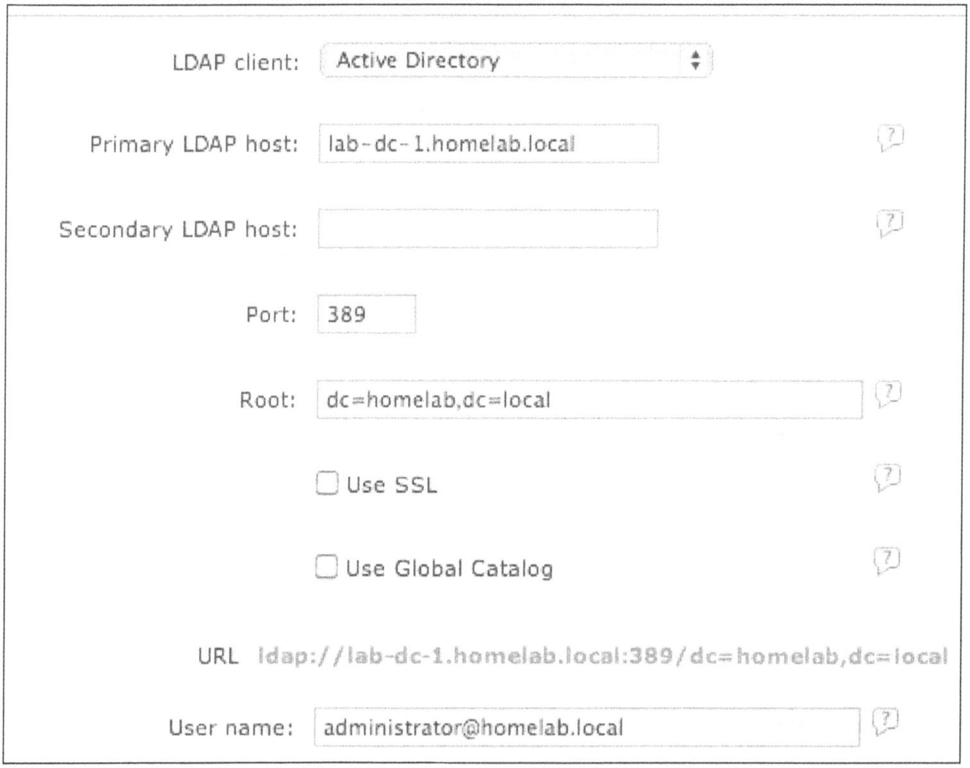

Optionally, you can choose the **Use SSL** option, which secures communication, needs an SSL certificate, and requires the Orchestrator Configuration service to be restarted. You will need to import the SSL certificate, which can be done under The **Network | SSL Certificate** tab. In the **SSL Certificate** tab, select a certificate and click on **Import**. Once it's done, restart the **Orchestrator configuration service** under **Startup options**.

To be able to use LDAP over SSL, make sure you've covered the following points:

- SSL access is enabled on the primary and secondary LDAP servers
- The LDAP Server Signing Requirements group policy is disabled on the LDAP server
- You have verified that the certificate you are going to use is valid for server authentication

If you select the **Use Global Catalog** option, it will allow LDAP referrals in case the LDAP client is the **Active Directory**. In this case, the LDAP lookup port number will be changed to `3268` and Orchestrator will follow LDAP referrals when searching for users and groups in subdomains.

Orchestrator needs access to read your directory structure, so you will need to specify credentials that can be used to connect to the LDAP server. This is done in the **User name** textbox in the configuration interface under LDAP.

Possible formats to specify the username in **Active Directory** are as follows:

- Bare username format: for example, `user`
- Distinguished name format: `cn=user,ou=users,dc=company,dc=org`
  - This format can be used with Sun and eDirectory. Do not use spaces between the comma and the next identifier.
- Principal name format: `user@company.org`
- NetBEUI format: `COMPANY\user`

Specify the password in the **Password** field.

In the next fields, you will need to specify **User lookup base** and **Group lookup base**. These are the containers that Orchestrator will use to look for users and groups.

Click on **Search** and type a top-level domain or organizational unit. For example, if you search for the word `company`, you'll be able to find `dc=company,dc=org`.

Click on **LDAP connection string** for the discovered branch to insert it in the field.

In the next field, define **vCO Admin group**. Members of this group will have administrative privileges for vCO. There are two global roles defined in Orchestrator: Developers and Administrators. Developers have editing privileges on all elements. Administrators have full privileges; they can manage permissions or discharge administration duties on a selected set of elements to any other group or user. These two groups must be contained in **Group lookup base** as shown in the following screenshot:

Password:	
User lookup base:	dc=homelab,dc=local	Search
Group lookup base:	dc=homelab,dc=local	Search
vCO Admin group:	cn=vcoadmins,cn=users,dc=homelab,dc=local	Search
Request timeout (ms):	5000
	☐ Dereference links
	☐ Filter attributes
	☐ Ignore referrals
Host reachable timeout (ms):	5000

Once options in the preceding screenshot are configured, you can click on the **Test Login** tab and type in the user credentials to see if this user can access the Orchestrator smart client. Once a user logs in successfully, the system also checks if this user is a member of the Orchestrator Administrators group.

Further settings can be used to customize LDAP search queries so that the LDAP search is more effective. The settings are as follows:

- **Request timeout (ms)**: It determines the time period in milliseconds between Orchestrator sending a query to the server and the server to perform the search and return a reply.

- **Dereference links**: This option, when checked, means that all links will be followed before performing a search operation. This option must be selected (during LDAP configuration if Sun Java Directory Server is being used) as reference links are not supported there.

- **Filter attributes**: This option makes the search faster by not returning attributes. However, some extra LDAP attributes may need to be used for automation later.
- **Ignore referrals**: It disables referral handling, which means that the system will not display any referrals.
- **Host reachable timeout (ms)**: It determines the timeout period in milliseconds for destination host status checks.

Once all the options have been configured, click on **Apply changes**.

Occasionally, you may encounter an LDAP error message and experience problems with connecting to the LDAP server. In this case, it will be useful to know the meaning of the LDAP error codes. The most common errors are listed in the article at the following link:

```
http://pubs.vmware.com/vsphere-50/index.jsp#com.vmware.vsphere.vco_
install_config.doc_42/GUID-0864F51D-5896-4A31-8E6B-1B3309DC5C32.html
```

Database connection

As mentioned before, Orchestrator requires a database. You will need to configure the connection parameters to be able to connect to the database. Keep in mind that the credentials for authentication to the SQL server, in most cases, are different from those for authentication to LDAP servers.

Before configuring the database connection, make sure you've covered the following points:

- The new database has been set up for use with the Orchestrator server.
- The SQL Server Browser service is running if the SQL Server database is used.
- For the Oracle database, set the `NLS_CHARACTER_SET` parameter to `AL32UTF8` before configuring the database connection and building the table structure for Orchestrator. This setting is crucial for an internationalized environment.

To configure a database connection, go to the Orchestrator configuration interface, and click on **Database**.

Select the **Database Type**. Orchestrator supports Oracle, SQL Server, and SQL Server Express. In the next fields, specify the following connection parameters:

- **User name**
- **Password**
- **DB server**
- **Database Host IP address** or **DNS name**

- **Port**
- **Database name**
- **Instance name (if any)**
- **Domain**, if applicable as shown in the following screenshot:

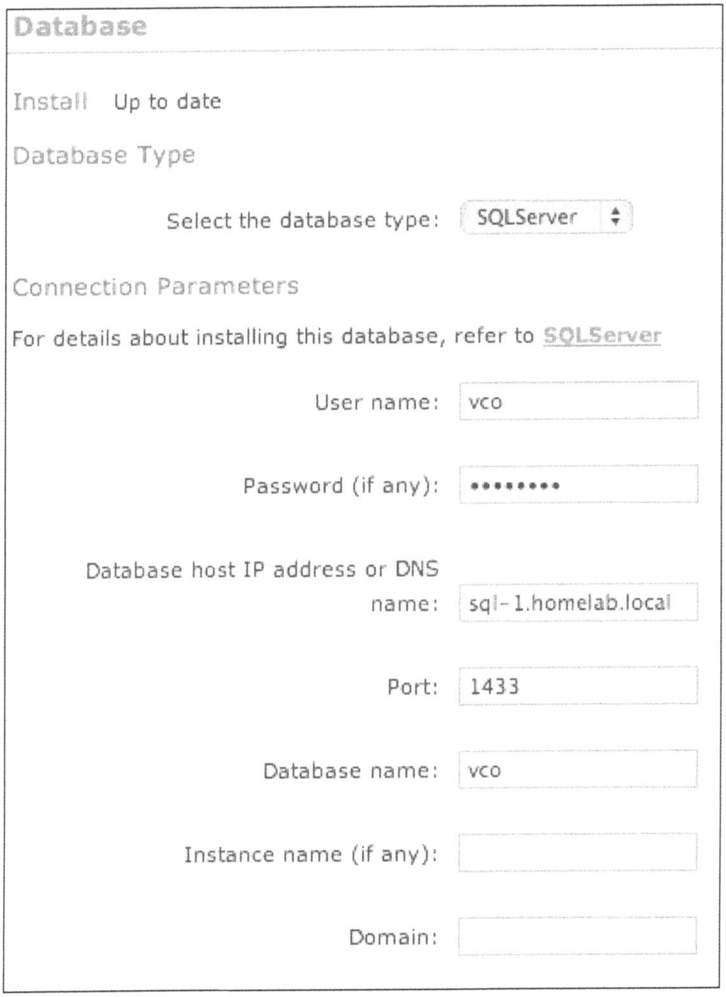

```
Database

Install   Up to date

Database Type

              Select the database type:   [ SQLServer    ⬍ ]

Connection Parameters

For details about installing this database, refer to SQLServer

                       User name:   [ vco                    ]

                  Password (if any):   [ ••••••••             ]

      Database host IP address or DNS
                           name:   [ sql-1.homelab.local  ]

                           Port:   [ 1433                 ]

                  Database name:   [ vco                  ]

              Instance name (if any):   [                      ]

                         Domain:   [                      ]
```

If the specified parameters are correct, you will get a message that connection to the database has been successful. This indicates that the connection to the database works; the next step is to install or update the database. If you choose to install a new database, a new table structure will be created. If you choose to update the database, the table structure for the database used with the previous version of Orchestrator will be updated.

Once the database is populated, you can reset the database access rights to db_dataread and db_datawrite.

> If you change the Orchestrator database after configuring and installing the default plugins, you must click on the **Troubleshooting** tab and force plugin reinstallation by clicking on **Reset current version**. This operation deletes the install_directory\app-server\server\vmo\plugins_VSOPluginInstallationVersion.xml file, which contains the versions of the plugins already installed, and forces plugin reinstallation.

If you use SQL Express, you'll need to configure the database to use TCP/IP. The steps are as follows:

1. Go to **Start | All Programs | Microsoft SQL Server 2008 R2** and then **Configuration Tools**, and click on **SQL Server Configuration Manager**.
2. Expand the list to the left of the configuration manager.
3. Click on **Protocols for SQLEXPRESS**.
4. Right-click on **TCP/IP** and select **Enable**.
5. Right-click on **TCP/IP** and select **Properties**.
6. Click on the **IP Addresses** tab.
7. Under **IP1, IP2**, and **IPAll**, set the **TCP Port** value to 1433.
8. Click on **OK** and restart SQL Server.

Server certificate

Any Orchestrator deployment requires a certificate. Orchestrator uses the server certificate to perform the following tasks:

- Sign all packages before they are exported by attaching your certificate's public key to each one.

- Display a user prompt after users import a package that contains elements signed by untrusted certificates.

You can use either a self-signed certificate or one obtained from a certificate authority. It's considered best practice to avoid using self-signed certificates. It still can be an option for internal-only use or temporary use, such as testing.

A self-signed certificate can be created from the configuration interface under **Server Certificate**. Click on **Create certificate database** and **self-signed server certificate**, type the correct information, choose a country from drop-down list, and click on **Create**.

Orchestrator creates a certificate that is unique to your existing environment. Its details can be viewed in the Server Certificate window. The certificate's private key is stored in the `vmo_keystore` table of the Orchestrator database.

You may need to use a certificate signed by a trusted certificate authority to provide an acceptable level of trust to third parties. A CA guarantees that you are who you claim to be by signing your request with their certificate, which is trusted worldwide. You can use the certificate signed by a CA to confirm that a package was created by your server.

To obtain a certificate from a certificate authority, you will need to create a Certificate Signing Request (CSR), submit it to a CA, obtain your certificate, and install it in the Orchestrator.

To create a CSR, log in to the **Orchestrator configuration** interface, go to **Server Certificate**, generate a CSR, and click on **Export certificate signing request**. You will be prompted to save the CSR in a file.

Once it's done, you will need to provide this CSR to the certificate authority of your choice. This procedure may vary from one CA to another. In general, they will require some kind of proof of your ownership of the domain and/or proof of your identity.

After validation, the CA returns your certificate that must be imported back to Orchestrator. To accomplish this, click on **Import certificate signing request**, which has been signed by the CA, and select the file sent by the CA you had chosen.

For migration or backup purposes, there is an option to export and import the server certificate. Under **Server Certificate** in the configuration interface, click on **Import certificate database** or **Export certificate database**. In both cases, you will be prompted for a password. Because the private key is stored in `vmo_keystore`, you will be prompted to save `vmo-server.vmokeystore` when exporting the certificate.

In certain cases, you may need to use a different SSL certificate for signing your packages instead of the one used for the initial Orchestrator configuration. In this case, you will need to export all packages and change the Orchestrator database. The steps to accomplish this are outlined as follows:

1. Export packages:
   ° Click on the **Packages** view in the Orchestrator client, right-click on the **package to export**, and select **Export package**
   ° Select a location to save the package and leave the **View content**, **Re-Packageable**, and **Edit element** options selected

It is important to make sure you don't sign the package with your current certificate because it will become unavailable if it's encrypted once the certificate database is deleted.

2. Create a new database and configure Orchestrator to work with it. For more information about setting up the Orchestrator database, refer to the *Database connection* section.

You may need to export the Orchestrator configuration and backup the database first.

3. Create a new self-signed certificate or import a server certificate signed by a certification authority as described in the previous section.

4. Reinstall the default Orchestrator plugins:

   ° In the Orchestrator configuration interface, click on the **Troubleshooting** tab

   ° Click on the **Reset current version** link and restart the Orchestrator server

5. Re-import your packages:

   ° Click on the **Packages** view in the Orchestrator client. Select **Import package** from the drop-down menu

   ° Browse to **select the package to import** and click on **Open**

   ° Click on **Import** or **Import and trust provider**

   ° Click on **Import checked elements**

Plugin configuration

Under the **Plug-ins** tab in the configuration interface, you can choose which plug-ins will be available. To access this setting, you are required to enter the username and password of a user who is a member of the Orchestrator Administrators group. Therefore, LDAP configuration is a prerequisite for plug-ins configuration.

You can check plugins that need to be enabled and uncheck those that need to be disabled as shown in the following screenshot:

The **Mail** plugin is installed with Orchestrator by default and is used for e-mail notifications. It can be configured under **Mail** in the configuration interface. Select **Define default values** and fill in the required text fields listed in the article at the following link:

```
http://pubs.vmware.com/vsphere-50/index.jsp#com.vmware.vsphere.vco_
install_config.doc_42/GUIDAF60409B-3E97-4512-8A6C-C2DF3F0B5F95.html
```

SSH plugin configuration can be done under **SSH** in the configuration interface. Click on **New connection**, and in the **Host name** field, type the host address that will be accessed via Orchestrator.

Once you click on **Apply changes**, this host will be added to the list of SSH connections.

Optionally, you can configure the entry path on the server — click on **New root folder**, enter a new path, and click on **Apply changes**.

Orchestrator uses the credentials of the currently logged in user to access other hosts via SSH; therefore, the username and password will not be required.

With vCenter Server 5.0.1 plugin, you can set up the Orchestrator connection parameters to your vCenter Server instances.

In the configuration interface, select **vCenter Server 5.0.1** and click on **New vCenter Server Host**. From the available drop-down menu, select **Enable**, then fill in the fields **host name**, **IP address**, or **port**, optionally, and check the **Secure channel** checkbox to establish a secure connection to your vCenter Server.

Keep a default value in the **Path** textbox; enter the **User name** and **Password** that Orchestrator will use to connect to the vCenter Server host. Orchestrator uses these credentials to monitor the vCenter web service and to operate Orchestrator's system workflows. Therefore, this user needs to have administrative privileges extending to the top of your vCenter hierarchy. The following screenshot shows an example of setting up the Orchestrator connection parameters to your vCenter Server instances:

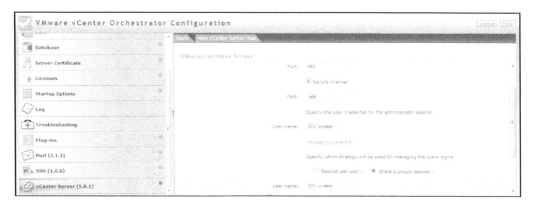

Select the method you will use to control users' access to the vCenter host and apply the changes. Available options for the method are listed in the VMware documentation article at the following link:

```
http://pubs.vmware.com/vsphere-50/index.jsp?topic=%2Fcom.vmware.
vsphere.vco_appliance.doc_42%2FGUIDBCE18F5F-08BB-45AD-9AAD-
6A4335F17457.html
```

Once the default plugins are configured, you may need to install additional plugins. There are two types of files that can be deployed: .vmoapp and .dar. The difference between them is that a .vmoapp file can contain a collection of several .dar files and can be installed as an application, while a .dar file contains all the resources associated with one plugin only.

The .vmoapp files are installed from the **General** tab in the Orchestrator configuration interface and the .dar files from the **Plug-ins** tab.

For `.dar` plugin installation, under **Install new plug-in**, click on the magnifying glass icon, browse, and select the `.dar` file, click on **Open**, and then click on **Upload and install** as shown in the following screenshot.

The installed plugin file will be stored in `install_directory\app-server\server\vmo\plugins`.

The procedure for the `.vmoapp` plugin installation is the same as a `.dar` plugin installation; however, it is performed in the **General** tab. Click on **Install application**, and you'll be prompted for the location of `.vmoapp` file. Once you choose the file, open it, and click on **Install**. New plugin tab will appear in the Orchestrator configuration interface.

Each time a `.vmoapp` plugin is installed, a validation is made on the server configuration. In most cases, additional configuration steps are required. They can be performed on a tab that the new application adds to the Orchestrator configuration interface.

Installing Orchestrator as a system service

Orchestrator can be installed as a system service. Once it's done, you will be able to start, stop, and restart the service from the Orchestrator configuration interface.

This can be accomplished from the configuration interface under **Startup Options**. Click on **Install vCO server as a service**, and then click on **Start** to start it.

If the Orchestrator server doesn't start, make sure that the server it's installed on has at least 4 GB of memory and that the database is running on a separate, dedicated server. For a standalone installation, this requirement comes down to 2 GB.

Administering vCenter Orchestrator

vCenter Orchestrator can be administered using the Orchestrator client. It's an easy-to-use desktop application that allows you to perform daily administration tasks such as importing packages, running and scheduling workflows, and managing user permissions.

To access it, go to **Start** | **Programs** | **VMware** | **vCenter Orchestrator Client**. In the **Host name** field, type the IP address that Orchestrator is bound to. This IP address is set in the configuration interface on the **Network** tab. Log in using the credentials that were set under the **LDAP** tab in the configuration interface.

Depending on the certificate installed on the Orchestrator server, you may receive a certificate warning. The table in the article at the following link describes each option that's offered:

```
http://pubs.vmware.com/vsphere-50/index.jsp?topic=%2Fcom.vmware.
vsphere.vco_appliance.doc_42%2FGUID-D0C69C5A-5CA1-4B4B-A5E1-
5888ACBDF64C.html
```

An Orchestrator client consists of multiple views that allow us to manage different objects of Orchestrator. A quick review of available views is provided in the later section.

Under **Tools** | **User preferences**, you can customize different aspects of Orchestrator client behavior. These settings are saved in the `\Documents and Settings\ Current_User\.vmware\vmware-vmo.cfg` file. The `.vmware` folder will be created the first time you connect to the running Orchestrator server.

The table in the article at the following link lists the available configuration options:

```
http://pubs.vmware.com/vsphere-50/index.jsp?topic=%2Fcom.vmware.
vsphere.vco_administer.doc_42%2FGUID-4AE205B3-ED6C-4DFE-99C2-
CC058F82BDCB.html
```

Under the **My Orchestrator** view, you can see a summary of the most recent Orchestrator server activities such as recently modified elements, pending and running workflows, running policies, completed workflows, and workflows that are waiting for user interaction.

In this view, common administrative tasks can be performed as well, such as running a workflow, importing a package, and setting root access rights.

Under the **Configuration** view, you can create configuration elements that allow the defining of common attributes across the Orchestrator server:

- The **Packages** view allows administrators to add, import, export, and synchronize packages.

- The **Scheduler** view shows all scheduled workflows in the system. Workflows can be sorted by name or status.

- The **Workflows** view provides access to the Orchestrator workflow libraries. In this view, you will be able to view information about each workflow, create, edit, and run workflows, and interact with the workflows.

- The **Actions** view provides access to libraries of predefined actions and allows you to duplicate, export, and move the actions across modules in a hierarchical list of actions.

- In the **Resources** view, you can import external objects such as images, sysprep files, custom scripts, and HTML and XML templates, and use them as resource elements in workflows and Web Views.

- The **Inventory** view displays the objects of the plugin applications that are enabled in Orchestrator.

- Under the **Web Views**, you can create, publish, and export Web Views to a working folder for modification or as templates that can be used to create a new Web View. This view can be used to access Orchestrator functions from a Web browser.

- The **Web Operator** view allows users to run the workflows from a browser. It allows users to use certain Orchestrator functions without installing the Orchestrator client. To start the Web Operator view, go to **Web Views** in Orchestrator client, right-click on **weboperator**, and select **Publish**.

Then, open the web browser and go to `http://orchestrator_server:8280`. On the home page, click on **Web View List**. Click on **weboperator** and log in with your Orchestrator username and password.

Expand the list of workflows and click on a workflow in the hierarchical list to see additional information in the right-hand side pane.

From there, you can also select whether to run the workflow now or at a later time. The table in the article at the following link gives more details about each option:

`http://pubs.vmware.com/vsphere-50/index.jsp?topic=%2Fcom.vmware.`
`vsphere.vco_develop_web_views.doc_42%2FGUID-1E96A38D-B86B-4F10-ABBC-`
`5485FC71C8CE.html`

Overview of workflows

A **workflow** is a set of actions and decisions that run in a certain sequence until a certain result is reached. Orchestrator offers a set of workflows designed for different management tasks that perform these tasks according to best practice. There are also libraries of actions that can be used in your own workflows.

Examples of tasks that can be performed are provisioning virtual machines, backing up, performing regular maintenance, sending e-mails, performing SSH operations, managing the physical infrastructure, and so on.

Workflows can be scheduled to run at a certain time or when a certain event occurs. Workflows can be started by other workflows.

Workflows can be created in the Integrated Development Environment (IDE) interface of the Orchestrator client. From this interface, you are able to access libraries and run workflows on the workflow engine.

The standard library of workflows contains workflows that allow you to automate operations in virtual infrastructure. It contains the folders listed in the VMware documentation at the following link:

```
http://pubs.vmware.com/vsphere-51/index.jsp?topic=%2Fcom.vmware.
vsphere.vco_using_client.doc%2FGUID292D7B55-7581-4536-964C-
0F75DEEEFAFF.html
```

Workflows in the standard library are read-only. You need to create a copy if there is a requirement to customize one for standard workflows.

You can limit users' access to workflows by setting permissions. This is done under the **Permissions** tab when editing workflow. Click on the **Add access rights** link to define permissions. From there, you will be able to add users or groups and select the level of permission.

The levels of permission are defined in Orchestrator as shown in the article at the following link:

```
http://pubs.vmware.com/vsphere-50/index.jsp?topic=%2Fcom.vmware.
vsphere.vco_administer.doc_42%2FGUID953E20D8-8A26-4105-B2C3-
ABD8F486D840.html
```

Each workflow has a set of credentials assigned. Credentials used by a workflow to run depend on the way this workflow is started. Details can be found in the VMware documentation article at the following link:

```
http://pubs.vmware.com/vsphere-50/index.jsp#com.vmware.vsphere.vco_
administer.doc_42/GUID67DC3E20-0AB0-4E0A-9AEB-862B5585949C.html
```

Workflows may contain global constants and global variables also called attributes. Constants are read-only attributes while variables are writable attributes. Attributes are used to pass values between workflow elements and can be defined by defining in one of the following ways:

- Define attributes when you create a workflow
- Set the output parameter of a workflow element as a workflow attribute
- Inherit attributes from a configuration element

When a workflow starts, it may require input parameters, that is, arguments supplied by an application, another workflow, or action. Input parameters have the following properties: name, type, and descriptions; and once passed to a workflow, they cannot be changed.

Output parameters are values that a workflow returns when it runs. They are usually the result of running a workflow.

Under the **Schema** tab of the workflow, you can view the workflow schema, which is a flow diagram of interconnected workflow elements.

Each time you run a workflow, a workflow token is created. This token represents a specific instance of running or completed workflow with its set of input parameters. These parameters are called token attributes.

The token can be in one of the states listed in the article at the following link:

```
http://pubs.vmware.com/vsphere-50/index.jsp#com.vmware.vsphere.vco_
administer.doc_42/GUID-7C4E3ED2-4377-4780-982B-C654AC273ADE.html
```

If there is a workflow that is waiting for user interaction, you will see it under the **Waiting for input** tab in the **My Orchestrator** view. Double-click on it, right-click on **workflow token**, and select **Answer**. Provide the required information so that the workflow can resume.

Resource elements and actions

Workflows and Web Views may require external objects, or attributes, that once imported into Orchestrator, are called **resource elements**. Examples of resource elements are image files, scripts, XML templates, HTML files, and so on.

To import an object, go to the **Resources** view, right-click on one of the resource folders, and select **Import resources**. You will be prompted to select a resource.

Once imported, elements can be organized into folders. The maximum size of a resource element is 16 MB.

Resource elements can be viewed under the **Resources** view in the Orchestrator client. If you click on a resource element, you will be able to see information about it in the right-hand side pane. Click on the **Viewer** tab to display the contents of the resource element.

Existing resources can be changed by right-clicking on the element and selecting **Edit**. The **General** tab comprises **name**, **version**, and **description text fields**. The **Permissions** tab contains access rights for users and groups. You can make the appropriate changes and click on **Save and Close**.

Resource elements can be updated in Orchestrator if the source file has been modified by right-clicking on the element and selecting **Update resource**.

There is also an option to export elements, which is available when you right-click on the resource element that you need to export.

You can add resource elements to workflows as attributes using the **General** tab in the **workflow edit** mode. You will be able to search for available attributes under the **Select a type** dialog box by typing `resource` in the **Filter** box.

Actions are individual functions that are used to build workflows. They can take multiple parameters and return a single value. Actions can call any object or method available in Orchestrator, either ones that Orchestrator comes with or imported ones, using a plugin.

Actions take input parameters from workflow attributes. These attributes can also be set by other elements of the workflow when they run.

Actions can be created in the **Actions** view by right-clicking on the appropriate module and selecting **Add action**. You will be prompted for name of the action. Once it's done, you can right-click on the action and select **Edit**. On the **Scripting** tab, you will be able to write an action script. Then, you can set the action permissions and click on **Save and Close**.

Actions can be duplicated, exported, imported, and moved across modules in the hierarchy. All these actions are done by right-clicking on the action or the appropriate module.

Summary

VMware vCenter Orchestrator is an automation tool that provides a set of workflows that can be used for automating configuration and managing vSphere infrastructure. It uses vCenter Server APIs that cover almost every operation.

Orchestrator can be installed either together with vCenter Server or separately. There are also options to upgrade from previous versions and export the configuration during migration.

There is a list of configuration tasks that have to be done after Orchestrator installation, before Orchestrator can be used. It includes but is not limited to LDAP configuration, database connection settings, certificate installation, plugin configuration, and service configuration.

Workflows are a set of actions and decisions that run in a certain sequence until a certain result is reached. Orchestrator offers a set of workflows for different management tasks that perform these tasks according to best practice.

Workflows and Web Views may require external objects, or attributes, that, once imported into Orchestrator, are called resource elements. Examples of resource elements are image files, scripts, XML templates, HTML files, and so on.

Actions are individual functions that are used to build workflows. They can take multiple parameters and return a single value.

Index

L

LDAP authentication, VMware vCenter Orchestrator
  configuring 280
  LDAP search queries, customizing 282
limits, resource allocation 193
Linked Mode group
  about 30
  configuring 31
  prerequisites 31
  vCenter Server, adding 32
  vCenter Server, removing 32
Linux guest OS
  VM drive, extending 98, 99
  VMware Tools, installing 104
local storage 45
lockdown mode, ESXi security
  enabling 184-187
LSI Logic Parallel adapter
  about 86
LSI Logic SAS adapter 86
LSI Parallel storage adapter 44
LUN
  about 49
  considerations 49

M

Managed Object ID (MOID) 139
management layer, VMware vSphere 16
management suite
  additional modules, installing 29
  installing 24-30
  Linked Mode group 30
memory ballooning 271
memory pressure metric 270
Microsoft Cluster Server (MSCS) 86
multipathing 53

N

network adapters
  configuring 58, 59
Network-attached storage (NAS) 47, 48
networked storage 45
Network File System (NFS) protocol 47
networking

  about 57
  configuring 58, 59
  setting up, with redundancy 65
  virtual switches 59
Non-Uniform Memory Access (NUMA) 213

O

objects, Update Manager
  compliance scanning 241
  remediating 242-244
  scanning 241
Open Virtualization Format (OVF) 22
OVF template
  about 119
  importing, from GUI 119
  importing, into older versions of vSphere 120
  USB support 122
OVF Tool
  using 119

P

patch management 9
path failover 53
permissions, built-in users
  Dcui user 176
  root user 176
  Vpxuser 176
permissions, in vCenter
  about 173
  inheritance 173
  object permissions 174, 175
physical adapters, ESXi host management
  Fibre Channel (FC) 44, 46
  Fibre Channel over Ethernet (FCoE) 44
  iSCSI 46, 47
  NAS 47
  RAID 44
  SCSI 44
physical storage, ESXi host management
  local storage 45
  networked storage 45
planned downtime
  about 132
  HA and redundancy features, using 132
  migration, with vMotion 134, 136

Thank you for buying
Implementing VMware vCenter Server

About Packt Publishing

Packt, pronounced 'packed', published its first book "Mastering phpMyAdmin for Effective MySQL Management" in April 2004 and subsequently continued to specialize in publishing highly focused books on specific technologies and solutions.

Our books and publications share the experiences of your fellow IT professionals in adapting and customizing today's systems, applications, and frameworks. Our solution based books give you the knowledge and power to customize the software and technologies you're using to get the job done. Packt books are more specific and less general than the IT books you have seen in the past. Our unique business model allows us to bring you more focused information, giving you more of what you need to know, and less of what you don't.

Packt is a modern, yet unique publishing company, which focuses on producing quality, cutting-edge books for communities of developers, administrators, and newbies alike. For more information, please visit our website: www.packtpub.com.

About Packt Enterprise

In 2010, Packt launched two new brands, Packt Enterprise and Packt Open Source, in order to continue its focus on specialization. This book is part of the Packt Enterprise brand, home to books published on enterprise software – software created by major vendors, including (but not limited to) IBM, Microsoft and Oracle, often for use in other corporations. Its titles will offer information relevant to a range of users of this software, including administrators, developers, architects, and end users.

Writing for Packt

We welcome all inquiries from people who are interested in authoring. Book proposals should be sent to author@packtpub.com. If your book idea is still at an early stage and you would like to discuss it first before writing a formal book proposal, contact us; one of our commissioning editors will get in touch with you.

We're not just looking for published authors; if you have strong technical skills but no writing experience, our experienced editors can help you develop a writing career, or simply get some additional reward for your expertise.

vSphere High Performance Cookbook

vSphere High Performance Cookbook

Prasenjit Sarkar

ISBN: 978-1-78217-000-6   Paperback: 240 pages

Over 60 recipes to help you improve vSphere performance and solve problems before they arise

1. Troubleshoot real-world vSphere performance issues and identify their root causes

2. Design and configure CPU, memory, networking, and storage for better and more reliable performance

3. Comprehensive coverage of performance issues and solutions including vCenter Server design and virtual machine and application tuning

Implementing VMware Horizon View 5.2

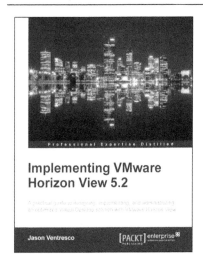

Implementing VMware Horizon View 5.2

Jason Ventresco

ISBN: 978-1-84968-796-6   Paperback: 390 pages

A practical guide to designing, implementing, and administrating an optimized Virtual Desktop solution with VMware Horizon View

1. Detailed description of the deployment and administration of the VMware Horizon View suite

2. Learn how to determine the resources your virtual desktops will require

3. Design your desktop solution to avoid potential problems, and ensure minimal loss of time in the later stages

Please check **www.PacktPub.com** for information on our titles

VMware ThinApp 4.7 Essentials

ISBN: 978-1-84968-628-0   Paperback: 256 pages

Learn how to quickly and efficiently virtualize your applications with ThinApp 4.7

1. Practical book which provides the essentials of application virtualization with ThinApp 4.7

2. Learn the various methods and best practices of application packaging and deployment

3. Save money and time on your projects with this book by learning how to create portable applications

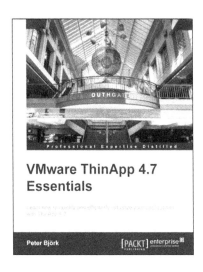

VMware View Security Essentials

ISBN: 978-1-78217-008-2   Paperback: 130 pages

The insiders guide on how to secure your VMware View Environment

1. Discover how to correctly implement View connection, security, and transfer servers

2. Understand all the firewall rules and the basics of multi-layered security

3. Secure all your connections between client and desktop

Please check **www.PacktPub.com** for information on our titles